SOCIAL ORDER AND MENTAL HEALTH

The Florida Health Study

Social Order and Mental Health

The Florida Health Study

by

JOHN J. SCHWAB, M.D.,

Professor and Chairman, Department of Psychiatry and Behavioral Sciences, School of Medicine, University of Louisville

ROGER A. BELL, ED.D.,

Associate Professor, Department of Psychiatry and Behavioral Sciences, School of Medicine, University of Louisville

GEORGE J. WARHEIT, PH.D.,

Professor of Sociology in Psychiatry, University of Florida

and

RUBY B. SCHWAB, B.S.

BRUNNER/MAZEL, *Publishers* • New York

Library of Congress Cataloging in Publication Data
Schwab, John J.
Social order and mental health.

Includes index.
1. Social psychiatry—Florida. 2. Psychology, Pathological—Etiology. 3. Epidemiology 4. Social history—Florida. 5. Florida—Social conditions. I. Bell, Roger A., joint author. II. Warheit, George, joint author. III. Ruby B. Schwab, joint author. IV. Title.
[DNLM: 1. Mental disorders—Etiology. 2. Socioeconomic factors. 3. Mental disorders—Occurrence—Florida. WM31 S398sa]
RC455.S323 362.2'09759 78-13105

ISBN 0-87630-185-5

Published by
BRUNNER/MAZEL, INC.
19 Union Square, New York, N. Y. 10003

MANUFACTURED IN THE UNITED STATES OF AMERICA

Man is, at one and the same time, a solitary being and a social being. As a solitary being, he attempts to protect his own existence and that of those who are closest to him, to satisfy his personal desires, and to develop his innate abilities. As a social being, he seeks to gain the recognition and affection of his fellow human beings, to share in their pleasures, to comfort them in their sorrows, and to improve their conditions of life. . . . It is quite possible that the relative strength of these two drives is, in the main, fixed by inheritance. But the personality that finally emerges is largely formed by the environment in which a man happens to find himself during his development, by the structure of the society in which he groups up, by the tradition of that society, and by its appraisal of particular types of behavior. The abstract concept of "society" means to the individual human being the sum total of his direct and indirect relations to his contemporaries and to all the people of earlier generations.

ALBERT EINSTEIN*

* In: *Ideas and Opinions*. Based on *Mein Weltbild*. Carl Seelig (Ed.). Sonja Bargmann (Trans. and Rev.). New York: Bonanza Books, Division of Crown Publishers, Inc., 1954, 153.

Foreword

Let no one who merely glances at the careful statistical tabulations in the text infer that this book is but another demographic survey of an isolated Florida county—or least of all, in Alan Gregg's poignant phrase, that the "statistics are human beings with the tears wiped off." John Schwab and his colleagues have dealt intelligently, insightfully, and above all, humanely with the historic, ethnic, economic, political, and cultural changes that have profoundly influenced the physical, mental, and interpersonal welfare of over one hundred thousand differentially stressed human beings. Clinically the study is a superb demonstration that the adjective "social" in "social psychiatry" is redundant; all iatric diagnoses, prognoses, and therapies must include the comprehensive perspectives elucidated here. Ergo, the findings are important not only for the region studied, but for countless heterogeneous communities in our nation and elsewhere.

The Introduction previews the volume, but does not do justice to its variegated contents. All of us interested in human welfare will find that *Social Order and Mental Health* epitomizes careful research design and a rich source of psychologic, psychiatric, and sociocultural illumination, conveyed with literary grace and heuristic clarity.

I recommend it highly as a memorable adventure in intriguing and informative reading.

JULES H. MASSERMAN, M.D.
President
American Psychiatric Association

Contents

Introduction

The 1978 Report of the President's Commission on Mental Health announced that about 25% of all Americans suffer from mental health problems. Epidemiologists have maintained a scientific interest in the prevalence of mental disorder for years. However, more general concern about the numbers of persons in the community who are at high risk for mental illness and the adequacy of institutions to meet human needs fluctuates, mounting at times of societal unrest. At such times there is fear that the prevalence of mental illness is rising, possibly reflecting social instability.

This volume reports the results of a study of mental health risk in an entire county in North Florida. The county was typical of many in our country that have been undergoing rapid social change. Our major objectives were to assess the number of persons in the general population who were at risk for mental disorders and to search for possible sociocultural factors associated with varying degrees of risk.

The motivation to undertake this six-year project stemmed from growing concerns about the persons needing, but only sometimes receiving, psychiatric care. Although I entered psychiatry in the early 1960s, I retained my initial interest in internal medicine and, for a few years, devoted my professional efforts to the care and study of general medical patients with emotional distress. During that time, I became increasingly aware that all illness arises in a social setting and that both illness and the type of treatment received are influenced by the prevailing social and cultural climate.

In the late 1960s, civil rights, "isms," women's liberation, and various protests reflected our societal turmoil and focused attention on broad social issues that affected groups and individuals. Some of these problems were surfaced by medical patients referred for psychiatric consultation. One was a middle-aged, male veteran of both World War II and the

Korean Conflict who had a peptic ulcer that he attributed to worry about what would happen to his son who was a Conscientious Objector. Many mothers were both anxious and depressed about the changing mores and their daughters' sexual activities. Young medical patients told repeatedly that no one understood them; drugs provided at least temporary relief. At every turn, an observer could see that the elderly, the poor, and many of the blacks were caught in a frightening web, entrapped by the social system, by circumstance, and by their own dilemmas. Meanwhile, Alachua County seemed to be changing before one's eyes. The county seat, Gainesville, was becoming a regional center for education, medicine, and technology.

In 1969, we received a five-year research grant from the Applied Research Branch of the National Institute of Mental Health (Grant No. 15900) to: 1) study possible relationships between the social processes that were occurring in the County and risk for mental illness, and 2) evaluate mental health needs and the utilization of services. In developing the project, we leaned heavily on the two other major investigations of mental illness in the community conducted since World War II—the Stirling County and the Midtown Manhattan Studies. They provided fundamental guidelines for our research. Thus, we were building on the achievements of others, hoping that the results would ultimately add to knowledge about the ways to treat and prevent that human distress we call mental illness.

In Chapter 1 we present the rationale for the study. Alachua County seemed to be a favorable setting because, like many others in the Southeast, it was undergoing such rapid change that the social order appeared to be altering for the first time in over a century. Thus, the place and the time offered an unusual research opportunity. Moreover, we were able to study a population that contained a large number of blacks. Chapter 2 describes the historical background of the region with a focus on the caste system's prescriptions and proscriptions for behavior. Chapter 3 gives the characteristics of Alachua County and its population.

In Chapter 4 we discuss the major handicaps confronting psychiatric epidemiologists—how to define and measure risk for mental illness in the community. Then we explain the development of our construct, Social Psychiatric Impairment (SPI), and the research design.

In Chapter 5 we present the respondents' scores on scales assessing psychopathology and symptom patterns. Data on impairment of functioning and interpersonal distress are reported in Chapter 6. The respondents' reports of psychosomatic ailments and physical illnesses and the extent of concurrence of these dysfunctions with SPI are given in Chapter 7. In Chapter 8 we compare needs for mental and physical health care with the utilization of services.

Chapters 9 and 10 are devoted to the presentation of data on more theoretical considerations—the respondents' perceptions of the social changes that were occurring, their aspirations, intergenerational social mobility, and migration—and the relationships between them and the degree of risk for mental illness in individuals and groups.

Chapter 11 reports the results of the follow-up study of about one-third of the original sample, conducted in 1973. This study enabled us to present findings on the changing health status, "incidence and remission" as measured by a standardized scale developed for use in Stirling County, the Health Opinion Survey (HOS). Chapter 12 summarizes some of the theoretical and clinical implications of this epidemiologic study.

We know that in a work such as this it is always simpler to discuss impairment rather than health, the abnormal instead of the normal, just as it is easier to describe pain than pleasure. We are hoping, however, that the results will have utility for researchers' attempts to explain and predict behavior.

Acknowledgments

This volume presents the results of the work of many researchers, interviewers, and graduate students. Dr. Charles E. Holzer, III, Dr. Nancy H. McGinnis, and Ms. Lynn Robbins assisted us with almost every phase of the project 1969-1974. Dr. Gary Spencer, Dr. Kenneth Hodge, Dr. Don Lund, Ms. Patricia Farris, and Ms. Judith Brown made significant contributions to the research. During the years 1969-1974, more than 40 interviewers and research assistants worked on the project; it has provided data for 11 Master's theses and 12 Doctoral dissertations.

Mr. Neal D. Traven analyzed the data presented. We are particularly grateful to Mrs. Helen M. Russell who labored arduously over the manuscript and also assisted with the editing. Dr. Gladys Busch, Ms. Elizabeth Lin, Ms. Stacy Garrett, Ms. Mary Ann Pate, and Ms. Sherri Chandler helped with the data analysis, library work, and typing.

I am grateful to my colleagues on the faculty and staff of the Department of Psychiatry and Behavioral Sciences in the School of Medicine at the University of Louisville. They cooperated in many ways and also realized that I was heavily involved in this work that consumed a disproportionate part of my time and energy in the winter and spring of 1978.

JOHN J. SCHWAB, M.D.

SOCIAL ORDER AND MENTAL HEALTH

The Florida Health Study

1

The Florida Health Study: Introduction and Rationale

How the structure of a society promotes the well-being of its members or, conversely, produces social discontent and emotional distress has been the concern of philosophers even before Aristotle defined man as a political animal. The basis for social organization is conjectural, but throughout the world, human beings live in social groups and their societies are stratified. Individuals and subgroups are hierarchically ranked according to various standards, e.g., prestige, or wealth, or the given society's values and ideals. Even groups regarded as primitive have developed numerous and often complex taboos, customs, and controls to maintain social order.

OBJECTIVES

The major objective of this work is to examine some of the relationships between social processes and the mental health and illness of members of various social groups. It reports the findings of research carried out in North Florida, a section of the United States known for its distinctive social structure, at a time when the century-old social order was undergoing dissolution—1969 to 1975. Until World War II, the social order in the Southeast was structured by a rigid caste system developed during the Reconstruction Era; it maintained racial segregation and insured political and economic domination of the region by the propertied class, especially the white gentry who traced their heritage to the ante-bellum South. This caste system influenced every aspect of daily life—etiquette, customs, and life styles. Thus, it affected the quality of life in the community, the character of familial and other interpersonal relationships, and, particularly, basic drives and feelings such as aggression, sex, guilt, and self-esteem.

But the social, political, and economic life of the region was transformed in just a little more than 20 years, between the 1954 Supreme Court decision ordering school desegregation and Jimmy Carter's victory in the Presidential election of 1976. C. Vann Woodward states that the second reconstruction of the South occurred in the 1960s (1). And Orfield notes that: "[N]o nation has accomplished without war or revolution, a social transformation as profound and as rapid as that implied by the partial integration of the schools of the South" (2). The change has been dramatized by the series of black-white confrontations that have obliterated the long-standing "separate but equal" doctrine and resulted in enfranchisement for southern blacks. Other tangible changes in the region have been the rapid population increase, a marked rise in family annual income, and the economic vitality illustrated by the growth of southern cities and the development of natural resources. In a sociological analysis entitled "The Changing South: National Incorporation of a Region," McKinney and Bourque document that the South "has been changing *more rapidly* than the rest of the nation during the last forty years" (3). The accelerated rate of change has been paralleled by a breakdown of the old social order.

RATIONALE

The main reasons for conducting a social psychiatric study of an entire county in the Southeast were that both the timing and the setting offered unusual opportunities to appraise relationships between the structure of society and the individual's well-being. We began the study in 1969 and completed most of it by 1975, a period when the social order was in the throes of change and when we could isolate a number of different groups and conjecture how the tumultuous sociopolitical events were associated with varying states of mental health and illness. Some of these groups consisted of persons who had been conditioned by the social order existing prior to World War II; of others whose identities were shaped by the dramatic events of the 1950s and 1960s; and of still others, the newly emerging élite—mainly entrepreneurial and technologically-oriented newcomers. Furthermore, the County had a relatively large black population, over 20%, enabling us to look at changing black-white relationships in the desegregation era. In addition, the rapid rate of social change in the County allowed us to study critical social processes such as the rural-urban shift, the deprived-affluent imbalance, and the intergenerational conflict.

The heterogeneous composition of the County's population increased the potential significance of the study. The percentage of blacks was large enough to permit us to evaluate the extent of "the mental illness problem" in a sizeable black population, as well as to make meaningful black-white comparisons. Students constituted almost one-fourth of the total population and provided valuable data on the effects of the "generation gap." The rapid increase in the County's population, particularly since World War II, supplied us with new residents whose attitudes, convictions, and standards could be compared with those of long-time residents or natives. Thus, in a county that was representative of many in the Southeast, we were able to look at mental health and illness in groups that had struggled with major contemporary issues—the black-white confrontation, the generation gap, and the new versus the old.

The Epidemiologic Background

Another major reason for undertaking this research was that there have been only a few large-scale epidemiologic studies of mental illness in the general population in North America. The two best-known are the Stirling County Study, carried out in Nova Scotia in the 1950s and 1960s, and the Midtown Manhattan Study, conducted in the 1950s (4-8). These epidemiologic investigations of psychiatric disorder sought to determine the number of mentally ill in the community, the untreated as well as those who were obtaining treatment, and to evaluate associations between certain sociocultural processes and mental illness rates. Both reported that more than 50% of a random sample of respondents suffered from some degree of psychological disorder and that, minimally, 31% in Stirling County and 23% in Midtown Manhattan showed demonstrable evidence of being impaired by mental illness.

The frame of reference for the Stirling County Study was based on the premise that the degree of measurable community integration-disintegration was directly associated with higher or lower rates of mental illness. A fundamental assumption was that the sociocultural environment influences an individual's "essential psychical condition." The Stirling County researchers ranked communities for degree of integration-disintegration according to indices that reflected the extent to which these conditions interfered with or fostered an individual's ability to satisfy his essential striving sentiments. They found that psychiatric disorder was significantly more common in disintegrated than in integrated communities.

The Midtown Manhattan Study investigators conceptualized a stress-strain model of mental illness. They postulated that stress (noxious or potentially noxious factors such as loss or adversity) leads to personality deformation—strain; but the quality and intensity of the reaction to stress are determined in part by the availability and utility of mediating factors and coping resources. Low socioeconomic status (SES) was seen as stressful; on the other hand, high SES could serve as a buffer against stress or supply options that palliated its effects. Their findings showed that the number of stressful events sustained by an individual was directly related to the presence and degree of impairment and that higher rates of impairment were related to lower SES.

These major efforts in psychiatric epidemiology supplied a background and a general method of procedure for our research in the Southeast. However, neither the Stirling County nor the Midtown Manhattan Study was conducted in an area that contained a sufficient number of black respondents to make black-white comparisons. Furthermore, each was carried out in a locale that is vastly different from the one we investigated. The large, relatively tranquil Nova Scotia county studied by the Leightons was populated predominantly by descendants of Old English and French Acadian stock. Midtown was "a typical 'Gold Coast and Slum' area with high population density and a heterogeneous population . . . 99 per cent white. . . . The national backgrounds of the Midtowners (traced back to the country of birth of their grandparents) . . . varied, but [were] principally European" (9). Because those areas differed greatly from each other and especially from the Southeast—geographically, demographically, and socioculturally—the results obtained from those investigations could not be generalized to our region of the country.

Our Approach

When we designed our comprehensive epidemiologic study of Alachua County, Florida, in 1969, we had three specific aims: 1) to ascertain the prevalence of social psychiatric impairment and the number of persons with reported psychosomatic and other physical illnesses in the County; 2) to evaluate the need for health care, especially mental health care, since a Community Mental Health Center was to be developed in 1971; and 3) to look at relationships between social processes—such as intergenerational social mobility, social change, racial distance, and migration—and the presence or absence of indicators of mental illness. Because the rapidly growing County was in the throes of social change, we were particularly interested in possible associations between disruptions of the social order and a greater or lesser number of symptoms and other impairments in various groups that were achieving or losing status.

SOCIAL AND CULTURAL CHANGE

To study associations between social change and behaviors indicative of mental health or illness, the researcher must investigate a particular community at two points in time. Such studies should be carried out both before and after a significant event.* Or, they can be conducted at about 20 year intervals to evaluate differences in the generations. Since we had only a three-year follow-up, we looked carefully at the "generations" in an effort to obtain a historical grasp of reactions to social change.

The importance of the concept of the generation was propounded by Ortega y Gasset who believes that history can be understood only by studying generations (11). This point of view has been emphasized recently by the novelist John Fowles in his latest work, *Daniel Martin* (12). Fowles thinks that, at least in Great Britain and North America, the 20th century began in 1945 and that there are significant observable characterologic differences between Anglo-Saxons who came of age in the pre- and post-war eras.

The rapid social changes occurring throughout the world are the outstanding developments of this century. Social change involves shifts in hierarchical rankings within the social structure, geographic mobility and urbanization, and a host of political and economic processes, including the redistribution of occupational patterns. Culture change refers to modifications and variations of life styles, values, and beliefs as they pertain to patterns of human interaction and to the utilization of objects of material culture, especially the technological. Previously, in accord with the influence of Darwinism, social and cultural changes were seen in an evolutionary perspective, but today, tempered with skepticism, we attribute change in a given society to the influence of external social forces, disequilibrium within the society, diffusion, and particularly innovation. For groups as well as individuals, social and cultural changes bring benefits, but they also disrupt established patterns of behavior and thus create uncertainty.

Attempting to study a topic such as social change and mental illness is immensely difficult because of numerous theoretical and methodological

* For example, David and Deborah Rosen have been studying small communities in the Shetland Islands that are being changed by the discovery of North Sea Oil (10).

issues. Researchers usually limit their efforts to comparisons of aggregate data about the community, such as comparisons of statistics on employment or income with data about mental hospitalization, suicide, or homicide rates. But sociologic indices of change refer solely to populations and allow us to draw inferences only about what is happening to humanity at the aggregate, not the individual, level. In reality, the winds of change blow unevenly; some individuals adjust and some advance by exploiting the changes, whereas others stand still or even retreat. Some benefit from rapid social change, moving up on the income, occupation, and education ladders, attaining a higher social position and seemingly enjoying the fruits of these successes. But others who cannot or do not attempt to adjust to the rate of change often experience a relative or absolute decline in social and other statuses. Change produces conflict within the individual as well as between groups. As Murray says: "A personality is a full Congress of orators and pressure groups, of children, demogogues, communists, isolationists, war mongers. . . . Caesars and Christs, Machiavellis and Judases, Tories and Promethean revolutionists" (13).

Sociologic indices of change, such as those showing rising economic status for the general population, prompt questions that can be answered only by data obtained from a study of the persons and families involved. To what extent are advances in socioeconomic status associated with the "good life," satisfaction, and mental health? Is social immobility or a decline in financial or occupational status—conventionally judged as evidence of inferiority or failure—associated with a lack of well-being, dissatisfaction, and mental and physical distress? Our study attempts to provide at least partial answers to such questions. Instead of relying on aggregate data, we chose a more direct approach; each individual was questioned about his or her perception of 14 social changes (ranging from racial unrest and pollution to people being more unfriendly and life moving at a faster pace, causing pressures) and whether the change was "upsetting." Then we correlated the responses with ratings for risk for mental disorder as measured by social psychiatric impairment (SPI).

Rapid social change, in itself, usually produces significant alterations in the social order. But the change which occurred in the South during the 1950s and 1960s was accelerated by the power of the Federal Government, especially Supreme Court decisions that were often enforced by Federal marshals and, on occasion, by mobilization of National Guard units.

SOCIAL ORDER

Social order is such a fundamental characteristic of all societies that it is considered to be an innately human proclivity. Bertrand Russell mentions that our concepts of order and even our view of order in nature have a social origin. A person lives, "[N]ot on his own but in a society. Even at the most primitive level this involves some kind of organization, and from this source the notion of order is drawn. . . . Some regular changes in nature, such as the sequence of day and night, and the cycle of the seasons, were no doubt discovered a very long time ago. Still, it is in the light of some human interpretation that these changes were first understood" (14).

The "instinctual" basis for social order is advanced, at least implicitly, by Wilson in his recent provocative work, *Sociobiology* (15). An underlying tenet of sociobiology is that there is a genetic basis for social behavior; one of the fundamental behaviors is altruism—preservation of the genes by preservation of the species. For example, social insects serve the entire community, some going so far as to give their lives to protect the colony from invaders. Thus, it can be conceived that DNA controls life, insuring the survival of the genes through the survival of the group, which in turn almost always entails the maintenance of some type of social order.

All societies develop social control processes to maintain social order. The concept of social control was advanced by E. A. Ross in the 1890s. He stipulated that the individual's capacities for sympathy, sociability, resentment, and a sense of justice contribute to social order, but these capacities alone are insufficient to maintain it (16). Society also engages in "moral engineering," using as control mechanisms public opinion, police and the legal system, belief and religion, education and custom, art and ceremony, and even illusion. In "Sorcery, Sin, and the Superego: A Cross Cultural Study of Some Mechanisms of Social Control," John Whiting points out that social control provides for the regulated satisfaction of primary drives such as aggression, hunger, and sex. It cannot be maintained merely by positive reinforcements and negative sanctions. Therefore, throughout the history of mankind, cultural mechanisms such as customs and taboos have been elaborated and built into the child-rearing practices that function as basic social control processes in the adult (17).

Social Order in the South

Until the legal and political upheavals of the 1950s, the South had the most highly developed and inflexible social order in the United States. The plantation system and the institution of slavery had created a landed aristocracy. Following the Civil War and the 10-year period of racial equality that ended when the Federal troops were withdrawn in 1876, the pre-war formal social order was reestablished and enforced by the caste system. For years the social order consisted of strictly defined, hierarchically-arranged groups. The white gentry, usually plantation owners descended from the aristocracy of the ante-bellum South, occupied the top rung of the ladder. Just below them were the new industrialists, the nouveaux riches whose notorious sweatshops—the textile and tobacco mills started in the 1890s—had made them wealthy in just one or two generations. They aped the landed aristocracy and sought access to that status by marriage or by purchase. Next were the middle-class whites—politicians, professionals, administrators, and businessmen. The very large fourth level contained the numerous poor whites who eked out a marginal existence by sharecropping, tilling their own thin land, or working in textile, tobacco, or other mills. This group, largely non-unionized, voted faithfully to keep the political power in the hands of the white upper classes who reigned supreme. The millions of blacks were in a different caste, regarded as racially inferior—a second-rate species that was strictly segregated and not franchised.

There was little social mobility; the caste lines were impermeable barriers. Intermarriage between blacks and whites was illegal, and even the class lines that separated the white groups were usually, but not absolutely, firm boundaries. But, in the 15 years between 1955 and 1970, many of the legal and illegal social control mechanisms that had stabilized this social order were not only ruled invalid by the Federal Government, but also, largely destroyed.

The social order in the South was further splintered by the rapid social changes occurring in the 1960s. These were highlighted by the emergence of new elitist groups with power, particularly the educated, mobile newcomers who were oriented toward the values of the wider society, not just those of the region. The blacks, who had previously been a homogeneous group, began to stratify as they attained some degree of political equality and limited access to economic opportunities.

Thus, at the time our research program started, the long-established social order was in a state of flux. The second reconstruction of the

South had been almost accomplished. The external conditions of life in the Southeast differed greatly from those observable even 15 or 20 years earlier. There was increased prosperity, evidenced by new businesses and the rapid construction of condominiums, suburbs, and roads. The highly visible manifestations of racial segregation were disappearing—signs noting "Colored Only" over drinking fountains and rest rooms had been at least partially obliterated by paint. The old social order was being transformed, shaped by both political events and by the new élite. Such drastic social changes are exceedingly complex; because of the rapidity of the change, residual forms endure and variations of the highly-structured previous orders develop. We had an unusual opportunity, therefore, to evaluate mental health and illness, satisfactions, tensions, and conflicts in various groups—the old, upper-class Southeasterners, the nouveaux riches, the rapidly expanding white middle class, the remaining poor whites, and the blacks, who also constituted a number of socially heterogeneous subgroups.

The region felt the momentous national events that had occurred during the 1960s—the Vietnam War, dissent, women's liberation, and changing roles and statuses—as well as forced desegregation. Consequently, we were able to appraise respondents' perceptions of social change processes, individual and family satisfactions and dissatisfactions, and the symptoms of mental and physical disorders, during a period of rapid social change.

Although the external conditions of life in the region had changed rapidly, internal dynamics changed slowly. Many persons' attitudes and values had been shaped by the caste system; they clung tenaciously to the sentiments cherished by the old social order. Others, particularly the educated newcomers, advocated change. We hypothesized that certain groups would be at high risk for mental disorders and that others, particularly those who appeared to benefit from the changes, would report significantly fewer mental symptoms and impairments of function.

THEORETICAL BACKGROUND FOR THE STUDY

The theoretical basis for our study of social order and mental health was derived from concepts of marginality described by Park and Stonequist. In their early work they emphasized that the marginal person, typically a mulatto, but also migrants and others suspended between two cultures, was in the midst of culture conflict. The psychological effects of such dilemmas are "spiritual instability, intensified self-consciousness, restlessness, and *malaise"* (18). Stonequist also points out that "double consciousness" results from identification within two clashing cultural traditions (19).

With dramatic changes in the social order, previously secure groups had only marginal prestige and some of the groups that were already marginal, economically and educationally, were losing their precarious status. Although conditions for blacks were improving, some of the hard-won gains had been acquired only after a 10-year struggle that had left its scars. Moreover, enforced desegregation was primarily political; for the blacks, economic opportunity and cultural advancement proceeded at a much slower pace. Some socioanthropologic concepts hold that boundaries are essential requisites for mental health; we conjectured that with social change blurring boundaries that had existed for centuries, some groups—both black and white—would be at high risk for mental illness.

Social change, in itself, can be anxiety producing if for no reason other than that the familiar has been supplanted by the new. With the nationwide shifts in standards and mores occurring during the 1960s, guidelines for gauging behavior were losing their validity. Uncertainty, as well as marginality, therefore, was a fundamental consideration in our study. In Chapter 3, "Alachua County and Its People," we will describe the characteristics of various groups hypothesized to be at either high or low risk for mental illness.

In summary, one of our major goals was to identify individuals who reported manifestations of mental illness and to appraise some social change processes associated with mental health risk. In this volume we will present the major findings from more than five years of research in a country typical in many ways of the changing South. To give the results applicability and meaning, we need to obtain a grasp of the social and physical environment and of the emotional climate in which the respondents lived. To do this and to understand the social structure in the South today, we must know the story of its development. As Cash perceived in 1941, history has shaped both the conscious and unconscious "mind of the South" which to some extent is still continuous with the past (20). In the next chapter, therefore, we will look briefly at two centuries of Southern history and focus especially on the caste system's influence on groups and behaviors that relate to mental health or illness.

REFERENCES

1. WOODWARD, C. V., *The Strange Career of Jim Crow*. 3rd Revised Edition. New York: Oxford University Press, 1974.
2. ORFIELD, G., *The Reconstruction of Southern Education*. New York: Wiley-Interscience, Division of John Wiley and Sons, 1968, 355.
3. MCKINNEY, J. C., and BOURQUE, L. B., "The Changing South: National Incorporation of a Region," *American Sociological Review*, Vol. 36, No. 3, June 1971, 399.
4. LEIGHTON, A. H., *My Name Is Legion*. New York: Basic Books, Inc., 1959.
5. HUGHES, C. C., TREMBLAY, M-A., RAPOPORT, R. N., and LEIGHTON, A. H., *People of Cove and Woodlot*. New York: Basic Books, Inc., 1960.
6. LEIGHTON, D. C., HARDING, J. S., MACKLIN, D. B., MACMILLAN, A. M., and LEIGHTON, A. H. *The Character of Danger*. New York: Basic Books, Inc., 1963.
7. SROLE, L., LANGNER, T. S., MICHAEL, S. T., OPLER, M. K., and RENNIE, T. A. G., *Mental Health in the Metropolis—The Midtown Manhattan Study. Vol. I.* New York: McGraw-Hill Book Company, Inc., 1962.
8. LANGNER, T. S., and MICHAEL, S. T., *Life Stress and Mental Health. Vol. II of the Midtown Manhattan Study, T.A.C. Rennie Series in Social Psychiatry*. Glencoe, Ill.: The Free Press of Glencoe, 1963.
9. Ibid., 67.
10. VOORHEES-ROSEN, D., and ROSEN, D. H., "Shetland: The Effects of Rapid Social Change on Mental Health," presented at the VI World Congress of Psychiatry, Honolulu, Hawaii, August 31, 1977.
11. ORTEGA Y GASSET, J., *Man and Crisis*. New York: W. W. Norton and Company, 1958.
12. FOWLES, J., *Daniel Martin*. Boston: Little, Brown and Co., 1977.
13. MURRAY, H. A., "What Should Psychologists Do about Psychoanalysis?", *Journal of Abnormal and Social Psychology*. Vol. 35, 1940, 150.
14. RUSSELL, B., *The Wisdom of the West*. Garden City, N.Y.: Doubleday and Company, Inc., 1959, 14.
15. WILSON, E. O., *Sociobiology*. Cambridge, Mass.: The Belknap Press of Harvard University Press, 1975.
16. ROSS, E. A., *Social Control*. New York: The Macmillan Company, 1901.
17. WHITING, J. W. M., "Sorcery, Sin, and the Superego: A Cross-Cultural Study of Some Mechanisms of Social Control." In: Ford, C. S., *Cross-Cultural Approaches*. New Haven, Conn.: Human Relations Area Files Press, 1967, 147-168.
18. PARK, R. E., "Human Migration and the Marginal Man," *The American Journal of Sociology*, Vol. 33, No. 6, May 1928, 893.
19. STONEQUIST, E. V., *The Marginal Man*. New York: Charles Scribner's Sons, 1937.
20. CASH, W. F., *The Mind of the South*. New York: Alfred A. Knopf, 1941.

2

The Historical and Social Background

Part I—History of the South

INTRODUCTION

Cash described the "mind of the South" as a frontier mind and likened it to a "tree with many age rings . . . but with its taproot in the Old South" (1). The South has run the gamut of historical and social experiences—colonization, national leadership, slavery, the plantation system, Civil War, defeat, political humiliation, the caste system, extensive illiteracy, poverty, and finally, industrialization (2). These experiences shaped a regional consciousness characterized by provincial and paradoxical elements: for the whites, a curious mixture of conformity and individualism, pride despite deprivation, and a romanticized sense of history. But for the blacks, the history of the South has meant servitude, learning how to survive, shuffling, inferiority, and, finally, resistance that culminated in courageous struggles for equality.

Historians agree that until recently the South has had a sectional identity that was shaped by its history. But that sectional identity was fragmented by the disruption of the social order and the convulsing rate of change occurring during the 1960s. To understand the people in our study, we need to review the variety of experiences that have molded their sentiments and attitudes. Historically determined sociocultural processes have placed various groups in relatively advantaged or disadvantaged positions, resistant or vulnerable to the changes that would be accompanied by adaptive or maladaptive reactions. In this chapter we shall sketch the history of the Southeast, since many of the people we studied were descendants of immigrants from Georgia and the Carolinas. Then we shall look in more detail at the caste system, its prescriptions and proscriptions for behaviors, and its consequent influences on mental health or illness. Finally, we shall present data on racial attitudes and racial distance obtained during the study and compare them with the results of other studies conducted during the last 50 years.

HISTORY

The early settlers who populated the area from Virginia to the Carolinas came almost exclusively from Great Britain. Spaniards and French had dominated a few areas on Florida's Atlantic Coast and the Gulf Coast from Pensacola to New Orleans, but their influence penetrated the interior only in the bayous of Louisiana and Mississippi. In the 17th and 18th centuries, political and economic factors stimulated the rapid colonization of the Southern seaboard states. The British were anxious to establish military bases as far south as possible to form a buffer against the growing Spanish control of the New World. And the shortage of land in 17th century England, attributable to the growth of the population, the demise of the feudal system, the Enclosure Acts, and disruptions accompanying the religious and civil wars, had created serious social and economic distress. English monarchs gave huge tracts of land to royal favorites and to the second and third sons of the nobility, precluded from inheriting a portion of the family estates by the law of primogeniture. In company with entrepreneurs, they enticed the poor and the misfits to emigrate, frequently as indentured servants.

The Southern Colonists

The colonists were not a representative cross-section of British society. A few, usually the landowners, were related to the nobility. Some were enterprising middle-class business men searching for economic opportunity. Fewer in the South than in the North were seeking freedom from the religious and political intolerance of the Stuart and Cromwell regimes. However, a small refugee group of Huguenots had settled in South Carolina and a small Moravian group had immigrated to North Carolina. Many of the immigrants were the remnants of defeated Irish and Scottish armies, felons, prostitutes, and marginal groups—those who had the choice of exile or prison. Furnas quotes Abbot Smith's summary: "[The Colonies] were a haven for the godly, a refuge for the oppressed, a challenge to the adventurous [but] particularly [in regard to] indentured servants . . . also the last resort of scoundrels . . . men and women who were dirty and lazy, rough, ignorant, lewd, and often criminal" (3). Even before the Revolution, prominent Americans were concerned that the Colonies had become a dumping ground for Britain's unfit and unwanted. For example, in 1760, Benjamin Franklin called the frontiersmen the "refuse of both [French and English] nations, often of the worst morals and the least discretion" (4).

Colonizing of Georgia

The colonization of Georgia, the last of the 13 original colonies to be established, is important for the background of our study because, a few generations later, the descendants of these settlers moved into northern Florida. In 1732, James Oglethorpe and a group of trustees obtained a royal charter for the new colony that was to extend south and west of the Savannah River. He was guided by political and humanitarian motives to curtail the influence of the Spanish in Florida and the French in Louisiana and to rehabilitate many of the British poor who were languishing in debtors' prisons. After the founding of Savannah in 1733, the colony was peopled by immigrants from the British Isles, largely the poverty-stricken Scots and Irish. Although the colony did not prosper during the next few decades, by the time of the Revolution it was populated by immigrants from Virginia and the Carolinas and was considered to be one of the richer of the first 13 colonies. When Florida was acquired from Spain by a treaty ratified in 1821, many of these land-hungry settlers streamed southward.

Genetically, it would appear that the colonists were not well endowed. But the laws of natural selection may have been influential. It is estimated that about 15% of the emigrants, presumably the less fit, died in the crowded, squalid sailing ships. And the mortality rate was high during the first few years after arrival, especially among those who were frail, lacked social adaptability, or had no material advantages. Survival required carving a home out of the wilderness and enduring the sun, the mosquitoes, and new diseases for which they had no immunity.

The Anglo-Saxon uniformity of the region, evidenced by the vast kinship networks and the similarity of proper names, has been noted by many writers. In *The South Today,* Walker Percy notes that almost everybody in Mississippi is a cousin (5). It has even been postulated that the Anglo-Saxon homogeneity is genetically responsible for the supposed "degeneracy" of the South.

DEVELOPMENT OF A CLASS SYSTEM

Especially in the Carolinas and later in Georgia, a class system developed within a generation or two. The port cities, such as Charleston and Savannah, became thriving commercial centers where first, backwoodsmen traded their pelts and later, farmers sold tobacco and cotton for shipment to the British Isles. A small, prosperous mercantile class emerged. After the Indians were pushed west and south, the land-hungry colonists deforested huge areas to plant rice, tobacco, and eventually, cotton. As the plantations grew, a landed gentry became established.

The Plantation System

This monolithic economic system based on a single crop—King Cotton—could not have developed without slavery. It was a profitable but wasteful system; a few became affluent while thousands received bare survival rations. Throughout the 18th century, thousands of slaves were imported from the West Indies and West Africa. By 1776 there were 450,000 slaves in the southern states and by the time of the Civil War there were more than 3 million. Within two generations after the invention of the cotton gin in 1793, the plantation system was fully established in most of the Southeast and was spreading rapidly. By the time the Missouri Compromise was reached in 1820, and all of the states of the Old South except Florida had been admitted to the Union, it had penetrated beyond the Mississippi River. The speed at which this massive economic and social system developed is nearly unprecedented. Moreover, this particular economic system structured the entire social order—a class-caste society composed of an aristocracy, a landed gentry, mercantile groups, a small middle-class, yeomen farmers, the marginal backwoodsmen in the hill country, and the slaves.

The usual pattern for the settler who later became a slaveholder was for a young man and his family gradually to increase their land holdings and slaves. By working arduously, an ambitious man and/or his sons could go from poverty to aristocracy in a short time. In less than a hundred years, a true upper class developed where there had been a pioneer society. But even at the time of the Civil War, the number of Southern slaveholders was relatively small. Despite the opulence displayed in the major cities and on the showplace plantations, as a region, the South was considerably poorer than the North. The great majority of the population was composed of poor whites who eked out a minimal existence in the hills or on bits of bottom land.

The Civil War

The economic and social systems that had developed during two centuries were shaken, but not drastically altered, by the Civil War.

The pre-existing social order persisted with only minor modifications. A few of the northern carpetbaggers became propertied landowners and the former slaves became tenant farmers whose "serfdom" was insured by the "furnish" system. The vast political and economic power of the North strangled the growth of Southern industry, and the rate of social change in the South was relatively slow. Perhaps most importantly, with the failure of Reconstruction in 1876, the caste system perpetuated the myth of Negro inferiority and offered the blacks very restricted educational and economic opportunities. As long as the economy of the South was dependent almost exclusively on cotton—from the invention of the cotton gin until World War II—there was, in Galbraith's words, a "forced equilibrium of poverty for all but the very few" (6). Although cotton production in the South was greater in 1877 than it had been before the Civil War, "Even if all income had been distributed to the sharecroppers, poverty would still have been acute" (7).

Part II—Class and Caste

Our concern with social order and mental health requires that we look closely at the class-caste system that has dominated the social history of the South. We view social order as both the hierarchical structure of groups within a society and as the process whereby this structure can be maintained or modified. Both class and caste systems shape the behavior of individuals and groups. Marx emphasized the importance of status within the social class system: "It is not the consciousness of men that determines their being, but, on the contrary, their social being that determines their consciousness" (8). A caste system is a finely tuned mechanism that both conditions and trains individuals to live within its boundaries. Thus, it determines mental patterns and controls the expression of emotions. Myrdal summarizes:

> [In the South, the] thousand and one precepts, etiquettes, taboos, and disabilities inflicted upon the Negro have a common purpose: to express the subordinate status of the Negro people and the exalted position of the whites (9).

DEFINITION OF CLASS AND CASTE

At this point we should define class and caste. The members of a class system are on a continuum with changing status always a possibility.

In contrast, the caste system is discontinuous—change in position can take place only within one's own caste and movement between castes is interdicted. A class system controls behavior much more implicitly and inconsistently than a caste system which regulates behavior not simply by custom, but also, by stipulating exactly what is permitted and what is forbidden.

On an open continent, with unbounded economic opportunity, American society became stratified—hierarchically ranked in terms of wealth, privilege, prestige or power. In addition, one of the most rigid and grievous caste systems in modern history developed in the South. It was based solely on the "color line" that, according to Blumer, "defines the approach of each racial group to the other . . . [and] limits the degree of access to each other [on] an axis of dominance and subordination" (10). Use of the "color line" to demarcate social groups occurred in a historic context that should have impeded the development of the caste system. The intellectual outlook and Western society's sentiments in the 18th century glorified rationalism, progress, and above all, the rights of man. The United States was dedicated by the founding fathers to be a classless, unfettered society devoted to the principles of liberty.

SLAVERY

Both the principle and the fact of slavery were in conflict with the American ideal and, indeed, the basic charters of our government. Dissensions about the slavery question almost disrupted the Constitutional Convention in 1787, threatening even the founding of our nation. Jefferson and others agonized over the means whereby the slavery issue had been evaded in the framing of the Constitution. During the first half of the 19th century, the issue became increasingly vicious and threatening. In the 1830s, when slavery was at its height, de Tocqueville wrote: "The most formidable of all the ills that threaten the future of the Union arises from the presence of a black population upon its territory; and in contemplating the cause of the present embarrassments, or the future dangers of the United States, the observer is invariably led to this as a primary fact" (11). Many leaders in the North hoped that slavery could be confined to a few Southern states and that as it became economically unprofitable it would eventually disappear. But the profits resulting from the invention of the cotton gin and the rapid industrialization of the North provided marked economic advantages for the Southern planters who supplied the raw material—cotton—and for the manufacturers in New England and Great Britain.

The institutionalization of slavery which formed the basis of the caste system succeeded in the United States despite an unfavorable intellectual climate and at a time when slavery was being abolished in other parts of the world. Perhaps this incongruity can be traced to the relative fragility of sentiments and ideals when they compete with economic forces that offer privilege and wealth. But such conflicts must be resolved in the minds of those facing the dilemmas, at least temporarily. Regarding the black along a spectrum ranging from the most humane view of him as a child to the malevolent concept of him as a primitive, savage, lower-order being was probably the fundamental rationalization for slavery. And some whites in the South appear to have believed that they were bettering the lot of the savage. For example, James Truslow Adams wrote: "[W]ould the 12,000,000 of negroes in the United States today (sic) prefer that their ancestors had never been enslaved and that therefore they themselves, if alive, should at this moment be living as savages or barbarians in the African jungle?" (12).

DEVELOPMENT OF THE CASTE SYSTEM

Although emancipation provided limited social and political freedom for the Southern Negroes, it did not alter the common opinion that they were somehow subhuman. This belief provided the basis for the intricate and covert caste system which succeeded the simpler, openly acknowledged, system of slavery. Dollard points out that the caste system maintained "the essence of the old status in the South" (13). Thus, a rigidly orchestrated, harshly enforced set of social and economic regulations was developed as a way of keeping Negroes as slaves while preserving the fiction that they were free.

A caste system is used to maintain social order. It trains the individual, regulates behavior, rewards compliance, and punishes nonconformity. Davis and Dollard explain: "In the personal experience of a white person or of a Negro in the South, the caste controls appear as sanctions defining the conditions under which he may reach the basic biological and social goals. They are experienced as privileges and punishments which facilitate or block the road to certain basic goals" (14).

Economic and Social Psychological Aspects of the Caste System

The system operated as the economic and social control processes that preserved and perpetuated the social order by affording advantages to the privileged and by controlling basic drives—aggression and sex. Consequently, the caste system's rewards and punishments were both material and psychological. For middle- and upper-class whites, the major advantage was economic—rampant exploitation of blacks and, to only a slightly lesser extent, of the poor whites. The poor whites were rewarded by somewhat more advantageous positions as long as the Negroes could be restricted to the lowest-paying and most menial jobs. Psychologically, the color line supported even the poorest white man's conviction that he was free and superior. About him, at every hand, his "inferiors" were visible. That barrier, the color line, not only furnished ego support, but also buttressed the poor white's identity. The conditions of oppressive poverty, illiteracy, and disease did not bar the poor white from a consortium with the white gentry, businessmen, and entrepreneurs. And, indeed, these diverse groups, often bearing similar surnames, could recall that they were blood-related.

Furthermore, the poor whites could express their frustration by aggression, releasing basic drives. In 1944, Myrdal described the violence which whites were allowed to display toward blacks: "It is the custom in the South to permit whites to resort to violence and threats of violence against the life, personal security, property and freedom of movement of Negroes" (15). Until recently, the whites' aggression toward the blacks, as well as that of blacks against blacks, went unpunished. The legal system operated according to the "quadruple standard"—Anglo-Saxon law for white against white; lynch law for black against white; pseudo-law for white against black; and no law for black against black.

Although the caste system forbade miscegenation and restricted the middle-class white males' sexual exploitation of black women, the sexual adventures of lower-class white males with blacks were accepted. It was understood that white youth, regardless of class, would and could use black women as a sexual outlet.

Among the whites, the caste system's material disadvantages were felt by the poor. Maintaining the caste system automatically involved allegiance to the social order which for the numerous poor whites meant belief in the system and acceptance of lower-class status—a life of hardship and disease.

The psychological disadvantages for whites were obsessive fear, ambivalence, and guilt. Although there were only three slave rebellions, Southern whites were haunted by the fear of black uprisings. Such fears of aggression and reprisal appear to contain a substantial element of projection, possibly stemming from guilt.

The ambivalences can be traced to close associations maintained by the whites with individual blacks who had been mammies or trusted house and field servants and also to the ever-present contradiction between democratic ideals of equality and the harsh realties of oppression. Styron observes: "White Southerners like and love individual Negroes and sometimes Negroes in general; they apparently also hate them" (16). The clash between sentiments of liberty—"the land of the free"—and the obvious segregation and exploitation of the blacks created inner contradictions that were only salved, not resolved, by denial and rationalization. According to Myrdal such contradictions produce threats to moral integrity and "all of the confusion, the ambiguity, and inconsistency which lurks in the basement of man's soul. . . . Out of the strain comes a sense of uneasiness and awkwardness which always seems attached to the Negro problem" (17).

Southern novelists, Faulkner in particular, have portrayed segments of Southern white society as being haunted by guilt attributable to the economic and sexual exploitation of the blacks for almost two centuries. Thus, the deprived conditions of the blacks and the obvious inequities of the caste system produced disquiet—fear, ambivalence, and guilt—and required that the whites rationalize, deny, and repress in order to maintain some degree of inner harmony.

The caste system afforded the blacks few, if any, material advantages. Until the 1950s, the economy of the Southeast relied primarily on agricultural production. The pre-Civil War plantation existed in only a slightly changed form as a tenant farm, tilled by sharecroppers. The owner supplied the land and the materials; the tenant and his family provided the labor in return for a share of the profits from the sale of the crop. Sharecropping was a way of life for rural Negroes, an extension of the old plantation system with a change of terminology from slave to tenant. Nevertheless, the blacks did develop a class structure within the caste that was based on economics and also, until recently, on skin color and hair type. Relative whiteness and straightness of hair assigned one arbitrarily to a higher status. Kardiner and Ovesey conclude that: "This class structure differs in no way whatsoever from its prototype in white society" (18). Earlier, Myrdal stated that the Negro upper classes "have their social status and, indeed, their existence as an upper class only *by virtue of their relationship to the lower classes of Negroes*" (19). Thus, the lower-class black has historically been the bottom layer of both the class and caste systems.

In order for a caste system to remain functional, it must accord some privileges, at least as compensations, to those who are stamped "inferior."

Freedom for instinctual expression and, indeed, for emotional expression could be viewed as the major compensation for the blacks as long as it was limited to interactions within caste boundaries. Legal and police authorities not only connived with black aggression against black but also considered their violence to be a normal outlet as well as evidence of inferiority. The violence inflicted by blacks against blacks, illustrated by the high homicide rate and typified by numerous slashings and cuttings, is characteristic of the behavior of oppressed people described by Fanon. He attributed the intraracial aggression among colonized Algerians prior to the War of Liberation—comparable to the experience of the blacks in the South—to the degraded quality of life, oppression, and frustration (20).

Movement out of the caste system was limited for blacks. Migration to the North was only a partial escape and "passing as white" was difficult. In *Born to Rebel,* Mays states that the Negro who came of age in the South in the early part of this century had to obey two imperatives in order to stay alive. These were to: 1) stay out of "trouble," and 2) "live in the world without being part of it—stay free in the mind and not succumb to the environment" (21).

The Caste System and the Black Personality

It is possible that the effects of slavery and the caste system have influenced the blacks psychologically as well as socioeconomically. In *Racism and Psychiatry,* Thomas and Sillen point out that epidemiology has been misused to rationalize the caste system, that white psychiatrists have attempted to delineate a specific Negro personality pattern, and that often studies of mental illness in blacks have tended to overemphasize the pathological elements and make generalizations which implied that, as a group, they lacked personality integration (22).

Witmer, Greene, O'Malley and others expressed concern about the increasingly large numbers of Negroes who were admitted to state hospitals in the decades following the Civil War (23-25). According to 1860 Census figures, there were only 766 "colored insane" in the United States; in 1880 there was 6157. In 20 years the rate quintupled from 16.9 to 91.2 per 100,000. At the time, most Southern psychiatrists attributed this striking increase to the removal from dependency status and the necessity to meet the stresses and strains of a competitive existence. It was even suggested that slavery had had a beneficial influence on blacks' mental health. But E. M. Greene pointed out that the harsh conditions of life for Southern Negroes in the 1870s and 1880s were largely responsible for the increased admissions to State hospitals in the South. The only jobs available to the blacks demanded arduous manual labor and the skimpy wages barely purchased the minimal necessities of life. Consequently, mental illnesses produced by trauma and malnutrition were common. Moreover, the State hospital was the last refuge for the infirm and the elderly who were unable to work—the family could not afford to feed an "extra mouth." The census data indicate that the blacks, as well as others, were using the State hospitals as social welfare facilities. Epidemiology was and is misused when admission rates to state hospitals are thought to reflect incidence or prevalence rates in the general population and it is abused when generalizations about racial differences in mental illness are drawn from such data. Only community studies with random samples of the population can furnish prevalence data because those admitted to public hospitals are selected groups.

Based on psychoanalytic studies of 25 blacks in the early 1950s, Kardiner and Ovesey conjecture that a "degradation of self-esteem" was a prominent aspect of the Negro personality (26). They believe that there is a "basic Negro personality" which is not innately characteristic of the race but which developed as a reaction to oppression. Some of the characteristics of the basic personality were revealed by Rorschach studies which disclosed qualities of imitativeness and denial and the equation: "aggression + control = emotional flatness" (27). In *The Mark of Oppression,* they conclude that this "basic Negro personality is, however, a caricature of the corresponding white personality, because the Negro must adapt to the same culture, must accept the same social goals, but without the ability to achieve them. This limitation in social opportunities accounts for the difference in personality configuration" (28).

We think, however, that despite pervasive racial discrimination and flagrant oppression, many blacks have displayed a capacity for adaptation which has not only enabled them to survive but also to find and utilize compensations in their daily lives and often develop their creative capacities. This strength in the face of adversity can be interpreted only as evidence of an integrated personality structure and mental health.

In 1969, Anne Moody, writing her story as a black girl "coming of age in Mississippi," vividly describes the sanctions against Negroes (29). She explores the myth of the passive Negro humbly accepting his station and states flatly that the only thing preventing expression of the pent-up emotions was total unrelenting fear of the white retaliation that was sure to come. It took courage for a black person to register to vote or even to ask others to register while knowing that his house could be burned in the night or he could be killed at any time.

The Change

In the 1960s the picture was changing in North Florida. It appeared that blacks were undergoing an intensification of racial consciousness. The blacks were not accepting white standards as they had in previous generations. Consequently, the whites were not able to maintain their "de facto" prestige in the black community. Derogatory terms such as "Whitey," etc. were being used publicly where formerly they were unspoken, at least in the white community. The shifting standards of beauty, toward the "natural" Afro look in both men and women and the disappearance of "process hairdos" intended to straighten hair illustrate this change.

In "Georgia Boy Comes Home" Louis Lomax describes a return to Valdosta, Georgia, less than 100 miles north of Alachua County (30). In that 1965 trip he noted the differences in his encounters with whites—differences that involved speech, gesture, and posture. The encounters were characterized by restraint on the part of both the blacks and whites and a general relaxing of the former strictures on Negro behavior. But even though he felt free and equal, he could express himself openly only when he was in the company of blacks.

Such containment of emotion requires excessive self-control, often secured at the price of inner turmoil or psychosomatic illness. "Playing it cool" serves to maintain self-esteem and manifest some degree of aggressive masculinity in the face of frustration and conflict—interracial or intergenerational.

Reports of Anger

In our study, each of the 1645 respondents in the random sample was asked how often he or she became "really angry"; 68% reported "seldom or never," 27% reported "sometimes," and 5% reported "often" or "all the time." Significantly more of the younger than older respondents, regardless of race, reported feeling anger. There were no statistically significant race or sex differences.

On the item questioning how the respondent expressed anger, significantly more whites than blacks reported verbalizing it or using facial contortions whereas significantly more blacks reported "withdrawing or doing nothing." There were no significant racial differences on expression of anger by aggressive acts toward other persons or objects.

Part III—Racial Distance

PREVIOUS SURVEYS

To evaluate possible changes in racial attitudes during the last few decades, we looked at the results of previous surveys of racial distance. In 1928, Bogardus conducted a nation-wide survey of 1725 respondents (31). He found that only 1.4% of the whites would accept interracial marriage; about 9 to 12% would accept blacks as friends or neighbors, and approximately 40% thought it was all right for blacks and whites to engage in the same occupation. Almost one-third of the whites evinced very restrictive attitudes; one-fifth of all whites wanted to limit blacks to visiting status in the United States and one-eighth advocated their complete exclusion from the country. The 205 blacks generally displayed more accepting racial attitudes: 6% reported that interracial marriage was acceptable, 34% indicated willingness to socialize with whites, and 66% believed that it was all right for blacks and whites to be neighbors. The white Southerners expressed greater racial distance than the whites from elsewhere in the nation. Less than 1% accepted intermarriage, only about 10% wanted blacks as friends or neighbors, and 35% wanted to exclude blacks from the country.

In their 1963 survey, Brink and Harris found that white Southerners' racial attitudes were changing. They reported that 45% would not object to having their children go to school with blacks, 26% would accept a black family as a neighbor, and 9% had no objection to intermarriage (32).

OUR FINDINGS

We used a modified form of the Bogardus Racial Distance Scale to measure racial distance in Alachua County. We were also interested in possible relationships between the degree of racial distance (regardless of race) and our respondents' states of mental health and illness.* Warheit, et al. classified our random sample as shown in Table 2-1.

More than 66% of the blacks were assimilators, in contrast to about 20% of the whites, and only 2% of the blacks were either accommodators or avoiders as opposed to almost 20% of the whites. Assimilation and accommodation were endorsed more often by those who were young,

* In Chapter 9 we will present comparisons of racial distance and mental health illness ratings.

TABLE 2-1

Classification of racial distance by percentages of respondents.

Classification	Example	Respondents (N=1645) (%)
Assimilators	Accepting interracial marriage	33.5
Acceptors	Endorsing face-to-face relationships	50.5
Accommodators	Endorsing only secondary relationships such as attendance at schools and churches	6.1
Avoiders	Advocating complete segregation	9.8

male, students, educationally advanced, or in upper occupational statuses, regardless of race. As might be anticipated, whites who grew up in other parts of the country (Elsewhere) reported considerably less racial distance than those who had lived in the South all of their lives (33).*

Our findings indicated that racial attitudes toward acceptance and even assimilation had changed markedly in the 40 years since Bogardus conducted his study. The most marked differences appeared in comparisons of the various generations. More of those under age 30 reported acceptance of integration than those age 30 to 59, and especially 60+. We conjecture that these differences reflect the social changes that had transpired over three generations.

It would be a mistake, however, to overestimate the changes which have occurred in the public arena. The "color line" is still visible in the South; as a barrier, only its outer reaches have been broached. Certain aspects of the caste system have withstood the impact of sociocultural change. Although some blacks still "shuffled" and appeared to be eager to acquiesce, deference had been replaced to a considerable extent by quiet rectitude which preserved emotional and social distance.

Part IV—Social Change in the "New" South

Lacking in progress, tradition-bound, and predominantly rural, life in the South prior to World War II was frequently viewed by outsiders as an anachronism—out of step with American political and social ac-

* For specific purposes we divided our sample by geographic origin: Alachua, Other Florida, Deep South, and Elsewhere. See Chapter 10.

tivity. Southern towns were stereotyped as sleepy and rural areas as indolent. Clichés epitomized groups in the social order—"decadent" aristocrats, "white trash," the "happy" Negro, etc. The orientation was predominately rural and local.

Villages and small towns, usually the county seats, were loci of political and commercial activity. Only a few large centers could be designated as truly urban. Throughout vast areas, rural life styles prevailed and many traditions persisted unchanged from pre-Civil War days. The economy was primarily agricultural; black tenant farmers and migrant workers were trapped by the system. Legally the tenant was free to move and many did, but to most, the fear of even greater economic insecurity was a formidable obstacle to geographic mobility. The low level of education and skill and consequent disadvantages in competing, as well as the generally depressed economy of the 1930s, further restricted both geographic and social mobility for poor whites and blacks alike.

Around the turn of the century, cheap labor and ready access to raw materials had lured industrialists to build factories in what were to become infamous mill towns. However, because of absentee ownership, the absence of a cohesive working class that could fight for its rights, and the lack of both an industrial base and a tradition, industrialization proceeded slowly and the region reaped few benefits. Although employment by manufacturers increased twice as rapidly as in the country as a whole (more than 7% between 1929 and 1937), it was limited mainly to work in textile and tobacco mills at non-union wages (34). In 1940, the general level of industrialization in the Southeast was less than one-half that of the rest of the United States.

With the movement in the 1930s from farms to "public works," many of the men, particularly those in the generation that had made the move, had serious difficulties adjusting. They were not accustomed to working long hours in confined areas, regulating their lives by factory whistles, or taking direct orders from foremen and supervisors. There is some evidence to indicate that this loss of individualism was associated with increased emotional illness and psychosomatic disorders among the men, as well as among the women a generation or two later when their roles began to change.

In the 1940s, life in the South was characterized by novelists and social historians as tortured and decadent, dominated by pervasive poverty, malnutrition, disease, and cultural isolation. Cash concluded his 1941 volume: "In the coming days and probably soon, it [the South] is likely to have to prove its capacity for adjustment far beyond what has been true in the past" (35). Our study reports on this capacity for adjustment, as measured by mental health risk.

Like many other parts of our country, the Southeast has been undergoing extremely rapid social change since World War II. The magnitude of the rural-urban shift has been dramatic. In 1940, 65% of the population lived in rural areas; 35% in urban. The 1970 Census figures showed a reversal; 39% lived in rural areas and 61% in urban settings (36).

The urbanization of the Southeast has offered blacks opportunities to break away from previous restrictions. As early as 1940, Davis and Dollard found "caste taboos more numerous and the punishments for infractions more severe in the rural areas than in the city itself" (37). It would seem, therefore, that urbanization has furnished blacks with opportunities to develop new behavioral patterns.

The movement to urban areas accompanied the industrialization of the region. McKinney and Bourque's comparisons showed that Southern workers had moved out of "agriculturally-oriented jobs into professional, clerical, craft, and operative's jobs" at a much faster rate than elsewhere in the United States (38).

Indices of income and education also showed major changes. Per capita personal income in the South increased from $356 in 1940 to $2,559 in 1968, whereas in the rest of the nation it increased from $680 to $3,719 during the same period. McKinney and Bourque note that although incomes in the South still had not come up to national levels, they increased at a faster rate than elsewhere in the nation, particularly in the decade 1940 to 1950. Although educationally the South was about 10 years behind the rest of the country, McKinney and Bourque's 1971 projections of data on school enrollment showed that "the median education of persons 25 and over in the South should be very close to that of the non-South by 1980" (39).

These drastic changes were produced by a number of concurrent events. During World War II, many Northerners became acquainted with the South for the first time. Its favorable climate, undeveloped resources, relative abundance of unskilled labor, and improved communications lured tourists as well as industrialists and entrepreneurs into the area.

SUMMARY

The black-white issue probably has been the most significant force shaping the sectional identity of the South. First slavery, followed by the caste system, and then the impact of desegregation have distinctively marked the social and political history of the South for two centuries. But the conflicting emotions aroused by racial issues have resulted in elaborate denial systems and complicated mental gymnastics for whites and blacks and for the politically liberal and conservative alike.

The sentiments espoused by whites in the late 1960s included a conformity that developed in spite of the frontier background with its intense individualism and pioneer traditions. This defiant conformity can be attributed to the alliance of all whites against all blacks, regardless of wealth or education. It was reinforced by reminders of a historical cataclysm that, of all Americans, only the Southerners had shared—defeat in war. This Southern conformity embodied a conservatism intent upon maintaining the social order, particularly the caste system with its firm boundaries for segregation. Admixed with frontier individualism, it produced a secessionist ethos in the 1830s that, until recently, endured as a viable trend—exemplified by the formation of Thurmond's Dixiecrat Party in 1948 and Wallace's American Party in 1968. As late as 1965, Brogan noted that an intense desire to shut out the rest of the world was characteristic of the white South (40).

Many of the outward manifestations of the caste system have been disappearing with the rapid social change in the Southeast that followed World War II. Kardiner and Ovesey note that after emancipation, the Negro ". . . was given a nominal freedom, but without the opportunities for full participation" (41). We suggest that the same phenomena may be appearing as a result of civil rights gains in the 1960s—political equality but not concomitant economic opportunity. Our findings, therefore, must be interpreted in the light of the political, social, and economic changes occurring at the time our study was conducted.

To assess the degree of mental health and illness in a community in terms of social psychiatric impairment (SPI), we are compelled to maintain our awareness of the variety of sentiments that characterize the consciousness of the region. We have taken a brief look at the South as it was, is, and is becoming. We have examined briefly different groups' attitudes, interactions, and aspirations, as well as tensions, conflicts, and symptoms of mental illness, using a frame of reference that rests on self-concept theory and encompasses the dynamics of social change, particularly as they apply to a changing social order. In the next chapter we shall present a brief description of Alachua County and its inhabitants' characteristics and sentiments.

REFERENCES

1. Cash, W. F., *The Mind of the South.* New York: Alfred A. Knopf, 1941, x.
2. Mitchell, B., and Mitchell, G. S., *The Industrial Revolution in the South.* Baltimore, Md.: Johns Hopkins Univ. Press, 1930, ix.
3. Furnas, J. C., *Americans: A Social History of the United States 1587-1914.* New York: Putnam, 1969, 99.
4. See Reference 3, 39.
5. Percy, W., "Mississippi: The Fallen Paradise." In: W. Morris (Ed.), *The South Today, 100 Years after Appomattox.* New York: Harper & Row, Harper Colothorn Edition, 1966, 66-79.
6. Galbraith, J. K., *The Age of Uncertainty.* Boston: Houghton Mifflin Co., 1977, 289.
7. Ibid., 291.
8. Marx, K., and Engels, F., Cited in: Mills, C. W., *Images of Man.* New York: George Braziller, Inc., 1960, 101.
9. Myrdal, G., *An American Dilemma.* New York: Harper & Brothers Publishers, 1944, 66.
10. McKinney, J. C., and Thompson, E. T., *The South in Continuity and Change.* Durham, N.C.: Duke University, 1965, 322.
11. DeTocqueville, A., *Democracy in America, Vol. 1.* F. Bowen (Ed.). New York: Vintage Books, A. A. Knopf, Random House, 1945, 370.
12. See Reference 9, 44.
13. Dollard, J., *Caste and Class in a Southern Town.* Garden City, N.Y.: Doubleday and Company, 1949, 62.
14. Davis, A., and Dollard, J., *Children of Bondage.* Washington, D.C.: American Council on Education, 1940, 243.
15. See Reference 9, 558.
16. Styron, W., "This Quiet Dust." See Reference 5, 15-38.
17. See Reference 9, xlv.
18. Kardiner, A., and Ovesey, L., *The Mark of Oppression.* New York: The World Publishing Company, 1951, 62.
19. See Reference 9, 703.
20. Fanon, F., *The Wretched of the Earth.* New York: Grove Press, Inc., 1963.
21. Mays, B. E., *Born to Rebel.* New York: Charles Scribner's Sons, 1971, 23.
22. Thomas, A., and Sillen, S., *Racism and Psychiatry.* New York: Brunner/Mazel, Publishers, 1972.
23. Witmer, A. H., "Insanity in the Colored Race in the United States," *Alienist and Neurologist.* Vol. 12, 1891, 19-30.
24. Greene, E. M., "Manic-Depressive Psychosis in the Negro," *American Journal of Insanity.* Vol. 73, 1917, 619-625.
25. O'Malley, M., "Psychoses in the Colored Race," *Journal of Insanity,* Vol. 71, 1914, 309-336.
26. See Reference 18, 47.
27. Ibid., 337.
28. Ibid., 317.
29. Moody, A., *Coming of Age in Mississippi.* New York: The Dial Press Inc., 1968.
30. Lomax, L. E., "Georgia Boy Goes Home." See Reference 5, 50-65.
31. Bogardus, E. S.. *Immigration and Race Attitudes.* New York: D. C. Heath and Company, 1928.
32. Brink, W., and Harris, L., *The Negro Revolution in America.* New York: Simon and Schuster, 1963, 148.
33. Warheit, G. J., Swanson, E., and Schwab, J. J., "A Study of Racial Attitudes in a

Southeastern County: A Confirmation of National Trends." *Phylon*. Atlanta, Ga.: Atlanta University Press. Vol. 36, No. 4, 1975, 395-406.
34. McKinney, J. C., and Bourque, L. B., "The Changing South: National Incorporation of a Region," *American Sociological Review*, Vol. 36, June, 1971, 399-412.
35. See Reference 1, 429.
36. See Reference 34, 404.
37. See Reference 14.
38. See Reference 34.
39. Ibid.
40. Brogan, D. W., "The Impending Crisis of the Deep South." See Reference 5, 39-49.
41. See Reference 18, 384.

3

Alachua County and Its People

Alachua County has shared most of the region's historical and social experiences. Furthermore, it was in the process of being more completely transformed by the rapid social change than most of the Southeast except for the urban centers. The large State University, located at Gainesville, the county seat, attracted many young persons from elsewhere in Florida and graduate students from many parts of the country. The newly-arrived technologists associated with large companies that had located small research and development branches in Gainesville also had an impact as they enlarged the middle, upper-middle, and high socioeconomic status (SES) groups. Education, health, and agriculture were the predominant industries. Elements of both the Old and the New South gave the County variety and vitality.

GEOGRAPHIC CHARACTERISTICS

Alachua County occupies 965 square miles in North Central Florida. It is not a discrete ecological unit; on a map it appears to be about square—the county lines are largely artificial. Adjacent counties resemble it roughly in terrain but tend to be more rural and generally much poorer. Alachua itself consists of two ecological zones with differing soil types. The western section has the higher elevation and a soil favorable for raising cattle and growing tobacco and melons. The eastern half is less prosperous; in the northeast the topography is hilly and there are many small forests of pine. The southeast is low and swampy, dotted with marshes and small lakes that are popular fishing sites.

HISTORY AND SOCIAL CHARACTERISTICS OF THE COUNTY

Tradition has it that about 600 A.D. Indians settled the southern part of this area. Remnants of their pottery indicate they were an agrarian group. The first white men entered the area in 1528 and DeSoto went through it in 1539 on his way to the Mississippi. At that time the region was occupied by the Timuqua tribe who established a small village now known as Micanopy, about 10 miles south of present-day Gainesville. In 1774, the Spanish established missions nearby and began raising cattle. As the British colonized Georgia in the 18th century, the Seminoles and Creeks were pushed into Florida and Micanopy became the "chief town of the seminoles under the fierce Secoffee and his successors King Payne, Boleck, John Hicks, and Micanopy" (1).

The first permanent white settlement was established by Don Fernando de la Maza Arrendondo who had received a 24-square mile land grant from the King of Spain in 1819. His choice of Micanopy as his major settlement was influenced by "the wealth of cattle and horses possessed by the former inhabitants and the abundant crops they had been able to raise" (2). Through the efforts of Arrendondo and a land agent, Moses Levy, settlers from Georgia, Alabama, and the Carolinas began to populate the County. The Spanish influence waned; Florida, which had been seized by the British in the 18th century and later regained by the Spanish, was formally ceded to the United States by a treaty ratified in 1821.

The small town of Alachua, 10 miles northwest of Gainesville, was settled quickly in the 1820s and designated as the county seat by the Territorial Legislature in 1825. The other small towns were settled in the middle of the century. The County was organized as a legal entity in 1854 and Gainesville became the County Seat in 1856.

Furnas notes that after the extended Creek War, North Florida enjoyed a "marked expansion of the Dixie-style economy of slaves, cotton and some sugar. . . . Poor whites drifted across the border bringing their usual hand-to-mouth culture. It gave them a better living . . . where growing seasons were longer and game and fish more plentiful. But they retained the generic name crackers, (short for corncracker) of their Georgian heritage" (3). In the 1840s, health seekers from the North began to visit the North Florida region each winter. The area's reputation for having a healthy climate was spread by Union prisoners who returned to the North with tales of oranges growing wild and sunshine all year round.

During most of the latter part of the 19th century, the County was almost completely rural in character. The first railroad, opened in 1855, traversed Alachua from east to west, connecting Fernandina on the Atlantic Coast with Cedar Key and the Gulf Coast. Citrus, cotton, tobacco, corn, peanuts, and melons were the principal crops. Following the Great Freeze of 1886, the production of citrus declined drastically but cattle raising and farming continued to be the predominant occupations. Just before the turn of the century, the area became more accessible to Northerners. Coincident with the opening of Florida's eastern coast—the development of St. Augustine, Palm Beach, and other cities by Flagler and other entrepreneurs—and the exhaustion of northern Florida's virgin timber, the transportation pattern changed from east-west to north-south.

The Growth in Population

Alachua's population increased gradually during the latter part of the 19th century. Gainesville became The City; its continued growth and dominance of the region were assured when the land grant university was opened there in 1906.

Until the last few decades, Alachua had been a fairly typical Southern county. Its men and boys joined the Confederate armies and, just at the end of the Civil War, invading Northern troops defeated a small Southern force in a skirmish near Gainesville. There were a number of large plantations; remnants of slave quarters could still be seen in Gainesville and some outlying areas in the early 1970s. After the Civil War most of the blacks worked as tenant farmers until the University developed as a major educational institution and employer following World War II.

After 1945 the population of the County increased tremendously, concurrent with the development of the University as the educational, medical, and technological center of the region. The rapid growth is illustrated by the 271% increase in the total population, the 524% increase in urban population, and the rise in median family income from $1,310 to $8,329 between 1940 and 1970. Over 16,000 people moved into Alachua County during the decade of the 1960s alone.

Gainesville and Its Suburbs

The preponderant growth in the population occurred in Gainesville, and particularly, its suburbs. By 1970 its population was 64,510, of whom 12,044 were black (4). In most of the other towns, the population increase was negligible. Some even lost residents. During the 1960s, Gainesville developed as a "strip city," particularly along the major streets that bounded the University and led to the new, expanding suburbs. The area around the University, near the center of the city, was saturated with apartments, condominiums, and homes occupied mainly by students. The elite section of old Gainesville, just northeast of the center of the city, was deteriorating. Large old mansions were being divided into apartments for students and the growing "hippie" colonies.

Almost all of the blacks lived in the eastern and southeastern portions of the city where the quality of housing was generally poor. The white middle and upper classes lived mainly in the rapidly growing western and northwestern areas in affluent homes and new condominiums. Many of the blue-collar workers, young couples "just getting started," and persons in the lower-middle socioeconomic stratum lived in relatively new small houses in the northeastern section of the city. The poor whites lived in scattered pockets along the entire eastern fringe of the city.

By the time the preliminary County-wide field work for our study was being completed in 1970, the population pattern was similar to that of many rural and semi-rural counties in the United States, particularly in the South and mid-West. Approximately two-thirds of the total population lived in Gainesville; about one-third of the total rural population lived in the seven small towns concentrically located about 10 to 15 miles from Gainesville; the remainder lived in small, often secluded settlements or on the farms that extend throughout most of the County.

In 1970, of the 104,746 inhabitants in the County, 82.3% were white. Most of the balance were black—there were only a few Orientals and Indians. The percentage of blacks in Alachua and surrounding counties was slightly higher than that of the rest of the State. The population was basically young: about 31% under 18, 62% from 18 to 64, and 6% over 64. The median age was 23.4 years; only one other Florida county had a lower median age.

The percentage of married persons, 55.3%, was slightly lower than that for the nation which had 64.2% married males and 58.9% married females. Of the unmarried, 35.5% were single (never married), 3.3% were divorced, and 5.9% were widowed.

Economic Patterns

The average per capita income in 1970 was $3,193, slightly lower than the average in Florida, $3,741, or the $3,966 for the United States. But annual family incomes covered a broad range; although 27.2% of the families had annual incomes of less than $5,000, 27.3% had incomes in the $5,000-$8,999 category, 27.9% in the $9,000-$14,000 category, and 17.6% had annual family incomes greater than $15,000.

The University and the County, State, and Federal Governments were the principal employers. Consequently, Alachua had a fairly sizeable white middle-class population. Agriculture, however, was still prospering, especially as agri-business. In 1969 there were 906 farms in the County; the average size was 335.6 acres and the average farm with buildings was valued at $89,722. Throughout the County unemployment was low in 1970; only 2.1% of the total labor force of 43,720 (5). Many of the poor were receiving a low level of public assistance; e.g., in February 1972, 1226 elderly persons received an average payment of $66.93 and 1825 families received Aid for Dependent Children averaging $85.10 (6).

The quality of housing varied immensely. There were many upper-middle and upper-class homes in the new suburbs, some luxury condominiums, and stately farm houses. But there were numerous semi-secluded trailer parks, some of which were crowded and shabby. Ten percent of the housing units in the County lacked plumbing; most, but not all of these, were in the rural areas and were occupied by blacks.

Racial and Social Patterns

As we saw in the preceding chapter, racial distance had lessened significantly but, except for the greater University community, there was little evidence of racial integration. The enforced desegregation of the schools in the early 1970s was accompanied by turbulence and dispute. Throughout most of the County, the blacks lived in small, poor, isolated communities, centers of church and community life that were removed from the rapid change, contrasting life styles, and tensions that were evident in Gainesville where many of them worked.

In Gainesville, the sharply segregated black communities became known as dangerous for whites at night in the late 1960s. In addition to the latent black-white conflict, other groups were polarized. The rising crime rate in the 1960s was blamed on the growth of the "hippie" culture. (In addition to the almost 25,000 college students, Gainesville attracted numerous young persons who lived on the fringe of the University community.) Also, the large number of faculty and other University employees were regarded as "different" by the more conservative natives who were losing their power and prestige to the newcomers. With the rapid change in the County, we could observe dislocations in job patterns, status shifts, and intergenerational differences as well as changing values and norms.

Community Integration and Social Support Systems

We were also interested in the degree of community integration and the nature and extent of the respondents' social support systems. Alachua County is located in the "Bible Belt." Consequently, we were not surprised to find that many of the 1645 respondents in the major survey were Southern Baptists and a sizeable proportion belonged to fundamentalist churches. However, only 60% reported church attendance. Approximately 40% also reported membership in clubs and/or organizations. Club members were mainly in the 30-44 age group and in the upper middle or high SES groups. About 66% of the respondents, proportionately many blacks, females, older persons, and those in the middle, lower-middle and low SES quintiles, had close relatives living nearby. Over 80% reported they had close friends living in the community; about 75% of them reported that they could call upon friends for help in times of need.

The relationship between availability of social support systems and mental health or illness was emphasized decades ago by Emile Durkheim (7). He feared that the increasing secularization and loss of secondary institutions (les corps intermédiares) apparent in Western society at the turn of the century would produce anomie and have deleterious consequences. In his work, *Support Systems and Community Mental Health,* Gerald Caplan insists that "kin and kith supports" are needed for "continuing guidance and direction as well as self-validation" (8). Drawing upon more than three decades of experience in community mental health, he concludes that support systems "play a significant part in maintaining the psychological and physical integrity of the individual over time" (9).

Sentiments and Attitudes

Some of the respondents' sentiments and attitudes were reflected by their responses to the following questions or statements:

Q. How important is religion in helping you meet daily problems?
A. Very important—56%; fairly important—14%.

S. Life has changed so much in our modern world that people are powerless to control their own lives.
R. Disagree—46%.

S. There is a faster pace and pressure in everyday life.
R. Agree—68%.

Q. How do you like living in this community?
A. A great deal—60%; some—22%.

Q. What are your wishes and hopes for the future?
A. Improved standard of living—32%; happy family life—31%; good health—22%; opportunities for children—19%.

Q. What are your fears and worries about the future?
A. Ill health—21%; ill health of a family member—20%; inadequate standard of living—13%; unhappy family life—10%; war—10%.

Geographic Mobility

About 33% of our respondents had lived in Alachua for more than 20 years. However, many of the respondents were newcomers, 40% having lived in Alachua for less than five years and 17% for less than one year. Eleven percent had moved more than two times during the preceding year and 39% had moved two or more times during the previous five years.

Geographic Origin

As shown in Table 3-1, the respondents had diverse backgrounds. Therefore, we classified them according to their geographic origin, i.e., the place where they had grown up. Each of the four groups had differing sociodemographic characteristics. The Alachua natives tended to be older than the others; proportionately more were female, black, in either low or lower-middle SES quintiles, and either widowed or separated. Those from other parts of Florida differed markedly from the Alachuans; they were significantly younger, male, white, in either the middle or upper-middle SES brackets, and single (many were students). As a group, the respondents from the Deep South (Southeastern states excepting Florida) resembled the Alachuans; they tended to be older, black, female, in low SES, and a significantly high percentage were widowed. The group that had grown up Elsewhere in the U.S.A.* contained proportionately more people aged 30-44, white, in the two highest SES quintiles, and a significantly high percentage were married.**

As expected, these geographic groups showed marked differences in their educational achievements and occupations. Many native Alachuans

* Only 52 had grown up outside the U.S.A.; they were placed in the Elsewhere group.
** Of all the respondents in the high SES quintile, 56% were in this group.

TABLE 3-1

Respondents' geographic origins.

Geographic Origin	*Number*	*Percent*
Alachua County	451	27.4
Other Florida	469	28.5
Deep South	213	12.9
Elsewhere	512	31.1
	1645	100.0

had only a high school education or less, as did many in the Deep South group. In contrast, the Other Florida group contained many college graduates and a disproportionately large number of persons with postgraduate educations. A significantly large percentage of those in professional or managerial positions were in the Elsewhere group. In general, the native Alachuans and those from the Deep South were engaged in the more menial occupations.

In the analysis of our data, we shall look at these four geographic groups to evaluate the relationships between the changing social order and risk for mental illness.

Groups Hypothesized to Be at High Risk

One of the various groups that we hypothesized as being at high risk for mental illness was the old élite who had clung tenaciously to cherished attitudes and sentiments while struggling against desegregation and deploring the loss of traditional "Southern values." Before starting this project, the senior author interviewed a number of physicians and surgeons who had practiced in the County for at least 15 to 20 years to learn whether they thought their patients were expressing concern and symptomatic distress attributable to the rapid change. Several of the most respected practitioners in the community mentioned that alcoholism, in particular, was becoming an increasingly greater problem, especially for the middle-aged, upper-middle and upper class persons who had been residents of the County for many years, if not all of their lives. Before the mid-1960s they had controlled the political power, the country club and service organizations, and had their own exclusive social gatherings. The influx of well-educated, vigorous, young professionals—usually associated with the University—toppled the old élite from their dominant social position; as a consequence, many of them withdrew from civic or other activities and banded together in small groups to recall the "good old days" over "a few drinks."

Another group hypothesized to be at high risk consisted of the descendants of the pioneers who for generations had lived in the outlying areas of the County near the swamps and lakes. They have been immortalized by Marjorie Kinnan Rawlings in *The Yearling* and *Cross Creek* (10, 11). They eked out a minimal existence from fishing, hunting, and raising small gardens. Proud, stubborn, and poor, the men expressed a fierce independence. They lived close to nature and sought relative isolation to maintain their marginal existence. They were suspicious of strangers and feared exploitation as much as crowding; after all, their forefathers had been harassed for years by the English and eventually driven from the Scottish Highlands and Irish bogs by English armies. After working as indentured servants in the southern seaboard states, their ancestors sought freedom and privacy in the backwoods and on the frontier until they were pushed by the "advance of civilization" to the outer, undesirable areas of thinly populated counties. They were quick to take umbrage, to redress their grievances by resorting to gun and blade, but they were not mean in character; helping friends or a stranger who was lost or in need was "the natural thing to do." But with the growth of Gainesville and the rapid changes in the County, this group was losing even its remote lakes and marshes that now were serving as recreational areas where the city folk fished on weekends in their large, polluting motorboats.

With rapid social change, we thought that other marginal groups were being placed at risk. Some were the borderline persons who could not meet the demands and strictures of middle-class-dominated community life and consequently had sought refuge in small hamlets where idiosyncratic behavior was tolerated—where one could be thought of as only a little "tetched" or different. In the changing County, they had "no place to hide"; unusual behavior was more visible. Furthermore, the small family farm was disappearing, replaced in the southern part of the County by horse farms and in the west and north by cattle ranches and agri-business.

We hypothesized that desegregation and increasing stratification placed certain black groups at risk for mental illness. For example, during their formative years, young adult blacks were exposed to the sociocultural changes that transpired during the 1960s. As children and adolescents they had witnessed the turbulence of America and some had participated in the struggle for racial equality. But their opportunities for sharing in the life styles and material benefits displayed by the media were limited. Concurrently, the southern blacks' traditional cultural patterns were being assailed on two fronts: exploitation by the dominant white society and challenge by groups insisting on African heritage and Black Power who scorned accommodation to the caste system. Therefore, some blacks could be seen as experiencing conflict between competing parental restraints and growing pride in ethnicity. Such a situation produces cognitive dissonance and the dilemmas of the marginal man.

As the blacks began to obtain educational and other advantages as well as to sub-stratify, the lower-class whites were losing some material advantages, particularly job security. And just as importantly, if not more so, the poor whites were being deprived of the illusion that had shored up their self-esteem—their sense of racial superiority. The blacks' achievements, along with their greater visibility as persons at school, on the job, and in the community were shattering the Southern myth of Negro inferiority. With increasing racial equality, it was to be expected that the already marginal poor white group would be at even higher risk for mental illness.

Uncertainty

Uncertainty, as well as marginality, was evident in the community. With the growth of the University and the increase in the hippie population, Gainesville and its environs attracted groups of dissident youth who formed colonies. Initially these colonies located near the University, but as that area became saturated with new apartment buildings and businesses, these young people moved into the tarnished mansions or into rural settlements. By 1970, the city was known on the West Coast and in Denver, Atlanta, and Miami as a drug center. The crime rate was rising rapidly. In the middle- and upper-class sections of the city, houses that had been seldom locked previously were now protected with alarms and other security systems. Senior citizens, as well as others, feared intrusions and robberies.

Another source of uncertainty accompanying the change resulted from the nationwide shifts in standards and mores. The University students, many of whom hailed from more cosmopolitan centers such as Miami, Sarasota, and New York, advocated changes—legalizing the use of marijuana, trial marriage, and pacifism. Changing mores create uncertainty about guidelines for judging behaviors as normal or abnormal.

In summary, it seemed to us that the rapid social change was placing certain groups, especially the marginal, at high risk for mental illness. In contrast, it appeared that the rapid change was benefitting those prepared for it. The newcomers, particularly the well-educated persons in their 30s and 40s and those possessing material advantages, seemed to be advancing in status and prestige. Upper-middle or high socioeconomic status provides buffers that mediate the effects of stressors. Such groups, therefore, were expected to show little evidence of mental illness and other impairments, but whether their material and other gains were satisfying is another question and one we will examine.

Thus, our hypotheses center on marginality, uncertainty, socioeconomic status, and prestige for individuals and groups as the social order was being transformed by change—political, economic, and cultural—and the social hierarchy was shifting. Some gain from rapid social change but others become victims of "culture lag" (12).

REFERENCES

1. Davis, J. G., *A History of Alachua County*. Unpublished manuscript. 1959, 165.
2. Ibid.
3. Furnas, J. C., *Americans: A Social History of the United States 1587-1914*. New York: Putnam, 1969, 785.
4. *Florida Statistical Abstract 1972. 6th Edition*. E. C. Jones (Ed.). Gainesville, Fla.: University of Florida Press, 1972, 36.
5. Ibid., 308.
6. Ibid., 485.
7. Durkheim, E., *The Rules of Sociological Method, 8th Edition*. S. A. Solovay, and John H. Mueller (Trans.), G. E. G. Catlin (Ed.). London: Collier-Macmillan Limited, 1938.
8. Caplan, G., *Support Systems and Community Mental Health*. New York: Behavioral Publications, 1974, 11.
9. Ibid., 7.
10. Rawlings, M. K., *The Yearling*. New York: Charles Scribner's Sons, 1962.
11. Rawlings, M. K., *Cross Creek*. New York: Charles Scribner's Sons, 1942.
12. Ogburn, W., *On Culture and Social Change*. Selected papers edited with an Introduction by O. D. Duncan. Chicago: University of Chicago Press, 1964.

4

Development and Design of the Study

Part I—The Concept of Social Psychiatric Impairment

It is impossible to define health except in metapsychological terms.

SIGMUND FREUD (1)

Perhaps our most difficult task was to conceptualize and define the dependent variable—risk for mental disorder—in a measurable form that would be applicable to the heterogeneous population of the County and would possess a reasonable degree of scientific validity. In the first part of this chapter we shall look at different concepts of mental illness advanced by various disciplines and the development of our concept of social psychiatric impairment (SPI).

Epidemiologic investigations of mental health and illness in the general population are known to be imprecise primarily because of difficulties in case definition. Just counting the number obtaining treatment for mental illness provides data about a selected group. Some are self-selected, voluntarily seeking help because of symptomatic distress. Others are persuaded or compelled to seek help by others, e.g., a spouse or parent who has difficulty tolerating behavior which is troublesome or regarded as abnormal. A third group consists of those whose maladaptive behavior is so intrusive and deviant that public officials (the police and others) commit or otherwise send them for treatment. But the mentally ill who do not seek treatment or who do not have access to it are not counted. Therefore, to obtain meaningful data about mental illness, the investigator needs to survey a sample of the general population or take a census. However, these approaches are handicapped by difficulties with case definition and the measurement of mental illness in a form that has validity and reliability.

SOCIOCULTURAL FACTORS RELATED TO DEFINITION OF MENTAL ILLNESS

A number of sociocultural factors complicate attempts to define mental illness with precision. The definition is largely dependent upon individual and group norms and upon tolerance of deviant behavior. Behavior considered to be flagrantly abnormal in one cultural group, even blatant schizophrenic symptomatology or profound melancholia, may be tolerated in another. Moreover, in a particular society, behavior that is considered normal at one time may be thought abnormal a few decades later. Although there is no doubt that mental illness exists and can be found in every culture, the definition is influenced by cultural relativity and changing norms.

The age-old difficulty of defining mental illness is illustrated by Machado de Assis' classic story, "The Psychiatrist," written in the 1890s (2):

> A highly-esteemed psychiatrist in a Brazilian province was empowered to build a mental hospital. In seeking scientific criteria to determine who should be admitted, he reviewed his medical knowledge and searched the writings of philosophers and theologians. He found that obvious psychopathology was an insufficient criterion and concluded that mental illness was evidenced by a disturbance of reason or the mental faculties—a deviation from Aristotle's "golden mean." Using this criterion, however, it was necessary to confine most of the population because "imbalance" was so prevalent—characteristic of the majority. Therefore, he reevaluated his criteria and decided that perhaps the mentally ill were, in reality, the remaining few who appeared to be balanced, despite the chaos, revolution, and social unrest in the province. Eventually, almost everyone was hospitalized at one time or another, according to the criterion "in vogue" at the time. Realizing that scientific precision had not been achieved, the psychiatrist finally released all of the inmates and with supreme logic, incarcerated himself as the sole patient.

MENTAL ILLNESS: QUANTITATIVE OR QUALITATIVE?

The arguments about the definition of mental illness hinge on one central issue—is it a quantitative or a qualitative condition?

The Quantitative Concept

In *The Rules of Sociological Method,* Durkheim attempted to distinguish between the normal and the pathological (3). He recognized that health had been defined traditionally as adaptation of an organism to its environment, and morbidity as a disturbance of that adaptation. In searching for more objective criteria to differentiate the healthy from the morbid, he equated health with the average physical status for a given society at a given time in its history. He wrote:

> We shall call "normal" these social conditions that are most generally distributed [a statistical norm], and the others "morbid" or "pathological." If we designate as "average type" that hypothetical being that is constructed by assembling in the same individual, the most frequent forms, one may say that the normal type merges with the average type, and that every deviation from this standard of health is a morbid phenomenon. . . . Each species has a health of its own, because it has an average type of its own. . . . The healthy constitutes the norm par excellence and can consequently be in no way abnormal (4).

From Durkheim's viewpoint and from Weber's social action emphasis, mental illness can be defined as the incapacity of a person to perform institutionalized roles. Talcott Parsons states:

> [T]he primary criteria for mental illness must be defined with reference to the social *role-performance of the individual.* Since it is at the level of role-structure that the principal direct interpenetration of social systems and personalities come to focus, it is as an incapacity to meet the expectations of social roles, that mental illness becomes a problem in social relationships and that criteria of its presence or absence should be formulated (5).

Thus, sociological concepts of disturbed behavior (in those who do not have organic brain disease) are based primarily on societal norms and the capacity for institutionalized role performance. This is the basis for the quantitative point of view: Mental illness is defined as any behavior that is relatively uncommon—therefore abnormal—according to a given society's generally accepted standards at a particular time. According to this statistical model, the great majority described by the bell-shaped curve are considered to be normal. Those at one end of the curve are the mentally ill because they display aberrant behavior. Those at the other end are conceptualized as supernormal or "self-actualizing" persons. Medical sociologists and other social scientists use this model extensively because it allows them to study and classify behaviors according to their frequency and distribution in a society or a smaller group.

The Qualitative Concept

The qualitative concept of mental illness is espoused by the medical profession. Mental illness is an entity, an affliction. Sir Aubrey Lewis presented the case for this point of view succinctly and forcefully (6). He thought that mental illness should be defined by reliance on traditional medical criteria which utilize three types of data: 1) the subjective—how the patient feels, 2) the objective—observable disorder or dysfunction, and 3) the typological—recognizable clinical patterns.

Lewis asserted that "deviant maladapted non-conformist behavior is pathological only if it is accompanied by a manifest disturbance . . . at a discrete or differentiated level" (7). He explained that illness cannot be equated with maladaptation without risk of tautology. Social disapproval cannot be considered to be an accurate criterion for identifying mental illness because it varies according to group judgments. Non-conformity, likewise, is an inadequate criterion because it is usually expressed in terms of social role and biased by prevailing cultural and other factors.

Lewis accounted for the cultural influences on symptoms by noting that behavior must be described in terms that specify the social situation in time and place. He believed that although the concept of illness "has physiological and psychological components [it has] no essential social ones." But Lewis, as well as others, recognized that the medical model of health and illness presupposes norms, at least implicitly; each patient supplies his own individual norms which are then evaluated by the physician in terms of the more general ones established by the medical profession. Although illness is viewed as an entity, these problems with norms and the variability of the social setting imply relativity.

Cultural anthropologists have developed a modified version of the qualitative concept of mental illness. They view all behavior as adaptive; both normal and neurotic behaviors are conceptualized as accommodations to a social situation. Kardiner stressed that each culture has an "ideal" or "basic character type"; neurosis is determined by measuring behavior in the light of this "ideal type" as defined by the culture or social group (8). Thus, the abnormal are those who least approximate the "basic type."

Using a more functional approach, Dubois suggested that each culture prescribes a range of behavior for its members (9). Although she emphasized the concept of a "modal personality," abnormality is measured by the inability to perform societally prescribed functions. Wallace summarized the anthropological point of view: "What is recognized as pathological in behavior is usually a matter of common consensus within a society. But the standards of consensus vary from one society to another" (10).

Epidemiologic Approaches to the Definition of Mental Illness

As a result of the difficulties with the definition of mental illness, large-scale epidemiologic studies in North America have used different criteria for classifying or judging who is mentally ill. The rates-under-treatment approach was used by Faris and Dunham in Chicago; Hollingshead and Redlich in New Haven; Lemkau and his colleagues, and later, Pasamanick and his co-workers in Baltimore (11-14). These investigators considered the mentally ill to be those who were receiving care. This has been a fruitful approach that furnished valuable data about the utilization of private and public treatment facilities. It defines mental illness, at least by implication, as a clinical diagnosis made by a mental health professional. But, as we noted earlier, a serious and acknowledged limitation of rates-under-treatment studies is that they furnish no information about the many untreated in the community. Furthermore, they do not allow the investigators to make comprehensive evaluations of the relationships between social processes and mental illness.

In the Midtown Manhattan Study, Srole, et al. conceptualized mental health and illness as gradations on a continuum (15). They considered the presence of symptoms and incapacity to function as criteria of impairment. Thus, the unimpaired were defined as having no significant symptom formation and possessing a large group of capacities which imply an ideal level of health and are tightly linked to socially-acceptable norms. The most impaired were symptomatic and also seriously incapacitated, unable to function. The difficulties with this concept stem primarily from the value judgments required to determine what is adequate and what is inadequate. For example, capacities include: identification with ethical and moral values and a conservative handling of hostility and aggression. Such criteria are difficult to measure and also entail value judgments. The Midtown investigators found that 23.4% of their sample were impaired, 58.1% showed some evidence of symptom formation but little or no interference with life adjustments, and only 18.5% were well (16).

In the Stirling County Study, the Leightons and their colleagues used a more traditional clinical definition. To determine mental health risk they relied on psychiatrists' ratings based on criteria stipulated by the American Psychiatric Association's *Diagnostic and Statistical Manual I* for diagnostic categorizations and levels of effectiveness: work, emotional stability, mental and physical conditions, etc. (17). According to a four-point scale adapted from the *Manual,* they found that 30.5% of the sample suffered from a major psychiatric illness; 24.6% were given ratings of probable psychiatric disorder; 26.2% were considered doubtful; and 18.7% were probably well (18). Also, the sample was rated independently for impairment according to criteria established by the American Medical Association (AMA).*

IMPAIRMENT

In view of the limitations of the quantitative, qualitative, and clinical concepts of mental health and illness, many epidemiologists have measured impairments rather than illness. Impairment—limitation of function—is usually easier to measure than the presence or absence of mental illness. By definition it denotes being diminished in quantity, value, or strength and suggests deterioration. In medicine it is defined as a functional incapacity produced by disease or injury that interferes with a person's social and occupational adjustment. An AMA Committee has provided ratings of impairment based on a person's inability to function and, particularly, "loss of working or earning capacity" (20). Evaluating impairment involves assessing: perception, learning, thinking, remembering, feeling, emoting, and motivation. Impairment is rated specifically in terms of the percentage of loss of function affecting the whole person. Furthermore, the Committee states that "there is need for a frame of reference which has universal application. . . . A loss of function in mental illness is manifested by varying degrees of deterioration in *one or more* of the specific aspects of an individual's adjustment, i.e., regressive changes which are physiological, psychological, personal, and/or social" (21). This view of impairment supplies an

* Responses to the Health Opinion Survey (HOS), a 20-item symptom-function scale, were used by the Leightons, et al. as primary measures for determining "caseness" (19). Later, we will be discussing their use of this instrument in detail because we used it as one measure in the Florida Health Study.

essential unifying concept, that of regression—functioning at a simpler and less mature level than normal.

Assessing the Degree of Impairment in Community Studies of Mental Disorder

Assessing the degree of impairment in community studies of mental disorder can be viewed as an attempt to compensate for the limitations inherent in the concepts and definitions of mental illness. The investigator is not bound by the constraints of various models and can measure observable phenomena. Such phenomena are, fundamentally, evaluations of role expectations and performance which in turn are socioculturally established. Primarily, impairment involves one crucial point—the degree to which the capacity to work productively and consistently is decreased. In his 1960 World Health Organization report, "The Measurement of Levels of Mental Morbidity," Reid states that "one may have to accept an operational definition of the onset of mental disorder as a disturbance of feeling or behavior which is disabling enough to cause admission to hospital or an *inability to work effectively*" (22). (Italics ours.)

In his article on medical and sociological models used to assess mental health, Srole presents a diagram (Figure 4-1) that displays many of the problems confronting the investigator assessing mental health and illness in the community.

The populations in Cells A and D can be recognized by most criteria for measuring mental health or illness. Those in group C suffer from intrapsychic distress only, but manage to function at a level which is not considered to be abnormal or pathological; they are not identified when only impairment is used as the operational criterion.* Those in Cell B constitute many of the deviants who can be easily identified as having difficulty in role performance but who do not satisfy one of the essential criteria of the medical model—symptomatic distress. Most of them never seek psychiatric treatment. The few who do are usually considered to be refractory cases. Therefore, they are not noticed until they commit offenses that warrant removing them from society.

The concept of impairment bridges various definitions of mental illness and, because impairment is measurable, it can be used in epidemiologic studies. But assessing impairment is a compromise solution to

* It is possible that they might be more effective in their interpersonal and other role performances if they were not suffering from intrapsychic distress.

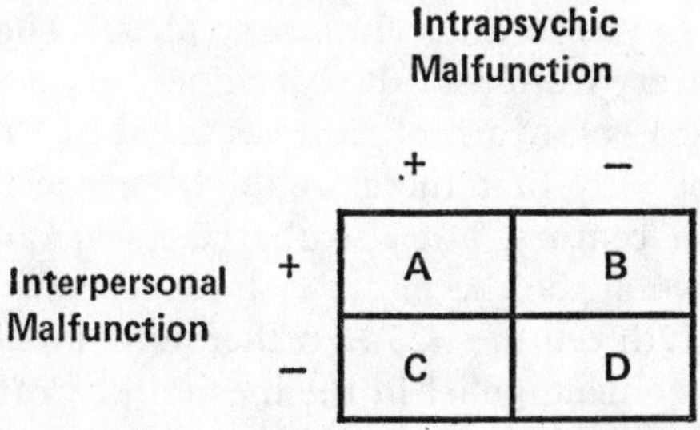

FIGURE 4-1. Relationships among symptoms and malfunctions. Source: Reference 23.

case definition and has some limitations that must be recognized. Specifically, it involves value judgments and thus may not be applicable to some subcultural groups.

SOCIAL PSYCHIATRIC IMPAIRMENT (SPI)

We did not think that a traditional definition of mental illness or impairment would suffice to meet our objectives in the Florida Health Study. We wanted to examine relationships between emotional distress with its impairments and social forces (the shape of things) and cultural trends (the style of things), as well as the more conventional demographic correlates of illness. Therefore, we attempted to broaden the definitions of impairment used by previous investigators to include dimensions other than symptoms and functioning, specifically, interpersonal distress.

Changes in the social climate influenced the formulation of our concept of SPI. Such changes are associated with shifting fashions in diagnosis. A dramatic example of such a change is the deletion of homosexuality as a mental disorder by the American Psychiatric Association. Furthermore, the new DSM-III is a radical revision of DSM-II (24). Such revisions are being made at an accelerated rate; DSM-I was published in 1952, DSM-II in 1968, and DSM-III circulated in draft form in 1977. Even before final publication, DSM-III is being criticized severely.

Development of an Operational Definition of Impairment

The development of an operational definition of impairment is influenced by the ethos of the time. From the viewpoint of organic historians such as Spengler and Toynbee, Western society has reached maturity and possibly is in a devolutionary phase. The Protestant Ethic is challenged on every front and the Machine Age has been supplanted by the technological era. Much of this was foreseen by Ortega y Gassett who predicted not only that there would be a generation gap in the middle of the 20th century, but also that the generation that came of age in the 1960s would be the most "critical generation" since the one born early in the 17th century (25). Furthermore, for the first time since the Age of Enlightenment, belief in the inevitability of progress has been supplanted by preoccupation with current realities and great expectations replaced by limited goals. Our modern world is characterized by urbanization, technology, the population explosion, and communications that expose individual and group behavior to the scrutiny of all.

It is no accident of history that role theory, which Parsons considers to be the most distinctly American contribution to sociology, developed coincidentally with the "passing of the frontier" (26). Social role has become a meaningful concept in the United States in this century. Achieved status is more important than ascribed status. Adherents to traditional values are diminishing in number as tangible and visible rewards are accorded to those who rapidly adopt changing functional value systems. For these reasons, we thought that the AMA concept of impairment would be too restrictive. It views impairment almost exclusively in terms of the individual and his pathology, failing to take into account the impact of sociocultural forces on that pathology, on its changing manifestations, and on prevailing, but transient, definitions of it.

Our view of the importance of sociocultural forces on impairment has been influenced by Ruesch and Brodsky's concept of social disability (27). They credit social disability as being a more critically important topic today than in the past because normative standards have become diffuse. Furthermore, population growth and the exposure resulting from mass communication reveal relatively imperceptible behavioral deviations which may be labeled impairments. Parsons notes that levels of mental pathology which were tolerated in a pre-industrial world have become intolerable under the stringent pressures of modern life (28). With these thoughts in mind, role expectations and capacities became important components of our view of impairment.

SPI Derived from Social Sciences and Psychiatric Models of Impairment

We derived our concept of SPI from the social sciences and psychiatric models of impairment. We think this synthesis is necessary in order to acknowledge the societal changes that are altering standards for appraising health and illness. All illness arises in a social setting and mental illness, to a large extent, is culturally defined. Differential rates of illness are associated with sociodemographic factors such as income, availability of treatment, and the type of therapy received—all of which are socioculturally determined.

Our concept of SPI extends beyond the limitations of a medical model of illness. It acknowledges the subjective, interpersonal, and larger social ramifications of personal distress, behavioral disorders with their interpersonal consequences, and deviance with its societal implications. It encompasses three dimensions of psychosocial distress: 1) traditional definitions of psychopathology; 2) levels of functioning at home, work, and in the broader social arena, and 3) the quantity and quality of interpersonal relationships. We defined SPI operationally as the disturbance felt by the individual, by his or her difficulties in functioning according to societal expectations, and by interpersonal distress.

The Strengths and Limitations of the Concept of Social Psychiatric Impairment (SPI)

We believe that the strength of the concept of SPI is that it does not reject completely a view of illness as an entity. It recognizes that impairment is largely a socially-defined condition and it takes into account the individual's interpersonal and other role performances. We derived it from clinical experience as well as from theoretical considerations; for example, many patients seek psychiatric care primarily for advice about interpersonal dilemmas. Moreover, we attempted to limit it to mental and behavioral symptoms and manifestations and to preclude indicators of psychosomatic or physical illness.

The limitations of the concept lie in the fact that it is new. Its emphasis on social role performance extends it into a murky terrain where boundaries are unclear. Thus, the concept can be considered diffuse. The inclusion of interpersonal distress as one of the major dimensions broadens the implicit definition of mental illness. And, obviously, it is difficult to determine its validity and reliability.

We used two methods to evaluate our respondents' states of mental health or illness. In the pretest, we relied on a qualitative approach; psychiatrists rated each respondent for the presence of SPI. In the major survey of 1645 respondents we used a statistical method for designating those at high risk for mental illness.

Part II—Design and Methods

In this section we shall describe the processes involved as our work proceeded from the conceptualization of our theoretical model to the conduct of our analyses. Specifically, we shall discuss the following topics: 1) the socioanthropologic field studies, 2) the rates-under-treatment studies, 3) the development of the Interview Schedule, 4) the validity and reliability—the pretest, and 5) the use of the Health Opinion Survey (HOS).

THEORETICAL AND METHODOLOGICAL ISSUES

As we have seen, the most difficult task confronting those working in the field of psychiatric epidemiology is that of defining the phenomena under investigation, i.e., what are mental health and illness and how can they be identified and distinguished from one another empirically? Regrettably, at present there are no commonly accepted definitions or field procedures; consequently, differing investigators often cannot replicate one another's efforts to establish the "true prevalence" of mental health and illness. In the absence of scientific consensus regarding definitions and procedures, each research group must consider the alternatives and choose among them. We were cognizant of the theoretical and methodological problems associated with the definition and measurement of mental health. The model we developed and termed Social Psychiatric Impairment (SPI) was designed to negate some of the salient criticisms of earlier studies in the field. We are aware, of course, that the goal of establishing standardized definitions and measurement procedures is a long way from achievement. But, the absence of consensus on these issues should not deter research efforts; the current state of the art will move forward only as investigators from a variety of disciplines approach the theoretical and methodological issues from their particular perspectives. From these efforts—disparate in approach but unified in purpose—we and others hope to supply an expanding body of knowledge that will at some future time provide the basis for a truly scientific synthesis.

As we began to develop the model of SPI, we prepared a comprehensive list of issues that confronted epidemiologists, e.g., the limitations of symptom lists to distinguish differences in mental health states; the confounding of mental illness by concurrent physical health problems or age; and the inadequacies of measures that did not provide meaningful data on mental health and social functioning. Also, we enumerated the methodological issues other investigators had confronted. These included response biases such as yea and nay saying, social desirability, and the problems associated with the recall of past mental and physical health conditions. We became keenly aware of the problems inherent in large, multidimensional studies. With these and other issues in mind, we constructed the model of SPI described in Chapters 5 and 6 and designed a series of studies that would provide information on the mental health and services utilization patterns of those living in the County.

SOCIOANTHROPOLOGICAL FIELD STUDIES

The construct (SPI) used as the major dependent variable included the notions of socialization, social roles, and role performance. These concepts are, of course, social structural in nature and culturally relative. And because we believe the manifestation of psychiatric symptoms is influenced by cultural processes, we conducted socioanthropological field studies to identify those factors associated with socialization, especially role expectations. These studies also searched for methods by which we could obtain information on social deviance, particularly as it is related to those aberrant thoughts and behaviors most indicative of mental health problems. Also we were interested in groups' health care patterns.

These field studies were conducted by doctoral students in the Department of Anthropology at the University of Florida. They were given assistance by their academic advisors, project supervisors, and nationally recognized scholars who served as short-term consultants. The content of their work, in addition to that related to social roles, deviance, and health-seeking patterns, closely paralleled the suggestions of Murdock, et al. in the *Outline of Cultural Materials* (29). The topics investigated included geographic and land use patterns, history, local norms, cultural participation, economic bases, social support networks, political structures, educational facilities and programs, racial and other social attitudes and behaviors, recreation, religion, kinship patterns, and a variety of others relevant to the development of the model of SPI.

As the socioanthropological data were secured, they were used primarily to assist the research staff in the construction of the Interview Schedules. Field reports were filed for use in the later analysis and interpretation of the rates-under-treatment and prevalence studies.

This field work, which took 18 months to complete, provided information on every "community" in the County. Some of these had clearly demarcated political and geographic boundaries while others were communities largely in the psychosocial sense, consisting primarily of persons "belonging" to one another.

RATES-UNDER-TREATMENT STUDIES

This second set of field studies addressed the following questions: 1) Who is seeking professional health care and health-related services in the County? 2) What are the conditions being treated? 3) What are the rates for differing social, demographic and geographic groupings? and 4) What services are being provided? We needed answers to these questions for two reasons. First, we recognized that rates of treatment for mental health problems constitute one method of estimating the prevalence of differing psychiatric disorders. Furthermore, we knew from earlier clinical studies that many persons being treated in general hospitals and clinics for physical health reasons were also being treated concurrently for mental health problems, usually with psychotropic medications.

The rates-under-treatment studies took about eight months to complete. The data were secured by obtaining a 10% sample of all medical patients being treated in hospitals during a one-year period of time. The only exceptions were females admitted for childbirth. In addition, we enumerated persons receiving mental health treatment in public hospitals, clinics, and agencies. We secured data on approximately 2500 adults who had utilized health and/or health-related services in the County during the calendar year prior to the commencement of the prevalence study.

THE DEVELOPMENT OF THE INTERVIEW SCHEDULE

Data from the socioanthropological and rates-under-treatment studies not only were useful as information sources in their own right, but also supplied the basis on which we could design and conduct the cross-sectional prevalence field survey.

Construction of the Interview Schedule was one of our most crucial research tasks; its development and testing took more than one year to complete. From the beginning, the theoretical construct of SPI shaped the design of the instrument. Moreover, we endeavored, insofar as possible, to utilize a general systems approach to guide our efforts. We made a conscious effort to give the Interview Schedule a dynamic, systemic interrelatedness. We believe that an organism is in a state of constant adaptation to its internal milieu, its interpersonal surroundings, and its broader social-cultural environment. Where feasible, we endeavored to build this theoretical assumption of dynamic adaptation into the Interview Schedule.

To begin constructing the Schedule, we analyzed a large number of interview instruments, questionnaires, patient data forms, and related materials from earlier research efforts. More than 2000 individual items drawn from many sources were listed, placed on 3 × 5 cards, and organized into theoretical topics which, on the basis of earlier research, clinical experience, and/or face validity, seemed to be most compatible. From an extensive analysis of these individual items we discovered there was a significant overlapping of item format and content. Also, many of the scales, symptom checklists, and indices were very similar. After completing these analyses, we constructed a pretest schedule; we placed the items in a logical sequence, but kept in mind their juxtaposition, in order to negate insofar as possible response biases such as yea and nay saying, response sets, and social desirability. After completion of the preliminary schedules, the interviewers who had been involved in the library research, item selection, and interview construction tested the Instrument with various subpopulations, i.e., the elderly, the disabled, the young, blacks, and others in the community. Then, the research staff evaluated each item both for content and format from the perspectives gained by the interviews in the community. Items were deleted, altered, or placed in differing sections of the schedule. In all, we conducted 10 such mini-pretests.

The Interview Schedule

In its final form, the Interview Schedule consisted of 317 separate items, many of which had multiple parts. Approximately 800 bits of information were contained in the following 12 major components of the instrument:

1) Social and demographic items such as age, sex, race, education, marital status, parents' occupation and education, patterns of residential mobility, and related variables.

2) Occupation items which included employment patterns, occupational history, periods of unemployment, job satisfaction, perceived job-produced stress, work preferences, and information on working mothers and housewives. Special sections of the occupation subcomponent included extensive data specific to housewives, students, the unemployed, disabled, or the retired.

3) Marital information concerning past and/or present marital statuses, marital satisfactions, problems encountered in the family setting, and perceived marital stressors. In addition, a separate subsection was devoted to the unmarried, the never married, and those previously married with minor children residing in their households.

4) A lengthy listing of items about respondents' patterns of social interactions with their immediate and extended families, the extent of contact, and satisfaction with the degree of contact. A corresponding set of items was included for friends; we were interested in surrogate family structures, particularly relating to blacks and to students, many of whom were sharing common living arrangements in family-like settings.

5) Information on religious beliefs and practices and on community involvement through formal organizations.

6) A set of items about perception of and concern about social changes.

7) Comprehensive psychosomatic and physical health inventories that included past or present illnesses, operations, major accidents, hospitalizations, medications, an extensive review of systems, and a self-rating of physical health.

8) A comprehensive mental health inventory consisting of more than 100 different items related to a broad spectrum of psychiatric syndromes and to dysfunctions. We included items about drug and alcohol use, sleep patterns, and self-ratings of mental health. We also included the 20-Item Health Opinion Survey (HOS) so that our results could be compared with those of others.

9) Health services utilization related to patterns of past or present health care and to sources, i.e., public or private providers.

10) An extensive list of questions about the mental and physical health and well-being of other family members and the kinds of services being utilized by them.

11) A number of scales that measured anomie, racial distance, etc.

12) A final section devoted to a modified version of the Cantril Self-Anchoring Striving Scale (30).

An examination of the components shows that the various sections of the Schedule were designed to obtain information based on the theoretical model which guided the research. We could secure information on each respondent's: 1) mental health from the large array of symptom lists, 2) social functioning as indicated by work and other social role performances, 3) interpersonal well-being as shown by ability to establish and maintain meaningful object relationships at primary and secondary levels, and 4) satisfaction with social status, physical and mental well-being, work, home, family, community and society at large. The Interview Schedule provided a comprehensive data base from which we could make determinations of each respondent's mental and physical health, functioning, social well-being, patterns of care, and satisfactions-dissatisfactions with the community, roles, and health care.

Sampling Procedures

The sample was drawn from a universe consisting of all the households in the County serviced by electric utility companies. The choice of these utility listings for preparing the sampling frame was made after extensive efforts to identify households by use of postal addresses, telephone and city directories, and voter registration lists proved to be inadequate. At the time of the survey, the seven companies serving the County claimed that about 98% of all homes had electrical hookups. From these lists, a sample of 2315 households was identified; this represented 7.5% of the total in the County. To select the individual households we drew, systematically, a random sample from the utility lists. Once the households were identified, individual respondents within them were selected by use of a method developed by Kish (31). Only adults 18 years of age or over were selected. Using this multi-staged, systematic, probability method supplied a sample closely approximating the social and demographic characteristics of the County as enumerated by the U.S. Bureau of the Census.

The Random Sample

Table 4-1 shows the demographic characteristics of the random sample for the major survery. The sample contains an unusually large number of young people because so many students lived in the County. There was a slightly higher percentage of females, both black and white, than

TABLE 4-1

Sociodemographic characteristics of the sample.*

Sociodemographic Characteristics	N	(%)
Age:		
16-22	270	16.4
23-29	315	19.2
30-44	411	25.0
45-59	332	20.2
60+	315	19.2

TABLE 4-1 *(continued)*

Sociodemographic Characteristics	N	(%)
Sex:		
Male	736	44.7
Female	909	55.3
Race:		
White	1267	77.6
Black	366	22.4
SES:		
Low	212	12.9
Lower-Middle	351	21.3
Middle	479	29.1
Upper-Middle	379	23.0
High	212	12.9
Marital Status:		
Single	295	17.9
Married	1009	61.3
Widowed	170	10.3
Separated	69	4.2
Divorced	102	6.2
Geographic Origin:		
Alachua	451	27.4
Other Florida	469	28.5
Deep South	213	12.9
Elsewhere	512	31.1
Education:		
Under 8th Grade	304	18.5
High School or Graduate	565	34.4
College or Graduate	521	31.7
Trade or Business School	41	2.5
Postgraduate or Degree	210	12.8
Place of Residence:		
Rural	314	19.1
Town	202	12.3
Urban	1128	68.6
Occupation:		
Prof./Prop. Lg. Business	66	4.0
Prof. II-Mgr., Prop., Small Business	281	17.1
Prof-Tech. III, Clerical	219	13.4
Craftsmen	117	7.1
Unskilled	242	14.8
Unemployed, Retired	93	5.7
Housewife	333	20.3
Student	288	17.6

* Not all respondents answered all questions.

males. The mean annual income was $8,806, although 15.9% had incomes of less than $3,000 per year. Almost 20% had less than an eighth-grade education, while at the other end of the continuum, 12.8% were post-graduate students or held higher academic degrees. Over one-third were engaged in professional, managerial, and technical occupations. Each subject was given an SES score ranging from 0 (low) to 99 (high). This was a composite score derived from indices of education, occupation, and income developed by the U.S. Department of Labor.* There was an almost normal SES distribution: 12.9% were in the low quintile, 73.5% in the lower-middle, middle, and upper-middle quintiles, and 13.6% in the high quintile.

The marital status profile shows that a relatively low percentage, 61.3% were married; 20.7% had been married but were now widowed, divorced, or separated. The average length of marriage for those married at the time of the survey was 16.2 years and for those previously married, 18.6 years. Thus, the sample represents a community with a fairly traditional, stable marital style of life.

Most of the respondents were Protestants, 84.9%. Of these, about two-thirds belonged to Fundamentalist churches, about one-sixth to conservative churches, and the remaining sixth to liberal Protestant churches. Only 9.2% of the sample was Roman Catholic and 2.6% Jewish.

An analysis of household types showed that 70.5% lived in a nuclear family unit; almost 5% lived in extended families, and 8.6% were singles who lived with non-related roommates. A seemingly high percentage, 14.5%, lived alone.

---

* The sociodemographic characteristics of the respondents in the five SES groups differed. In the lowest SES quintile there were many elderly persons, blacks, and the widowed or separated. A disproportionately large number were native Alachuans or from the adjacent states of the Deep South. A large number of respondents in this quintile were disabled, retired, or unemployed; a typical occupation was maid service. In the lower-middle quintile, the respondents tended to be either quite young or elderly. Many were blacks and a large number were widowed, separated, or single. Mainly, they were native Alachuans or from the Deep South. This category contained students, some housewives, and some of the unemployed or retired; many were waiters or small farmers. The middle quintile was composed predominantly of young, white, single or divorced persons, many of whom came from other parts of Florida or Elsewhere. This grouping contained many students; typical occupations were secretary or clerk. In the upper-middle quintile, many respondents were young adults, white, married or divorced; most came from Other Florida or Elsewhere. Many were employed in business, education, or health services. Disproportionately large numbers of those in the top quintile were aged 30-59, white, married, from Elsewhere, and employed as professors, physicians, technologists, or managers.

Refusal Rate

Of the 2315 households initially selected, 1967 persons, 85.0%, were successfully interviewed. The major reasons for nonresponse consisted of: refusals, 8.0%; respondents not found at home, 4.5%; addresses not located, 1.2%; and, respondents too ill to be interviewed, 1.3%. In every instance, vigorous efforts were made to contact respondents once they had been selected. The standard procedure for callbacks required a minimum of four return visits; often as many as eight attempts were made to locate and interview those selected. Some addresses could not be located because of faulty street listings—the largest city in the County had a major change in street names prior to the survey and in some instances appropriate alterations had not been made. Those too ill to be interviewed were suffering from a wide range of physical and/or mental health problems. Most persons in this group were quite aged, Basic social and demographic data, along with reasons for not completing the interview, were gathered on each person too disabled to complete the schedule.

THE PRETEST

Following the selection of the sample and construction of the Interview Schedule, we drew a subsample from the master sample to test the validity of the construct, SPI. We were concerned about its applicability to, and utility with, differing social and demographic groups. The pretest also gave us an opportunity to train the interviewers and to evaluate the field procedures.

For the pretest study of 322 respondents, all of the information pertaining to physical and mental health, functioning, and the quality and quantity of interpersonal relationships was abstracted from the Interview Schedule and assembled into individual protocols which were rated for level of SPI by three psychiatrists working independently. These raters were supplied with data on the respondents' physical as well as mental health and illness and with *all* of the replies to our questionnaire, i.e., positive, negative, indefinite ("don't know"). We hoped that these procedures would minimize the confounding of physical and mental illness and also give the raters a "balanced picture" of each respondent's symptoms, functioning, interpersonal networks, etc. The psychiatrists rated each respondents' protocol according to criteria which had been established beforehand.

Inter-Rater Agreement on Patient Sample

To validate our procedures, we interviewed over 100 psychiatric in- and outpatients in two hospitals, two clinics, and four private practices. The attending psychiatrists rated these patients for level of SPI according to our criteria. They used only their clinical knowledge of the patients; they did not have access to the patients' responses to our research interviews. Then our project psychiatrists independently rated each patient's protocol abstracted from the formal interview. All procedures were blinded. Of the 50 psychiatric outpatients, 49 were rated as impaired by their attending psychiatrists.* The attending psychiatrists rated 20 of their patients as more impaired and 9 as less impaired than did the project psychiatrists; there was *exact* agreement as to the *level* of SPI on 21 (42%) of the patients.

Inter-Rater Agreement on the Pretest Sample

Our three project psychiatrists were in total agreement on 58.5% of the ratings of the 322 respondents in the pretest sample. They were in total agreement on 75.5% of those ultimately judged not impaired. But they were in total agreement on only 20.4% of those ultimately judged to be impaired; they disagreed about the *level* of impairment (mild, moderate, or severe), not whether the respondent was impaired or not. Tolerating one level of disagreement by one of the three raters resulted in agreement on 100% of those ultimately judged not impaired and 90.3% of those judged impaired. The final ratings given each respondent were determined by majority agreement among the three psychiatrists and occasionally necessitated group discussions to obtain a final consensus.

Pretest Results

Of the 31% of the respondents rated as impaired, there were more persons under the age of 30 and over the age of 60 than those aged 30-59, more females than males, and more blacks than whites. We found the usual inverse relationship between impairment and income; 45% of the impaired had annual family incomes of less than $6,000 and about 12% had incomes above $20,000. Fewer of the married were impaired than the single, divorced, and particularly, the separated or widowed.

* The inpatients presented extensive psychopathology. Consequently, we did not think that including them would be a rigorous validation procedure—all of the raters found all of them to be impaired.

With two exceptions—the lower percentage rated impaired and the curvilinear relationship with age—the findings are consistent with reports from most community studies of mental disorder in North America.*

Predictors

We then determined which of the items in the lengthy Interview Instrument were significantly related to SPI and their relative strengths for predicting it. Some of the members of the research team, McGinnis and her colleagues, conducted a number of multivariate regression analyses to predict the psychiatrists' ratings. In the first equation, 14 sociodemographic variables such as age, sex, race, annual family income, and length of residence in the County accounted for 20% of the variance in the impairment ratings, i.e., the difference between being rated impaired or not impaired. Then we culled more than 150 items related to the dimensions of SPI, sociodemographic characteristics, and medical symptomatology to find the most powerful predictors. Of this group, 34 were used to construct a summary equation for the total pretest sample. Table 4-2 presents the summarized results—the 11 most powerful predictors of the psychiatrists' impairment ratings.

We were pleased to find that these 11 variables accounted for 68% of the variance in the ratings of the heterogeneous random pretest sample.** The extensive field studies, pretests, and validation procedures indicated that our Interview Instrument could be used to assess risk for mental illness in the community as measured by SPI. Furthermore, we found that our concept of SPI was not only meaningful, but also applicable. However, we modified it slightly; originally we had hoped that levels of aspiration and degree of satisfaction with one's everyday activities and circumstances could be incorporated into the concept of SPI. But more extensive analyses revealed that often there was no association between degree of satisfaction and indicators of mental health risk. Therefore, as a measure, SPI was limited to three dimensions:

* The 31% of our pretest respondents rated impaired (24.8% mildly and 6.2% moderately) is substantially less than the 81.5% reported in the Midtown Manhattan Study (32). It is also much less than reported in the Stirling County Study which rated 81.3% as having some degree of impairment (33).

** These 11 accounted only for the variance in the impairment ratings. They did not explain why the respondent was rated impaired or not impaired. The remaining 32% may be attributable to factors such as: certain interview items which the psychiatrists may have used in rating may not have met the statistical assumptions required by the methodology; the individual differences of the respondents; the subjectivity of the raters; and the sociocultural diversity within the pretest random sample.

1) The Bell Global Psychopathology Scale,
2) The Impairment of Functioning Scale, and
3) The Interpersonal Distress Scale.

TABLE 4-2

Regression equation for the total pretest sample in stepwise order. (N = 301)*

Items Accounting for at least 68% of the Variance	R^2(0.70)**
Felt like having a nervous breakdown or losing mind	0.33
Respondent's self-rating of health	0.49
Anxiety score***	0.54
Ill health affecting working capacity	0.53
Worry when no immediate problem	0.61
Use of tranquilizers, psychotropics	0.63
Trouble with throat	0.65
Geographic mobility	0.66
Deviation from normal weight	0.67
Restlessness	0.67
Healthy enough to do things one likes	0.68

* Pairwise deletion of missing observations reduced the original N from 322 to 301. There were 29 significant steps taken.

** The R^2 is the percentage of variance explained by the variable plus all the variables previously entered. Thus, "felt like having a nervous breakdown," etc. was the most significant. It alone explained 33% of the total variance. The next one added 16%, the next, 5%, etc. The last one was still significant but contributed only 1% to the total 68%. The remaining 23 variables contributed only an additional 2% to the total explained variance of 70%.

*** Normalized Z scores derived from standardized anxiety scales.

HEALTH OPINION SURVEY (HOS) SCORES

Although the validation procedures and our detailed analysis of the pretest indicated that we could use SPI as the dependent variable in the major survey, we added an additional measure—the HOS—as another dependent variable for a number of reasons. First, it is a standardized scale that has been used for almost 25 years in community studies of mental disorder. Second, although its limitations are widely recognized, it has an acceptable degree of validity. Third, its use in surveys of mental disorder in vastly different racial and cultural groups—white

Anglo-Saxon Protestants, French Acadians, Eskimos, and the Yoruba in Nigeria—indicated that it would have utility in our investigation of the heterogeneous population of Alachua County (34). Fourth, using the HOS would enable us to compare our findings with those obtained by other investigators in various parts of the world.

A comparison of the pretest respondents' SPI ratings and HOS scores showed that 31% were rated as being in the SPI category, whereas 25.2% had HOS scores in the possible or probable caseness range. We regarded SPI as a broader construct but since it was new and relatively untested we thought we should evaluate it with further comparisons with the HOS scores. Moreover, 44% of the pretest sample rated impaired by the psychiatrists had HOS scores in the normal range and 11% of those rated not impaired had HOS scores in the caseness range.

The Major Survey

In view of the difficulties in defining mental illness and the complexity of the rating process, we relied primarily on a statistical model of SPI and on HOS scores for the analysis of the major survey of 1645 respondents. Combining these approaches enabled us to look at the results of our major survey from both quantitative and qualitative views of mental illness. In that sense we followed Laughlin's Law of Relativity in Emotional Health: "[T]he 'normal' imperceptibly merges into the borderline, and the borderline into the neurotic. . . . Everyone has problems . . . at least at times. The difference between people in this area more often is one of quantity than of quality" (35).

In the next chapter we will examine some of the findings from the major survey—the 1645 respondents' scores on the Bell Global Psychopathology Scale and its subscales that identify symptom patterns. These analyses will present the extent of psychopathology in the Alachua County sample. In a subsequent chapter we will present the respondents' scores on the two other dimensions of SPI—impairment of functioning and interpersonal distress—and on the HOS.

REFERENCES

1. Freud, S., "Analysis Terminable and Interminable." In: J. Strachey (Ed.), *The Complete Psychological Works of Sigmund Freud, Vol. 23.* London: Hogarth Press, 1964, 216-253.
2. de Assis, M., "The Psychiatrist." In: W. L. Grossman, and H. Caldwell (Trans.), *The Psychiatrist and Other Stories.* Berkeley, Calif.: University of California Press, 1963.

3. Durkheim, E., *The Rules of Sociological Method. 8th Edition.* S. A. Solovay, and J. H. Mueller (Trans.), G. E. G. Catlin (Ed.). London: Collier-Macmillan Limited, 1938.
4. Ibid., 55-56, 58.
5. Parsons, T., "Definitions of Health and Illness in the Light of American Values and Social Structure." In: E. G. Jaco (Ed.), *Patients, Physicians, and Illness.* Glencoe, Ill.: The Free Press, 1958, 165.
6. Lewis, A., *The State of Psychiatry: Essays and Answers.* New York: Science House, Inc., 1967.
7. Ibid., 167.
8. Kardiner, A., Lingon, R., DuBois, C., and West, J., *The Psychological Frontiers of Society.* New York: Columbia University Press, 1945.
9. DuBois, C., *The People of Alor.* Minneapolis, Minn.: The University of Minnesota Press, 1944.
10. Wallace, A. F. C., "Anthropology and Psychiatry." In: A. M. Freedman, H. I. Kaplan, and B. J. Sadock (Eds.), *Comprehensive Textbook of Psychiatry-II, Vol. 1, 2nd Edition.* Baltimore, Md.: The Williams and Wilkins Co., 1975, 366.
11. Faris, R. E. L., and Dunham, W. H., *Mental Disorders in Urban Areas.* Chicago, Ill.: University of Chicago Press, 1939.
12. Hollingshead, A. B., and Redlich, F. C., *Social Class and Mental Illness: A Community Study.* New York: John Wiley and Sons (Sciences Editions), 1958.
13. Lemkau, P., Tietz, C., and Cooper, M., "Mental-Hygiene Problems in an Urban District," *Mental Hygiene,* Vol. 25, 1941, 624-646.
14. Clausen, J. A., and Kohn, M. L., "Relation of Schizophrenia to the Social Structure of a Small City." In: B. Pasamanick (Ed.), *Epidemiology of Mental Disorder.* Washington, D.C.: American Association for the Advancement of Science, 1959, 69-94.
15. Srole, L., Langner, T. S., Michael, S. T., Opler, M. K., and Rennie, T. A. C., *Mental Health in the Metropolis—The Midtown Manhattan Study. Vol. I.* New York: McGraw-Hill Book Company, Inc., 1962.
16. Ibid., 342.
17. Leighton, D. C., Harding, J. S., Macklin, D. B., Macmillan, A. M., and Leighton, A. H., *The Character of Danger.* New York: Basic Books, Inc., 1963, 131.
18. Ibid., 121.
19. Macmillan, A. M., "The Health Opinion Survey: Technique for Estimating Prevalence of Psychoneurotic and Related Types of Disorder in Communities," *Psychological Reports,* Monograph Supplement 7, Southern Universities Press, 1957, 325-339.
20. Committee on Rating of Mental and Physical Impairment, "Mental Illness—Guides to the Evaluation of Permanent Impairment," *Journal of the American Medical Association,* Vol. 198, No. 12, December 19, 1966, 1284-1296.
21. Ibid., 1286.
22. Reid, D. D., "The Measurement of Levels of Mental Morbidity." In: *Epidemiological Methods in the Study of Mental Disorders.* Geneva: World Health Organization, 1960, 31.
23. Srole, L., "Medical and Sociological Models in Assessing Mental Health." In: S. B. Sells (Ed.), *The Definition and Measurement of Mental Health.* Washington, D.C.: National Center for Health Statistics, U.S. Public Health Service, 1968, 48-65.
24. The Committee on Nomenclature and Statistics of the American Psychiatric Association, *DSM-II—Diagnostic and Statistical Manual of Mental Disorders, 2nd Edition.* Washington, D.C.: American Psychiatric Association, 1968.

25. Ortega y Gasset, J., *Man and Crisis*. New York: W. W. Norton and Company, 1958.
26. See Reference 5.
27. Ruesch, J., and Brodsky, C. M., "The Concept of Social Disability," *Archives of General Psychiatry*, Vol. 19, No. 4, 1968, 394-403.
28. See Reference 5, 181.
29. Murdock, G. P., et al., *Outline of Cultural Materials. 4th Revised Edition*. New Haven: Human Relations Area Files, Inc., 1961.
30. Cantril, H., *The Pattern of Human Concerns*. New Brunswick, N.J.: Rutgers University Press, 1965.
31. Kish, L., *Survey Sampling*. New York: John Wiley and Sons, Inc., 1965.
32. See Reference 15, 342.
33. See Reference 17, 128.
34. Murphy, J. M., "A Cross-Cultural Comparison of Psychiatric Disorder: Eskimos of Alaska, Yorubas of Nigeria, and Nova Scotians of Canada." In: W. P. Lebra (Ed.), *Transcultural Research in Mental Health*. Honolulu: University Press of Hawaii, 1972, 213-226.
35. Laughlin, H. P., *The Neuroses*. Washington, D.C.: Butterworths, 1967, 2.

5

Dimensions of Social Psychiatric Impairment (SPI): Psychopathology and Symptom Patterns*

The statistical model used to assess social psychiatric impairment (SPI) in our major survey was derived from the curves of error and theory of probability developed by Gauss in the early part of the 19th century to predict the velocity of molecules (1). In the 1830s the great Belgian astronomer and statistician, L. A. J. Quetelet, showed that the theory of probability could be applied to human characteristics such as height and weight (2). And in the latter part of the 19th century, Sir Francis Galton and, later, Binet and others, showed that a reasonably large population's intelligence scores were normatively distributed, described by the bell-shaped curve (3, 4). In this century, Sjöbring in Sweden, and then his former students, Essen-Möller and Hagnell, used the statistical model to assess the distribution of personality characteristics in random samples of the general population (5, 6).

The statistical approach assumes that the average is normal. Therefore, we labeled those who scored higher than one standard deviation above the mean on each of the various dimensions of SPI as high-risk respondents. At least by implication, the high-risk respondents were considered to be in need of mental health care. In contrast, those scoring more than one standard deviation below the mean (and meeting other criteria) were considered to be exceptionally healthy, the supernormal.

The Interview Instrument

The interview instrument administered to the random sample of 1645 adult respondents contained more than 100 questions about the presence of symptoms of various types of mental disorder:

* With the collaboration of Neal D. Traven.

1) the neurotic conditions—anxiety (worry and nervousness), depression (lowered mood, appetite and sleep disturbance, suicidal thoughts, etc.), obsessive-compulsiveness, and phobias;

2) more severe mental disturbances—depersonalization or feeling that everything is unreal, paranoid thinking centered on thoughts that others are following or plotting against the subject or that they are attempting to pick quarrels with him or her, trouble with memory and the difficulties produced by a memory disturbance, and hallucinations;

3) alcoholism.

The Bell Global Psychopathology Scale

From the pool of items, psychiatrists independently selected the 33 that they considered most clinically useful and that covered the various types of psychopathology being studied. These were evaluated by statistical measures and developed into the Bell Global Psychopathology Scale.* For the total sample the mean score was 23.3 (range 0-94,

* The Bell Global Psychopathology Scale was based on the following items:
Do you ever have loss of appetite?
Do you ever feel weak all over?
Do you ever have spells of dizziness?
Do you feel in good spirits?
Do you sometimes wonder if anything is worthwhile anymore?
Would you say you worry or get nervous when you don't have any immediate problem?
How often are you worried or nervous?
Do you have any strong fears about any particular animals or insects?
Do you have any strong fears about high places?
Do you have any strong fears about closed-in places?
Do you have any strong fears about driving or riding in a car?
Do you have any strong fears about being in crowds?
Do you have any strong fears about strangers?
In the last year, how often did you feel that you might have a nervous breakdown or that you might lose your mind?
Have you ever had periods of days or weeks when you couldn't take care of things because you couldn't get going?
When things don't turn out, how often would you say you blame yourself?
How often do you feel alone and helpless?
How often do you feel that life is hopeless?
How does the future look to you?
How often do you think about suicide?
How often do you have trouble concentrating or keeping your mind on what you are doing?
How often do you have unwelcome or strange thoughts or thoughts that frighten you?
How often do you find yourself doing the same things over and over to be sure that they are right?

standard deviation, 14.3); 246 respondents, 15.0%, scored 38+ i.e., in the high-risk range.*

SOCIODEMOGRAPHIC VARIABLES

Age

As shown in Table 5-1, we found a curvilinear relationship between age and high scores. This finding contrasts with the results from other surveys of mental illness in the community, almost all of which have reported a linear relationship with age—lower psychopathology scores in the younger age groups and significantly higher scores with advancing age. Our finding that the youngest respondents had the highest mean score is ominous. It supplied a data base supporting the increasing attention given to mental illness and, especially, suicide in young adults.

Sex and Race

As a group, females had a higher mean score than males, and blacks had a higher mean score than whites. Significant race-sex differences were apparent. Black females had a significantly higher mean score than either white females or black males whose scores did not differ significantly from each other. White males had a significantly lower mean score than

---

How often do you have trouble remembering things?
Does it [trouble remembering things] cause you difficulty?
How often do you feel that people are trying to pick quarrels or start arguments with you?
How often do you think people are following you or plotting against you?
How often do things not seem real to you or do you have feelings that you are not really here?
How often do you see or hear things that other people don't think are there?
Has drinking caused any trouble or problems for you?
Do you think you drink too much for your own good?
How often would you say you use alcohol to help you face your problems?
How often do you have trouble with sleeping?

* We examined both the reliability and validity of the Bell Global Psychopathology Scale. The reliability coefficient, Cronbach's Alpha, was 0.84. To assess validity, we administered the scale to 119 psychiatric inpatients and outpatients. Their mean score was 52.8, much higher than that of the Florida Health Study sample, 23.3. Of the patients, 84 (70.6%) scored in the high-risk range—above the empirically determined cut-off point for the random sample. Over one-half of the patient group who scored in the normal range had been diagnosed as schizophrenics; only 20 of 38 (52.6%) schizophrenics' scores were in the high-risk range. On the other hand, 33 of 34 (97.1%) patients diagnosed as depressive neurotics scored in the high-risk range. An extensive report on the Bell Global Psychopathology Scale is being prepared for publication.

TABLE 5-1

Scores on the Bell Global Psychopathology Scale by sociodemographic variables.

Sociodemographics	N	Mean ± s.d.	Sig.	% High (38+)
TOTAL	1645	23.3±14.3	—	15.0
Age:				
16-22	270	25.6±13.7		16.7
23-29	315	21.2±12.0		10.5
30-44	411	22.4±15.1	F (4,1638) = 4.16	14.8
45-59	332	23.9±15.0	p<.005	16.6
60+	315	23.8±14.8		16.2
Sex:				
Male	736	20.6±13.6	t (1643) = 7.05	11.1
Female	909	25.5±14.5	p<.0005	18.0
Race:				
White	1267	22.2±13.5	t (1631) = 6.29	12.7
Black	366	27.5±16.2	p<.0005	23.2
Race-Sex:				
White Male	574	19.8±12.7		9.6
White Female	693	24.1±13.9	F (3,1629)=29.64	15.3
Black Male	153	23.8±16.2	p<.0005	17.6
Black Female	213	30.1±15.6		27.2
SES:				
Lower	212	30.7±16.6		31.6
Lower-Middle	379	26.0±16.3		20.3
Middle	479	22.6±12.6	F (4,1640) =30.58	11.9
Upper-Middle	351	19.7±11.9	p<.005	8.8
High	224	18.9±11.7		6.3
Marital Status:				
Single	295	25.4±13.6		16.6
Married	1009	21.2±13.6		11.8
Widowed	170	27.3±15.3	F (4,1640) =17.96	22.4
Separated	69	32.4±17.6	p<.0005	30.4
Divorced	102	25.0±14.8		18.6
Geographic Origin:				
Alachua	451	26.0±15.6		21.1
Other Florida	469	22.8±13.5	F (3,1641) = 9.64	11.1
Deep South	213	24.0±14.9	p<.0005	19.7
Elsewhere	512	21.2±13.3		11.1

any of the other race-sex groups. More detailed analyses showed that the white respondents in the 16-22 age group had a much higher mean score than whites in other age groups. In contrast, among the black age groups there was much less variation.

Socioeconomic Status

We found a strong inverse relationship between socioeconomic status (SES) and mean psychopathology scores. Almost five times as many in the low SES as in the top SES quintile were in the high-risk category. Furthermore, controlling for SES washed out much of the observed racial differences. Within SES groups, the black males did not have a significantly higher mean score than the white males; however, the black females in the lower-middle and middle SES quintiles had a slightly higher mean score than the white females in corresponding SES groups.

Marital Status

The separated had a significantly higher mean score than those in the other marital statuses. The scores of the widowed, the singles, and the divorced did not differ much, but the married respondents had a significantly lower mean score than did the separated.

Predictors

A multiple regression analysis disclosed that of the 11 sociodemographic variables we considered, the only significant predictors of high psychopathology scale scores were: being young, female, and in the low SES group. Of these, being female and low SES were by far the most important. Age was a weak predictor, indicating that it was not only the older age groups who were at high risk. These variables explained only 10.7% of the variance in the scale scores.

High- and Low-Risk Groups

In summary, the especially high-risk groups were:

1) respondents in the two lower SES quintiles;
2) blacks, particularly females; and
3) the widowed and the separated.

The low-risk groups were:

1) white males;
2) respondents aged 23-29;
3) those in the highest SES quintile; and
4) the married.

SYMPTOM PATTERNS

Neurotic Conditions

Anxiety: Epidemiologic estimates indicate that the prevalence of anxiety severe enough to warrant treatment is very high, but estimates vary according to the criteria used for defining anxiety. For example, in 1961 Cattell and Scheier stated that a conservative consensus would show that about 20% of the American population needed treatment for disorders in which anxiety played a prominent role (7). However, in his 1972 review of "The Nature of Anxiety," Lader notes that "Anxiety is an ubiquitous phenomenon in everyday life," but that in the total population the prevalence of clinical anxiety states is 2-5% and in psychiatric patients, 7-16% (8). The importance of anxiety in medical practice is emphasized by Mendel who believes that it is the most common reason for a person to seek the help of a physician (9). Adams and Hope maintain that "as a clinical syndrome, the anxiety state outranks all other problems in general medicine" (10).

On our anxiety subscale, 15.3% of the respondents scored higher than one standard deviation above the mean. Proportionately more blacks and females scored in the high-risk range than did whites and males. Other groups with proportionately many scoring in the high-risk range were: those aged 60+, respondents in the lower-middle and especially the lowest SES quintiles, and the widowed or separated. Those groups with proportionately few respondents scoring in high-risk range were: aged 23-29, white males, or in the upper-middle and high SES quintiles.

Depression: The "age of anxiety" was succeeded by the "decade of depression" during the 1970s. In fact, it appears as if the prevalence of depression is reaching epidemic proportions. A few years ago the NIMH estimated that at least 8 million Americans were depressed. Some authorities think that even this large figure is conservative and that possibly as many as 12 million American adults are depressed. In the mid 1960s it was estimated that one in 10 would suffer sometime in life from depressive illness severe enough to require treatment; currently, one's life chances may be as high as one in six. G. W. Brown's recent study of women in London showed that 16% were depressed (11).

The seriousness of the problem of depression is illustrated by Lehman's contention that only one out of five depressed persons receives treatment, only one of 50 is hospitalized, and possibly, one in 200 commits suicide (12).

On our depression subscale, 14.5% of the sample scored in the high-risk range. As shown in Table 5-2, we found a curvilinear relationship between age and high mean depression scores. Proportionately more who scored in the high-risk range were respondents aged 16-22, 45-59, and 60+ than those aged 23-29.

The relationships between depression scores and age groups are particularly important. Until recently, most studies of depression in the general population or among medical patients reported a linear relationship between depressive symptomatology and advancing age. However, the results from some of our research, as well as that of other current investigators, indicate that many late adolescents and young adults are depressed. These findings are receiving widespread publicity in view of the sharply rising suicide rates for adolescents and young adults; the rate in the 15-24 age group has doubled in the last 20 years (13). One of the maxims of epidemiology is that the shifting of the age base for any chronic or recurrent illness toward younger age groups forebodes an increasing prevalence of the particular illness. Its validity has been demonstrated tragically by studies of the epidemiology of coronary heart disease, 1945 to 1975. Many more young men than expected were afflicted during those years when the death rate for ischemic heart disease for the total population rose sharply.

As we anticipated, females, as a group, had a significantly higher mean depression score than males, a finding consistent with the results of most studies of depression. The higher rate of depression in females than in males has been explained on genetic, psychodynamic, and sociocultural bases. It has been postulated that females are genetically susceptible because the trait is carried on the X chromosome and females have a double loading—the 23rd chromosome in females is XX whereas in males it is XY. Psychodynamically it is believed that females internalize aggression (and thus become depressed) to a much greater extent than males, who are more likely to "act out." And socioculturally, it is thought that the historically restrictive roles of females are conducive to depression. In contrast, the greater variety of roles available to males may offer them some protection against depression.

TABLE 5-2

Scores on the depression subscale by sociodemographic variables.

Sociodemographics	N	Mean ± s.d.	Sig.	% High (14+)
TOTAL	1645	8.1±5.4	—	14.5
Age:				
16.22	270	8.6±4.9		13.0
23-29	315	7.1±4.6		8.6
30-44	411	7.7±5.7	F (4,1638) = 5.46	15.3
45-59	332	8.5±5.5	p < .0005	15.4
60+	315	8.6±5.8		19.4
Sex:				
Male	736	7.3±5.2	t (1643) = 5.08	9.9
Female	909	8.7±5.5	p < .0005	18.2
Race:				
White	1267	7.7±5.2	t (1631) = 5.62	12.5
Black	366	9.5±5.9	p < .0005	21.3
Race-Sex:				
White Male	574	6.9±4.8		8.0
White Female	693	8.3±5.4	F (3,1629) = 18.69	16.3
Black Male	153	8.8±6.1	p < .0005	17.0
Black Female	213	9.9±5.7		24.4
SES:				
Lower	212	10.9±6.2		29.7
Lower-Middle	379	9.3±6.0		20.8
Middle	479	7.7±4.9	F (4,1640) = 36.43	11.7
Upper-Middle	351	6.6±4.3	p < .0005	8.3
High	224	6.3±4.4		4.9
Marital Status:				
Single	295	9.0±5.2		14.2
Married	1009	7.1±4.9		11.3
Widowed	170	10.0±5.9	F (4,1640) = 25.34	23.5
Separated	69	11.6±6.5	p < .0005	33.3
Divorced	102	9.2±6.2		18.6
Geographic Origin:				
Alachua	451	9.0±5.8		21.1
Other Florida	469	7.9±5.1	F (3,1641) = 7.78	11.9
Deep South	213	8.0±5.3	p < .0005	15.5
Elsewhere	512	7.4±5.2		10.5

Recently, Eisenberg, Radloff, and others have suggested that higher rates of depression in females are limited to married females, i.e., that unmarried females do not have higher depression scores than unmarried males (14, 15). For many women in contemporary society, marriage can entail diminished status, a restrictive role, limited opportunities for self-expression, numerous responsibilities, and few adult interactions other than with the husband. A common emotional reaction is depression. When we examined males' and females' depression scores, controlling for marital status, *both* single and married females had significantly higher scores than their male counterparts. But, we found no sex differences in the depression scores of the widowed, separated, or divorced—supporting only in part the views advanced by Eisenberg, Radloff and others. (See Table 5-3.)

Our results are consistent with most reports of the higher prevalence of depression among females than males in Western society; however, they also indicate that depression and marital status are complex subjects requiring further study.

As a group, the separated had a significantly higher mean depression score than the married. We think that roles and statuses are related to differences in groups' depression scores, but that other sociocultural factors, such as the presence or absence of social support systems, are also determinants of differences in males' and females' depression scores.

The blacks had a significantly higher mean score than the whites. For years the prevalence of depression in blacks was thought to be especially low; in fact, they were believed to be relatively "immune" to depressive illness, as evidenced by their low suicide rates. However, those early studies that also noted the much higher homicide rates among

TABLE 5-3

Mean depression subscale scores of males and females within marital status groups.

	Mean Depression Score				
Sex	Single N = 295	Married N = 1009	Widowed N = 170	Separated N = 69	Divorced N = 102
Males	8.5	6.6	8.0	11.3	9.1
Females	9.7	7.6	10.3	11.8	9.2
Sig.	$p<.05$	$p<.001$	n.s.	n.s.	n.s.

blacks than whites did not emphasize the inverse relationship between suicide and homicide in oppressed groups. Psychodynamically, depression is produced in part by the internalization of aggression. Thus, when there is evidence of the externalization of aggression, e.g., a high homicide rate or war, the frequency of depression is low. From a social psychiatric viewpoint, low suicide and high homicide rates in a group are fundamentals of the psychology of oppression. Recently, however, suicide rates among blacks have been rising sharply; currently they are higher for non-white females in the United States than at any time in history. Clinically, we have observed that social distance is a factor blocking the sensitivity of white doctors and nurses to their black patients' emotional distress, such as depression. Consequently, blacks' depressive conditions often are not diagnosed.

We found a particularly strong inverse relationship between SES and depression scores. Of those in the lowest SES quintile, 29.7% scored in the high-risk range for depression, in contrast to only 4.9% of those in the highest quintile. The relationships among SES, race, and depressive symptomatology warrant attention. In an earlier study, Warheit and his colleagues conducted detailed analyses of SES, race, and depression scores (16). Significant racial differences in the scores disappeared when they were controlled for SES; both whites and blacks in the lower SES quintiles had very high depression scores. Furthermore, multiple regression equations disclosed that low SES was the most important sociodemographic variable associated with high scores on their depression scale. For example, a given respondent's depression score would increase by approximately 2.4 points for every quintile reduction in his or her SES score. Thus, controlling for SES tended to erase racial differences on depression scores.

In summary, the high-risk group for depression consisted of: 1) respondents in low SES, 2) black females, and 3) the widowed or separated. The low-risk groups were made up of: 1) white males, 2) respondents in the two highest SES quintiles, and 3) those aged 23-29.

Phobias: Each respondent was questioned about specific fears of animals or insects, high places, confining spaces, riding in automobiles, being in crowds, and strangers; 15.5% of the sample scored high on the phobia scale. Age was not a significant factor, but sex, race, SES, and marital status were significant variables. As groups, proportionately many of those scoring in the high-risk range were: females, blacks, those in the low or lower-middle SES brackets, and the widowed or separated. The differences among the race-sex groups were striking: 38.5% of the black females had high phobia scores, in contrast to only 6.8% of the white males. A multiple regression analysis using age, sex, race, SES, and marital status as variables showed that being female and being black were strongly associated with phobias, whereas age, SES, and marital status were not.

Often, we found that multivariate and other detailed analyses that controlled for SES washed out racial differences in scale scores. However, on the phobia subscale, even the female, black, middle SES group had a much higher score than other demographic groups. Psychiatric theory considers phobias to be excessive, irrational anxiety states characterized by the displacement of anxiety toward specific objects or situations. But certain fears, even of phobic proportions, are so common that they are not necessarily regarded as abnormal unless they impair the person's functioning. The percentages of our random sample reporting the various phobias were:

Phobia	*Percent*
Animals or Insects	30.0
High Places	29.4
Confining Spaces	23.3
Riding in Automobiles	10.2
Being in Crowds	11.3
Strangers	10.6

Our findings should be viewed from a social psychiatric as well as from a psychoanalytic perspective. Fears of driving or riding in a car may have some basis in reality in view of the high motor vehicle accident rate. Some of the phobias can be linked to historical and cultural factors. Fear of animals (especially dogs) and of strangers may have had particular significance in Alachua County because dogs had been used in the South to track escaped slaves or, later, to protect property against blacks. Fear of strangers may be related to the formerly closed society's social order; almost all strangers were considered "suspect"—a threat to the system.

Agoraphobia (fear of being in crowds) is currently receiving a great deal of publicity and agoraphobia clinics are being opened in a number of cities. Recently, Fensterheim and Baer estimated that 12 per 1000 persons in the United States suffer from agoraphobia and that it is severe in 6 per 1000 (17). Our data indicate that this condition is much more common, reported by 11.3% of the adult population (a rate of 113 per 1000). Fear of being in crowds was reported significantly more often by females, especially black females, and by respondents in the low and lower-middle SES quintiles than by those in other sociodemographic groups. There were no significant age or marital status relationships. But in accord with our general hypothesis about the mental health of the Alachuans, significantly more of this group than those from Other Florida, the Deep South, or Elsewhere reported fear of being in crowds.

Obsessive Compulsiveness: In his review of the epidemiology of obsessive-compulsive neurosis, Nemiah states: "It is probably a rare person who has not at some time in his life experienced a fleeting bit of obsessional thinking or compulsive behavior. . . . The exact incidence of obsessive-compulsive neurosis is hard to determine. . . . Those who have studied the natural history of the disorder have found an incidence that is never higher than 5 per cent of all psychoneurotic patients, the percentage, of course, being lower if the total population includes patients with psychoses" (18). Nemiah notes that among patient groups there are no sexual differences in the frequency of obsessive-compulsive neurosis, but that many are unmarried and more are in the upper than the lower SES brackets. These findings have been obtained from studies of psychiatrists' and other physicians' practices, not gleaned from studies of the general population, and thus do not include the untreated obsessive-compulsive persons.

In our study, 13.9% scored in the high-risk range on the obsessive-compulsive subscale. Proportionately more young respondents, aged 16-22, females, and the single scored in the high-risk range than those aged 45-59 and 60+ males, and the married and the widowed as groups. We found no significant race or SES differences, but a disproportionately low percentage of respondents in the top SES quintile scored in the high-risk range.

These epidemiologic data are at variance with reports from psychiatrists' practices. It appears that patients obtaining treatment for neuroses, such as obsessive-compulsiveness, tend to come from the middle- and upper-social classes; obviously many of the poor and those in minority groups do not obtain mental health care for symptoms of obsessive-compulsiveness. Our results indicate that many younger respondents and many females, particularly black females, report obsessive-compulsive symptomatology. It is quite likely that this symptomatology is more common in the community at large than hitherto thought.* Its pervasiveness in all SES groups, and particularly among the younger respondents, supports Halliday's and Riesman and his colleagues' contentions that the obsessive character type is becoming more common, and by implication, that it is produced by the techno-environmental changes occurring in Western societies (19, 20).

INDICATORS OF MORE SERIOUS MENTAL DISORDERS

To evaluate the frequency and distribution of risk for more serious mental illness, we asked each respondent about depersonalization, difficulty with memory and related problems, paranoid ideation (feelings that people are picking quarrels and of being followed or plotted against), and hallucinations.

Depersonalization

In clinical psychiatry, complaints of depersonalization and derealization—sensing a distortion of the relationship between oneself and the environment—are usually expressed as a feeling that everything is different or unreal or that one has changed temporarily so that he or she is not in contact with what is happening. Recurrent symptoms of depersonalization are regarded as evidence of a serious neurosis, as symptomatology that is borderline in severity between neurosis and psychosis, or as an early manifestation of psychosis. Psychodynamically, depersonalization is considered to be a maladaptive defense against overwhelming anxiety.

Little is known about the prevalence of symptoms of depersonalization in the general population. Of the 1645 respondents, 1.6% reported feelings of unreality "often or all the time"; 19.9% scored higher than one standard deviation above the mean on the subscale. These feelings were reported significantly more often by the youngest respondents (aged

* Although the percentage defined as high risk was arbitrarily determined—scoring higher than one standard deviation above the mean—that percentage varies considerably: Anxiety—15.3%, depression—14.5%, phobias —15.5%, obsessive-compulsiveness—13.9%, depersonalization—19.9%, memory difficulties—19.9%, paranoia—9.4%, hallucinations—10.8%, and alcoholism—10.3%. Thus, although one or more standard deviations above and below the mean encompasses 31.7% of the sample and statistically we would expect that 15.8% would score above and 15.8% below the mean, we see that this distribution varies; for example, about twice as many respondents scored in the high-risk range on memory difficulties as on paranoia.

16-22), blacks, those in the two lowest SES quintiles, and the single or separated than by their counterparts. There were no significant sex or race-sex differences. Relatively low percentages of those aged 60+ or those in the highest SES quintile reported this type of distress.

In a later chapter, after the results of the follow-up study are reported, we will look at the health status of the respondents who were in the high-risk range on the depersonalization subscale and thus be able to evaluate the clinical importance of reports of this type of distress. For example, we are interested in the possibility that symptoms of depersonalization presage even more serious mental illness. Thus, we will be attempting, in Jeremy Morris' terms, to "complete the clinical picture" (21).

Difficulty with Memory

Of the sample, 19.9% scored in the high-risk range on the difficulty with memory subscale. As we anticipated, memory problems were significantly more prevalent among the older than younger respondents. Also, proportionately larger percentages of whites (particularly females), lower SES quintile persons, and the widowed reported memory difficulties than did other groups of respondents.

Memory difficulties usually increase with age and, to a variable extent, reflect declining intellectual powers. Also, memory difficulties enlarge the elderly person's sense of inadequacy and helplessness. They can dispose to the distress and added deficits of depressive and other conditions. Concern about memory difficulties leads the elderly to live in isolation; consequently, they have few social interactions and their sensory inputs fall below the threshold essential for emotional well-being. Consider, for example, the elderly person's dependence on public transportation. With memory difficulties, he or she is disinclined to make necessary trips, even for vitally needed medical care, to say nothing of small expenditures for business or pleasure. In our highly complex society, the memory difficulties experienced by the elderly are potentiated by the rapid rate of social change which, in itself, tends to be disorienting.

Paranoia

We were particularly interested in the results from the paranoia subscale because paranoid thinking encompasses a broad range—stretching from fears that have some basis in reality to frank delusions of personal danger. Furthermore, sociocultural factors can be influential determinants of a paranoid outlook. For example, in the Southeast, the blacks' fears of exploitation and bodily harm were reality-based, at least until recently. To determine whether the ideation is indicative of clinical paranoia or is culture-bound, one has to ascertain the norm for the subcultural group and also determine whether the disturbance in thinking, typical of paranoia, impairs the person's judgment, behavior, and functioning. Paranoia in subcultural or oppressed groups can be diagnosed only when ideation is abnormal according to group standards, is accompanied by other symptoms of mental illness that are not easily reversible, and/or is associated with impaired functioning.

Only 9.4% of the total sample scored in the high-risk range on the paranoia subscale. Proportionately more respondents aged 16-22, blacks (both males and females), the separated, and those in the lowest and lower-middle SES quintiles scored in the high-risk range than other groups. Very low percentages of those in the upper-middle and high SES quintiles (which contained very few blacks) scored in the high-risk range.

In all age groups—and especially for the younger respondents—the blacks' mean paranoia scale score was significantly higher than that of the whites. Classifying the sample into SES quintiles, however, showed that the mean paranoia scores for blacks were significantly higher than for whites in only the lower-middle and the middle quintiles.

A multiple regression equation showed that being black, young, in lower SES, or separated were significantly associated with higher paranoia scale scores. But these four variables explained only 8.2% of the variance. Controlling for SES did *not* erase the racial differences as it had for depression.

Finding that the blacks had a high level of suspicion is consistent with our expectations. For years they were an exploited group in the South; simply to remain alive required a high degree of vigilance and caution. Cash describes the extreme degree of violence inflicted by whites on blacks, especially during The Reconstruction Era and periods of economic decline (22). During Reconstruction, "[T]he old streak of brutality and cruelty began now to swell into definite sadism . . . . (that began) to generate, among both common whites and planters, a type of deliberate nigger-hazers and nigger-killers" (23). And during the Great Depression, the murder rate in southern towns was 23.1 per 100,000 in 1937; in contrast it was only 1.3 per 100,000 in New England and 4.7 in the Mountain States.

Hallucinations

Of our sample, 178 respondents (10.8%) reported ever having hallucinations. Proportionately larger groups of respondents aged 16-22, female, black, in the two lower SES quintiles, single or separated reported hallucinations than did those in other sociodemographic groups. Very few respondents in the upper SES brackets reported hallucinations. Most who reported hallucinations stated that they were uncommon but replied in the affirmative when asked whether they had occurred recently. Somewhat paradoxically, only 41 persons reported that their hallucinations disturbed them.

An intensive study of hallucinations in one of the small all-black communities in Alachua County by M. E. Schwab revealed that much larger numbers of two distinct groups—young adult females and elderly males—reported hallucinations than did others (24). The hallucinations reported by the two groups had vastly different characteristics and meanings. Among the young black females, the hallucinations were usually terrifying and associated with other indicators of psychopathology such as phobias and even more generalized emotional distress. In contrast, the hallucinations reported by the elderly males had a tranquil, placid character; usually they involved religious themes, resembled hypnogogic states, and could be interpreted as being "compensatory" phenomena.

We speculate that the relatively large number of young persons in the total sample, particularly the single, reporting hallucinatory experiences may be attributable to drug use. Of the total sample, 9.1% reported that on some occasion they had used drugs that had caused them to hallucinate. The use of hallucinogens was reported by significantly more young, white, male, middle SES, and single respondents than by those in corresponding groups (25).

Alcoholism

Determining the prevalence of alcoholism in the general population is complicated because the researcher must differentiate between the level of alcohol use that is socially acceptable in many societies and excessive drinking that too often produces behavior disorders and physical illnesses. In approaching this subject we had two objectives, first to ascertain the frequency and patterns of alcohol use, and second, to measure alcoholism according to our operational definition. In response to the question: "How often do you drink alcohol (beer, wine, whiskey)?" 65.2% reported that they drank; of these, 39.7% said that they did so "seldom," 36.8% "sometimes," 14.8% "often," and 8.8% "all the time." More males, whites, and particularly, upper-middle and upper SES respondents drank "frequently" than did females, blacks, and those in the low, lower-middle and middle SES quintiles. The respondents aged 30-44 and 45-59 reported drinking more often than those in the younger or older age groups. But those aged 60+ tended to be either "heavy" or "light" drinkers. Marital status was not significantly associated with the frequency of alcohol use (26).

Thus we found that there were significant sociodemographic patterns of alcohol use. For example, many upper SES respondents reported drinking often or every day but probing questions indicated that in many instances they consumed only small amounts of alcohol at a time. Therefore, we did not think that responses to questions about how often a person drank would provide accurate data on alcoholism. We restricted our operational definition of alcoholism to respondents' reports that alcohol use was related to problems in living. Our alcoholism scale consisted of three items:

1. "Has drinking caused any trouble or problems for you?"
2. "Do you think you drink too much for your own good?"
3. "How often would you say you use alcohol to help you face your problems?"

Of the total sample, 10.3% scored higher than one standard deviation above the mean. Proportionately larger percentages of the males, both black and white, and the divorced scored in the high-risk range than did respondents in other sociodemographic groups. Contrary to our expectations, there were no significant SES differences. Very low percentages of black females and the widowed scored in the high-risk range.

In an earlier study of respondents' use of licit and illicit drugs and alcohol we found the trends shown in Table 5-4.

We concluded that licit drug use was related, in part, to emotional distress; that illicit drug use was largely a youthful, white, male, middle-class cultural phenomenon; and that the frequent use of alcohol by higher SES groups indicated that it may be a characteristic of their life styles (27).

TABLE 5-4

Trends in the use of licit and illicit drugs and alcohol.

SOCIODEMOGRAPHIC CHARACTERISTICS		Stimulants, Hallucinogens, and/or Alcohol	Stimulants, Hallucinogens, and/or Alcohol (limited use)	Stimulants and/or especially Alcohol	Psychotropic Agents and/or Alcohol	Psychotropics and/or Sedatives	Sedatives	Sedatives and/or Hallucinogens	Licit and Illicit Drugs and/or Alcohol	Psychotropics, Sedatives, Stimulants, Hallucinogens, and/or Alcohol	Hallucinogens and/or Alcohol	No Discernible Trend
AGE:	Younger Persons	●										
	Middle Aged				●							
	Elderly						●					
SEX:	Male										●	
	Female					●						
RACE:	White*								●			
SES:	Lower		●									
	Middle	●										
	Upper			●								
MARITAL STATUS:	Single	●										
	Married											●
	Widowed					●						
	Separated							●				
	Divorced									●		

(Column group heading: DRUGS AND ALCOHOL)

NOTE: Dot indicates significant overrepresentation.

*** Larger percentages of whites than blacks. See Reference 26.**

PSYCHOPATHOLOGY SCORES AND GEOGRAPHIC ORIGIN

Since the County had experienced rapid growth and most of the respondents were not Alachua natives, we were particularly interested in these geographic groups' psychopathology scale scores and in possible differential manifestations of emotional distress. As shown in Table 5-1, on the Bell Global Psychopathology Scale, the Alachuans had a significantly higher mean score than those from Elsewhere. The respondents from Other Florida and the Deep South had scores very close to the mean for the total sample. Table 5-5 shows the significant findings on the subscales that gauged symptom patterns.

These findings reveal the extensive symptomatic distress of Alachuans, and to a much lesser extent, of the respondents from the Deep South. The significantly lower scores on the various subscales of those from Elsewhere than of the Alachuans support our hypothesis that the newcomers to the County had a better mental health status than the natives. Since the findings related to obsessive-compulsive symptomatology and to alcoholism in particular did not differ significantly among the geographic groups, we conjecture that the sociocultural associations with such disorders are more national than regional in character. Finding that memory difficulties were not related to any geographic group can be explained by the highly significant association between such disturbances and advancing age. Further explanations of these results depend upon more complete examination of possible associations between social factors and the respondents' mental health statuses.

SUMMARY

The respondents' scores on the psychopathology scale and its subscales lead to the following conclusions:

1) The curvilinear relationship between age and higher scores on a number of scales indicates that emotional distress is more prevalent among late adolescents and young adults than has been reported previously. It supports the contention that this age group was under stress probably attributable to the Vietnam War and to broader sociocultural factors that have prolonged their transitional social status. The stress was dramatized by "the generation gap" of the early 1970s.

2) Generally, the differences in the males' and females' scores are consistent with findings reported by other investigators who have studied mental health and illness in the community.

TABLE 5-5

Statistically significant associations between proportion of respondents scoring "High" on psychopathology (Px) subscales (symptom patterns) and geographic origin.*

GEOGRAPHIC ORIGIN	Anxiety	Depression	Phobias	Depersonalization	Paranoia	Hallucinations	Obsessive-Compulsive	Memory Difficulties	Alcoholism
	SYMPTOM PATTERNS								
Alachua County	H	H	H	H	H	n.s.	n.s.	n.s.	n.s.
Other Florida	n.s.	L	n.s.	n.s.	L	n.s.	n.s.	n.s.	n.s.
Deep South	H	n.s.	n.s.	n.s.	n.s.	H	n.s.	n.s.	n.s.
Elsewhere	L	L	L	L	L	L	n.s.	n.s.	n.s.

* H = Significantly Overrepresented; L = Significantly Underrepresented; n.s. = Not Significant

3) In many instances, the blacks' higher scores on the various scales were erased by controlling for socioeconomic status, indicating that lower SES—not race—was the truly significant association. Two exceptions were the blacks' high scores on the phobia and paranoia subscales; we speculate that this is a socioculturally determined finding that is traceable to the rigid social order, the enduring effects of the caste system.

4) The plight of black females was unusually severe. Repeatedly, they had significantly higher scores on the various scales than the three other race-sex groups. We think that their symptomatic distress reflected their role strain and lack of status—both racially and sexually—and concomitantly the deprivations they had suffered.

5) With only a few exceptions, especially scores on the alcoholism subscale, we found a highly significant association between lower SES and symptoms of mental disorders, consistent with other epidemiologists' results.

6) As a small, discrete group, large percentages of the separated respondents scored in the high-risk range on our scales. We think that

their transitional status may be responsible for this finding but it is impossible even to allude to the direction of such an association; preexisting symptomatic distress may have been responsible for the breakup of the marriage, for prolonged transitional status, or for the inability to develop or call upon potentially available social support systems.

7) As a group, the respondents from Alachua County had significantly higher scores on most of our indices of emotional distress than those who had grown up in other areas.

In the next chapter we will present our respondents' scores on the two other dimensions of SPI: impairment of functioning and interpersonal distress. Then we will discuss the three dimensions of SPI and the comparisons of the respondents in High Risk, Normal, and "Supernormal" categories. To scrutinize our findings more completely, we will then look at the sample's HOS scores and compare those in the caseness range with those in the SPI category.

REFERENCES

1. DAMPIER, W. C., *A History of Science and Its Relations with Philosophy and Religion, 4th Edition.* Cambridge, England: University Press, 1966, 229-230.
2. Ibid., 230.
3. GALTON, F., *English Men of Science: Their Nature and Nurture.* London: Macmillan, 1874.
4. BINET, A., Cited in: Nunnally, J. C., *Tests and Measurements: Assessment and Prediction.* New York: McGraw-Hill Company, 1959, 163.
5. SJÖBRING, H., cited in Essen-Möller, E., "Individual Traits and Morbidity in a Swedish Rural Population," *Acta Psychiat. et Neurol. Scand., Suppl. 100,* Copenhagen: Ejnar Munksgaard, 1956.
6. HAGNELL, O., *A Prospective Study of the Incidence of Mental Disorder.* Lund, Sweden: Scandinavian Univ. Books, 1966.
7. CATTELL, R. B., and SCHEIER, I. H., *The Meaning and Measurement of Neuroticism and Anxiety.* New York: Ronald Press, 1961.
8. LADER, M. H., "The Nature of Anxiety," *British Journal of Psychiatry,* Vol. 121, 1972, 481.
9. MENDEL, W. M., and SOLOMON, P. (Eds.), *The Psychiatric Consultation.* New York: Grune and Stratton, 1968.
10. ADAMS, R. D., and HOPE, J. M., "The Anxiety State and Psychasthenia." In: T. R. Harrison, et al. (Eds.), *Principles of Internal Medicine.* New York: McGraw-Hill Book Company, 1962, 390-397.
11. BROWN, G. W., BROWN, W. B., BHROLCHAIN, M., and HARRIS, T., "Social Class and Psychiatric Disturbance Among Women in an Urban Population," *Sociology,* Vol. 9, 1975, 225-259.
12. LEHMAN, H. E., "Epidemiology of Depressive Disorders." In: R. R. Lieve (Ed.), *Depression in the 70's.* The Netherlands: Excerpta Medica, 1971, 21-30.

13. *1977 The U.S. Fact Book: The American Almanac. 97th Edition.* New York: Grosset and Dunlap, 1977, 159.
14. EISENBERG, L., "Psychiatry and Society: A Sociobiologic Synthesis," *New England Journal of Medicine,* Vol. 296, No. 16, April 21, 1977, 903-910.
15. RADLOFF, L., "Sex Differences in Depression: The Effects of Occupation and Marital Status," *Sex Roles,* Vol. 1, 1975, 249-265.
16. WARHEIT, G. J., HOLZER, C. E., III, and SCHWAB, J. J., "An Analysis of Social Class and Racial Differences in Depressive Symptomatology: A Community Study," *Journal of Health and Social Behavior,* Vol. 14, December, 1973, 291-299.
17. FENSTERHEIM, H., and BAER, J., *Stop Running Scared.* New York: Rawson Associates Publications, Inc., 1977.
18. NEMIAH, J. C., "Obsessive-Compulsive Neurosis." In: A. M. Freedman, H. I. Kaplan, and B. J. Sadock, *Comprehensive Textbook of Psychiatry/II, Vol. 1, 2nd Edition.* Baltimore: The Williams and Wilkins Company, 1975, 1243.
19. HALLIDAY, J. L., *Psychosocial Medicine: A Study of the Sick Society.* New York: W. W. Norton, 1948.
20. RIESMAN, D., in collaboration with DENNEY, R., and GLAZER, N., *The Lonely Crowd: A Study of the Changing American Character.* New Haven: Yale University Press, 1950.
21. MORRIS, J. N., *Uses of Epidemiology, 2nd Edition.* Baltimore: The Williams and Wilkins Company, 1964.
22. CASH, W. F., *The Mind of the South.* New York: Alfred A. Knopf, 1941.
23. Ibid., 122-123.
24. SCHWAB, M. E., "A Study of Reported Hallucinations in a Southeastern County." Unpublished paper.
25. SCHWAB, J. J., BERGER, A., TRAVEN, N. D., and WARHEIT, G. J., "Licit and Illicit Drugs: Patterns of Use." In: Deniker, et al. (Eds.), *Proceedings of the Xth International Congress of the Collegium Internationale Neuropsychopharmacologicum.* Oxford, England: Pergamon Press Ltd., 1978, 1273-1281.
26. Ibid.
27. Ibid.

6

Dimensions of Social Psychiatric Impairment (SPI): Impairment of Functioning and Interpersonal Distress*

Part I—Impairment of Functioning (FX)

As we saw in Chapter 4, the definition of mental illness depends only in part on the presence of symptoms of emotional distress. Difficulties in functioning or an inability to perform essential roles also are integral, if not fundamental, components of our definition. In the Midtown Manhattan Study, both the presence of psychopathology and an inability to function were criteria of impairment (1). On a seven-point scale, the unimpaired were defined as having "no significant symptom formation," and the most impaired as having symptoms of mental illness and also as being "seriously incapacitated, unable to function" (2).

But concepts of mental illness that include impairment of functioning or inability to fulfill role expectations as integral to the definition must take into account both the tautologies and the value judgments involved. In most instances, ability to function tends to decline with advancing age. Furthermore, functioning and, particularly, fulfilling the obligations of one's role are judged according to a given society's standards and values. To evaluate functioning either as a manifestation or as a result of mental illness, the investigator needs measures that are meaningful and applicable to various subgroups in the population and that also allow for subcultural variability. For example, in Alachua County, it is common practice for many older blacks not to go to work on Mondays or on the day after a holiday. Judging this "absenteeism" as impaired

* With the collaboration of Neal D. Traven.

functioning indicative of mental disorder can be a reflection of white middle-class standards and biases. Consequently, our functioning scale was dependent upon the respondents' judgments and was linked closely with emotional distress. For example, the respondents were asked: "During the last year, were you unable to do your usual work because of worry or nervousness?" If the reply were other than "never," they were asked "About how many days?" (3).

To assess impairment of functioning—our second dimension of SPI—we used a nine-item scale containing the following items:*

Are you presently employed?
How often do you attend the main worship service of your church/synagogue?
About how many afternoons and evenings a month would you say you spend in club activities?
Has ill health affected the amount of work (housework) you do?
For the most part, do you feel healthy enough to carry out the things that you would like to do?
During the last year, have you ever had to stay at home or in bed because of worry or nervousness?
During the last year, were you unable to do your usual work because of worry or nervousness?
During the last year, were you unable to do your usual work at any time because of feeling that you might have a nervous breakdown?
During the last year, have you ever had to stay at home or in bed because of this feeling [of possible nervous breakdown]?

Deliberately, we did not include interpersonal items pertaining to familial and other roles and relationships; these were reserved for the third dimension of SPI—Interpersonal Distress. The range of scores was from 0 to 31. As shown in Table 6-1, the mean score for the total sample was 7.5, and the standard deviation was 4.3.

Of the 1645 respondents, 229 (13.9%) scored in the high-risk range. Those aged 60+ had a significantly higher mean score than those aged 30-44. Disproportionately many of the respondents in the following groups scored in the high-risk range: blacks, and the separated, widowed, and divorced. Disproportionately few of the white males and the married had high-risk scores. The inverse relationship between mean scale scores and socioeconomic status (SES) was even stronger than that found for the psychopathology scale scores. Disproportionately more respondents in the two lower SES quintiles scored in the high-risk range than did

* Cronbach's Alpha was 0.62.

TABLE 6-1

Scores on Impairment of Functioning Scale by sociodemographic variables.

Sociodemographics	N	Mean ± s.d.	Sig.	% High (12+)
TOTAL	1645	7.5±4.3	—	13.9
Age:				
16-22	270	7.6±3.4		11.9
23-29	315	7.1±3.1		7.9
30-44	411	6.7±4.0	F (4,1638) = 9.46	11.2
45-59	332	7.8±4.9	p<.0005	16.3
60+	315	8.5±5.3		22.2
Sex:				
Male	736	7.4±4.2	t (1643)= 1.12	11.5
Female	909	7.6±4.4	n.s.	15.7
Race:				
White	1267	7.3±3.9	t (1631) = 3.61	12.0
Black	366	8.2±5.4	p<.0005	20.5
Race-Sex:				
White Male	574	7.1±3.8		8.9
White Female	693	7.4±4.0	F (3,1629) = 4.90	14.6
Black Male	153	8.3±5.6	p<.005	21.6
Black Female	213	8.2±5.3		19.7
SES:				
Lower	212	10.3±5.6		34.9
Lower-Middle	379	8.3±4.8		19.8
Middle	479	7.2±3.7	F (4,1640) =44.63	9.4
Upper-Middle	351	6.5±3.0	p<.0005	6.6
High	224	5.7±3.3		4.9
Marital Status:				
Single	295	7.6±3.8		12.2
Married	1009	7.0±3.9		10.8
Widowed	170	9.0±5.9	F (4,1640) =12.39	27.6
Separated	69	9.0±5.2	p<.0005	26.1
Divorced	102	8.4±4.9		17.6
Geographic Origin:				
Alachua	451	7.7±4.8		17.3
Other Florida	469	7.2±3.8	F (3,1641) = 3.75	10.7
Deep South	213	8.2±5.0	p<.05	21.6
Elsewhere	512	7.2±3.9		10.5

those in the top SES quintile, few of whom scored in the high-risk range.

A multiple regression equation disclosed that only three sociodemographic variables were significant predictors of impairment of functioning scores; they explained 10.6% of the variance. Low SES was by far the most significant predictor, followed by race (black) and being divorced. We were surprised that advancing age was not significantly related to impairment of functioning. We think that low SES was such a strong factor than it absorbed the influence of advancing age; 34.9% of the lowest quintile respondents scored in the high-risk range in contrast to 4.9% of those in the highest quintile, but we should note that a disproportionately large number of those in the lowest SES quintile were elderly.

HIGH- AND LOW-RISK GROUPS

A detailed analysis of the Impairment of Functioning scale scores showed that the especially high-risk groups were: 1) aged 60+, 2) blacks (regardless of sex), 3) those in the two lower SES quintiles, particularly the lowest, and 4) separated or widowed. Only the respondents aged 23-29, or in the upper-middle and upper SES quintiles were in the low-risk category.

Impairment of Functioning and Geographic Groups

Contrary to our expectations, we found no statistically significant associations between the respondents' geographic origins and either high or low scores on the Impairment of Functioning scale.

Analysis of Psychopathology and Impairment of Functioning Scores

The findings presented thus far show that 246 of the respondents (15%), scored in the high-risk range on the Psychopathology scale and that 229 (13.9%), scored high on the Impairment of Functioning scale. However, these were not mutually exclusive groups. An analysis of the data shows that we had the following discrete groups: 1) high-risk scores on the Psychopathology scale only, 7.6%; 2) high-risk scores on Impairment of Functioning scale only, 6.5%; and 3) high-risk scores on both scales, 7.4%.

Thus, 21.5% of the total sample were in the high-risk range for mental disorder on scales measuring these two dimensions of SPI. Since accepted definitions of mental illness encompass both symptoms of emotional distress and impairment of functioning, we determined the extent to which these two dimensions, singly and in combination, were displayed by various groups. The only significant, differentiating characteristics of the groups scoring in the high-risk range on the psychopathology and functioning scales were: 1) on Psychopathology only—younger age; 2) on Impairment of Functioning only—older age; and 3) on both scales—middle and older age or lower SES.

Adding Impairment of Functioning to Psychopathology as a dimension of SPI especially increased the number of elderly in the SPI category. Also, it increased moderately the number of low SES respondents in the SPI category supporting the often-noted association between lower social class status and a greater prevalence of mental disorders. A tautology, however, should be noted: logically, impaired functioning would be related to lower SES and also to advancing age.

Part II—Interpersonal Distress (IX)

Clinical experience reveals that many persons seeking mental health care do so mainly for interpersonal problems. Although symptoms of mental anguish or impaired functioning might have been presenting complaints, frequently they turn out to be either consequences of interpersonal problems or of secondary importance. To detect such persons and delineate their problems as sharply as possible, we conceptualized interpersonal distress as a third dimension of SPI and developed a scale to measure it.* This scale contained 12 items pertaining to problems with marriage, children, friends, relatives, and other social relationships. We had comparable items for unmarried respondents. The items were:

How often does your family complain that you don't spend enough time with them because of work? (married and/or dependent children)

At the present time, do you have any close relationships with a person of the opposite sex? (non-married)

How would you say that you get along with your husband/wife?

Do/did you feel that you have/had many, some, or few problems in raising your children? (ever had children)

Do you have friends with whom you can talk about your most personal problems, fears, or hopes?

How often do you get upset, uptight or irritable with those around you?

---

* Cronbach's Alpha coefficient was 0.47.

Ties—Average of responses to:

How often do you get to see or talk to [close relatives nearby]?
How often do you get to see or are in touch with [close relatives far away]?
How often do you get together with [close friends nearby]?
How often, do you feel helpless to deal with your/your family's problems?
During the last year, did worry or nervousness interfere with your your family life?
During the last year, did worry or nervousness interfere with your social activities?
During the last year has this feeling [of possible nervous breakdown] caused problems with your family/personal life?
Does this feeling [of possible nervous breakdown] interfere with your social activities?

The range of scores was from 0 to 30. The mean score for the total sample was 8.8, the standard deviation 4.7. Of the respondents, 256, 15.6%, scored in the high-risk range. (See Table 6-2.)

Those in the two middle-age groups, 30-44 and 45-59, had significantly higher mean scores than the youngest respondents. Thus, the distribution tended to be curvilinear, but the configuration was opposite to that found for the psychopathology and impairment of functioning scores. The middle-age groups had the lowest mean scores on those scales but the highest mean scores on interpersonal distress.

Disproportionately more females, both black and white, than males had high-risk scores. Black females had an especially high mean score; 24.9% of this group scored in the high-risk range in contrast to 17.5% of the white females and only about 11% of the males, regardless of race. Disproportionately more blacks, as a group, had high-risk scores than the whites. The extensive interpersonal distress expressed by the black females can be attributed to the widely publicized "problems of the black family." For decades, particularly but not exclusively in the South, the black family has had a matriarchal character. The mother, or often the grandmother, took care of the children and also worked, often as a maid, outside the home. The nuclear family structure was disrupted by the caste system's restrictions on the black male's opportunities for employment. After the couple had a few children, the black male's already marginal wages were inadequate; frequently he "disappeared," leaving the mother to cope as best she could. We saw many instances of this situation during the late 1960s. The influence of desegregation and television's daily display of the niceties of the middle-class life heightened the black

TABLE 6-2

Scores on the Interpersonal Distress Scale by sociodemographic variables.

Sociodemographics	N	Mean ± s.d.	Sig.	% High (14+)
TOTAL	1645	8.8±4.7	—	15.6
Age:				
16-22	270	7.8±4.3		11.9
23-29	315	8.4±4.6	F (4,1638)= 6.49	13.3
30-44	411	9.4±4.9	p<.0005	17.5
45-59	332	9.3±5.0		19.9
60+	315	8.8±4.3		13.7
Sex:				
Male	736	8.2±4.5	t (1643) = 4.64	11.0
Female	909	9.3±4.8	p<.0005	19.3
Race:				
White	1267	8.7±4.5	t (1631) = 2.91	14.7
Black	366	9.5±5.3	p<.005	18.9
Race-Sex:				
White Male	574	8.2±4.3		11.3
White Female	693	9.0±4.6	F (3,1629) =10.99	17.5
Black Male	153	8.4±5.1	p<.0005	10.5
Black Female	213	10.3±5.3		24.9
SES:				
Lower	212	10.2±4.8		22.6
Lower-Middle	379	9.4±5.4		20.6
Middle	479	8.3±4.5	F (4,1640) = 8.14	11.7
Upper-Middle	351	8.4±4.4	p<.0005	14.2
High	224	8.5±4.0		10.7
Marital Status:				
Single	295	8.0±4.4		11.2
Married	1009	8.5±4.5		14.0
Widowed	170	10.0±4.3	F (4,1640) =18.87	17.6
Separated	69	12.3±6.2	p<.0005	37.7
Divorced	102	10.2±5.3		25.5
Geographic Origin:				
Alachua	451	9.2±4.8	F (3,1641)= 3.36	17.7
Other Florida	469	8.3±4.6	p<.05	14.1
Deep South	213	9.1±4.9		19.2
Elsewhere	512	8.9±4.5		13.5

women's aspirations for a greater degree of dignity as well as security. Many of them strove against overwhelming odds to maintain difficult marriages and achieve greater family stability.

Higher proportions of respondents in the two lower SES groups than those in upper SES groups scored in the high-risk range but we did not find an inverse relationship between SES and interpersonal distress scores. The only significant relationship was that those in the lowest quintile had a significantly higher mean score than those in the middle SES quintile.

The respondents' interpersonal distress mean scores varied with marital status. Disproportionately more of the separated, the divorced, and widowed scored in the high-risk range than did the married and the single respondents.

Predictors

A multiple regression equation showed that five sociodemographic variables were significantly related to high interpersonal distress scores: being female, being in the lowest SES quintile, and being separated, divorced, or widowed. However, they explained only a remarkably low percentage of the variance, 5.1%. We had anticipated that sociodemographic factors would have much more explanatory power for the interpersonal distress scale scores than they had for the psychopathology or functioning scale scores, but they had only one-half as much. We had assumed, for example, that: 1) the elderly would be missing needed social contacts and interactions and, as a consequence, report that they were distressed, and 2) many middle-SES respondents would indicate that failure (personal or familial) to meet stringently defined middle-class role obligations would be troublesome.

High- and Low-Risk Groups

A detailed analysis of the interpersonal distress scale scores showed that the especially high-risk groups were: 1) black females, and 2) the separated and the divorced. The especially low-risk groups were: 1) black males, and 2) those in high SES.

Interpersonal distress and geographic groups: The respondents from Alachua County had a significantly higher mean interpersonal distress score than did those from Other Florida. The high score for the Alachuans can be explained, at least in part, by the disproportionately large number of black females in the Alachua group. The low score found for the Other Florida respondents can be attributed to the sociodemographic composition of this group: many were the young and the single, groups that generally had very low scores on this dimension of SPI.

Interpersonal Distress as a Risk Measure

Assessing interpersonal distress broadened the SPI category. Particularly, it added some respondents from the two middle-aged groups, aged 30-44 and 45-59. These respondents had tended to have lower scores on the psychopathology and functioning scales than either the younger or older persons. Finding that respondents aged 30-59, especially females, had relatively high mean scores supports clinical observations that many persons in these groups seek psychiatric care primarily for interpersonal dilemmas. Studies using operational definitions of risk for mental illness that include only conventional indicators of psychopathology and loss of function may not identify persons with interpersonal distress as needing mental health care; or, they may include persons who have had to "develop" mental or psychophysiologic symptoms to justify their seeking treatment. On the other hand, there is little doubt that including the interpersonal distress scale widens our operational definition of risk for mental illness, extending its boundaries to include persons who have "problems in living," not just mental illness that fits a disease concept. But whether problems in living and mental illness are related, sequentially or otherwise, is a question that needs further investigation.

Part III—The Dimensions of SPI

An analysis of psychopathology, impairment of functioning, and interpersonal distress scale scores revealed the following groups:

SPI Dimension	Respondents N	%
Psychopathology only	76	4.6
Impairment of functioning only	82	5.0
Interpersonal distress only	110	6.6
Psychopathology and impairment of functioning	49	3.0
Psychopathology and interpersonal distress	49	3.0
Impairment of functioning and interpersonal distress	25	1.5
Psychopathology, impairment of functioning, and interpersonal distress	72	4.4
TOTAL	463	28.1

Table 6-3 presents the significant differentiating sociodemographic characteristics of respondents who had high-risk scores on these subscales (and combinations) of SPI.

The three dimensions of SPI tap symptoms and other indicators of risk for mental disorder in different segments of the population. The younger respondents tended to report psychopathology; the middle aged, interpersonal problems; and the older ones, impairment of function (often combined with mental symptoms). As a group, females tended more often than males to score in the high-risk range on two or more of the scales measuring the various dimensions of SPI. In particular, the plight of the black females was pervasive. Of the four race-sex groups they were at high risk on more of the dimensions of SPI, singly or in combinations, than any of the other three groups. Impairment of Functioning Only was the lone category in which they were not at high risk.

As we anticipated, many of the respondents in lower, and especially the lowest, SES quintiles, reported impairment of functioning with or without psychopathology and interpersonal distress. With the exception of interpersonal distress, those in the middle- and upper-SES brackets tended not to be at high risk on the various scales. A tendency to score high on two or three of the scales portrays the many dilemmas of the widowed, separated, and divorced.

Part IV—Comparison of the Social Psychiatric Impairment (SPI), Normal, and "Supernormal" Groups

Using the statistical approach we divided the total sample into three major groups: 1) those in the SPI category: 463 or 28.1%; 2) the normals: 994 or 60.4%; and 3) the "supernormals": 188 or 11.4%.* Table 6-4 shows these groups' sociodemographic distributions and significant associations.

Age

The relationships between age and SPI are consistent with the results of other large epidemiologic studies, almost all of which report a linear

* The "supernormal" group consisted of those who scored lower than one standard deviation below the mean on the psychopathology scale and had no scores higher than one standard deviation above the mean on either of the other scales.

TABLE 6-3

Social psychiatric impairment dimensions by sociodemographic characteristics*

SOCIODEMOGRAPHIC CHARACTERISTICS	SPI DIMENSIONS: Psychopathology Only	Functioning Only	Interpersonal Distress Only	Psychopathology and Functioning	Psychopathology & Interpersonal Distress	Functioning & Interpersonal Distress	Psychopathology, Functioning, & Interpersonal Distress	Healthy on All
AGE:								
Younger Persons	•							
Middle Aged			•					
Elderly				•				
SEX:								
Male								•
Female				•			•	
RACE:								
White								•
Black	•			•			•	
RACE-SEX:								
White Male								•
White Female								
Black Male		•						
Black Female	•		•	•	•	•	•	
SES:								
Low		•		•			•	
Lower-Middle							•	
Middle	•							
Upper-Middle			•					
High								
MARITAL STATUS:								
Single	•							
Married								
Widowed		•		•				
Separated			•				•	
Divorced			•				•	

* Dot indicates significant overrepresentation.

relationship between risk for mental disorder and advancing age. But as shown in Figure 6-1, we found a trend toward curvilinearity.

The relatively large number of respondents in the younger age group reporting symptomatology and distress may be indicative of their socio-cultural dilemmas, particularly intergenerational conflict and difficulties in adjusting to changing mores and standards. Or it may reflect the emphasis on self-awareness that was prominent in the United States during the 1960s when the youngest group in our survey was at a formative age. This trend toward curvilinearity is one of the major findings of

TABLE 6-4

Sociodemographic characteristics of SPI, normal and "supernormal" groups.

Sociodemographic Characteristics	N	SPI %	Normal %	"Supernormal" %
Age:				
16-22	270	26.3	70.0*	3.7
23-29	315	22.5	66.0	11.4
30-44	411	26.0	58.6	15.3
45-59	332	32.8	55.4	11.7
60+	315	33.0	54.3	12.7
Sex:				
Male	736	23.0	61.5	15.5*
Female	909	32.3*	59.5	8.1
Race:				
White	1267	25.5	62.3	12.2
Black	366	37.7*	53.8	8.5
Race-sex:				
White Male	574	20.9	63.6	15.5*
White Female	693	29.3	61.2	9.5
Black Male	153	31.4	53.6	15.0
Black Female	213	42.3*	54.0	3.8
SES:				
Lower	212	52.4*	41.5	6.1
Lower-middle	379	34.8*	53.8	11.3
Middle	479	21.5	67.8*	10.6
Upper-middle	351	22.2	64.7	13.1
High	224	17.4	67.0	15.6
Marital Status:				
Single	295	26.1	68.5	5.4
Married	1009	24.0	61.2	14.8*
Widowed	170	39.4*	54.7	5.9
Separated	69	55.1*	42.0	2.9
Divorced	102	38.2	51.0	10.8
Geographic Origin:				
Alachua	451	33.3*	56.1	10.6
Other Florida	469	23.7	66.3	10.0
Deep South	213	36.6*	51.2	12.2
Elsewhere	512	24.2	62.7	13.1
TOTAL	1645	28.1	60.4	11.4

* Significantly greater proportion than statistically expected.

our study and is supported by a growing number of reports of increased mental illness in adolescents and young adults published during the last few years.

Sex

Finding more females and fewer males than statistically expected in the SPI group is consistent with the results of other major epidemiologic studies. Usually, these differences are attributed to females' much higher rates for neurotic disorders; rates for psychoses tend to be about the same for both sexes (4). That higher proportions of females than males report neurotic distress but that there are no sex differences on reports of psychotic illness can be interpreted in a number of ways. Women may be more likely than men to admit neurotic symptomatology. In Western society, women tend to respond emotionally to stressors whereas men are more prone to "act out." Also, it is possible that problems associated with changing roles and statuses for women may be responsible factors.

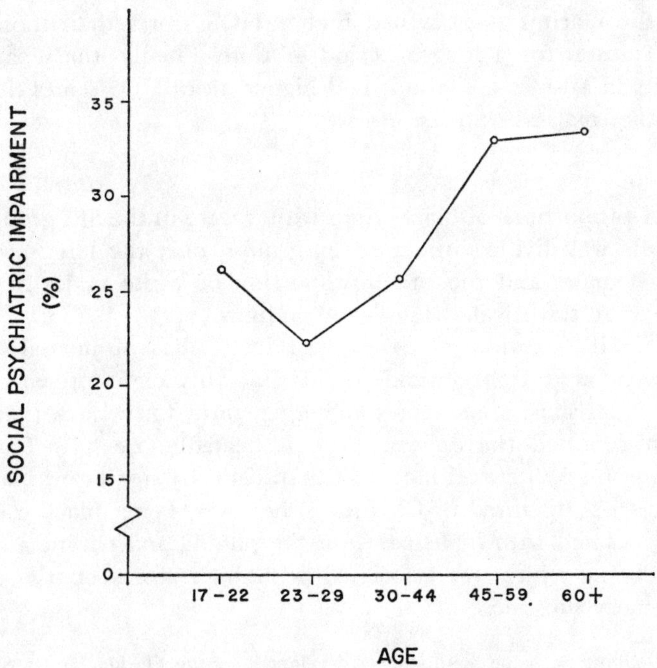

FIGURE 6-1. Percentage of respondents in the SPI category by age group.

The HOS scores of the 1645 respondents in Alachua County and more than 2000 in a three-county area in Central Florida were evaluated by Warheit, Holzer, Bell, and Arey (5).* They found that the females, regardless of race, in most marital statuses had higher scores than the males. A multiple regression equation showed that low SES and being female were the most significant predictors of high HOS scores.

During the last few years, a number of investigators have suggested that methodological factors such as response bias, role strain associated with lack of status and dissatisfaction in marriage, or discrepancies between females' expectations and opportunities for achievement during the current period of rapid social change are responsible for higher rates of mental illness in females than males (6). In particular, Gove maintains that being married accounts for the disproportionately higher prevalence of mental disorder in females (7). The findings of Warheit and his colleagues contradict Gove's contention (8). Changes in marital status were found to be associated with emotional distress, at least temporarily; such changes—getting married, divorced, separated, or being widowed—were seen as life crises. More of the respondents in the first year of any one of the marital statuses had higher HOS scores than those in the various statuses for a longer period of time. Finally, the separated respondents in all race-sex groups had higher mean HOS scores than those in the other marital statuses.

Race

Higher proportions of blacks than whites were in the SPI group. When the sample was divided into race-sex groups, only the large proportion of black females and the small proportion of white males in the SPI category were statistically significant findings.

In their 1969 review of 44 community studies of mental disorder, Dohrenwend and Dohrenwend found that only eight presented black-white comparisons; four reported higher rates for whites than blacks and four reported the opposite (9). Repeatedly, we have found that controlling for SES erased most of the statistically significant black-white differences. As discussed in Chapter 5, however, being black was significantly associated with high scores on the phobia and paranoia subscales whereas being white was associated with high scores on the difficulty with memory subscale.

---

* Using almost the same methodology developed for the Florida Health Study, Bell carried out a survey of 2029 respondents in a three-country area in Central Florida in 1972.

From a sociological perspective, the results showing that significantly more blacks than whites were in the SPI group can be attributed to the blacks' position in the class structure in the Southeast. They have been poorer, have had less political power, and have been targets of prejudice and discrimination for years. The institutional structures of American life have limited their freedom to compete for material goods. Throughout Alachua County, and in many places in the United States, the external conditions of life for the blacks appear to be deleterious; they have lived in substandard housing, have had access only to lower paying jobs, and many have been welfare recipients. Thus, their lives have been characterized by the powerlessness and deprivation often associated with mental and physical disorders.

SES

Significantly more of the persons in the lower than the upper SES quintiles were in the SPI group. Furthermore, we found an inverse relationship between SES and high-risk scores on almost all of our scales and subscales; the interpersonal distress scale was an exception. For more than 200 years epidemiologic studies thoughout the Western world (except in Sweden) have shown a strong relationship between lower SES and higher rates of mental disorder. These findings support the controversial social causation hypothesis—that material and cultural impoverishment produce both mental and physical illnesses. Kohn states that the poor are at triple jeopardy—harsh conditions of life, exposure to numerous stresses, and little access to mediating resources—for developing mental illness (10).

Marital Status

The SPI group contained significantly more separated or widowed persons and significantly fewer married than the normal or "supernormal" groups. Furthermore, on the subscales that measured various neurotic and other symptom patterns, proportionately more of the separated, widowed, and divorced (and occasionally the single) than the married respondents reported symptoms of anxiety, depression, depersonalization, paranoia, alcoholism, etc.

The "Supernormal"

Of the 188 respondents in the "supernormal" category, relatively many were males, 30-44 years of age, in the top SES quintile, or married.

Remarkably similar percentages of the Alachua County natives (10.6%), those from Other Florida (10.0%), from the Deep South (12.2%), or from Elsewhere (13.1%) were in the "supernormal" category. There were surprisingly few of the youngest respondents, aged 16-22 in this group; also there were few black females, low SES, separated, widowed, or single respondents in the "supernormal" category.

Part V—Comparison of Health Opinion Survey (HOS) Scores and SPI

The Health Opinion Survey (HOS), developed by Macmillan for use in the Stirling County Study, was derived from the Neuropsychiatric Screening Adjunct, which had been widely used during World War II to identify inductees who were at risk for mental illness (11). Macmillan's objective was to fashion "a rough measure of neurotic and related symptoms among rural community adults," an instrument that would "detect those adults whose responses to questions about their health approximated the responses of psychiatric patients and differed from responses of controls drawn at random from the community" (12). Macmillan validated the instrument for use in Stirling County. Psychiatrists independently examined patients and random samples of the population; their clinical findings correlated well with psychiatrically ill and ostensibly healthy respondents' HOS scores.

Since Macmillan's initial work in the early 1950s in Stirling County, the HOS has been validated a number of times on different populations. Spiro, Siassi, and Crocetti found that the HOS identified persons who were having difficulties in three major areas: 1) fears of a nervous breakdown, 2) impairment of work function, and 3) some somatization (13). These investigators think that the instrument does not distinguish precisely between the psychiatrically ill and the somatically ill, but they conclude that it is suitable for epidemiologic studies.

Tousignant and his colleagues believe that the HOS is biased toward physical illness, that it has problems of social desirability, lacks face validity, and has questionable correlations with clinicians' ratings. They think that the HOS screens three types of disorder: chronic mental illness, transitional stress situations, and poor physical health (14). The HOS, however, has been used widely by the Leightons and others in

Nigeria, among Eskimo groups, in studies in North Carolina, in Mexico and elsewhere (15).

In our study, the HOS was used with both the random sample of 1645 and the pre-test group of 322 respondents. To check the validity of the HOS, Kuldau, Warheit, and Holzer administered it to 237 patients entering the psychiatric in-patient units at two Community Mental Health Centers. These patients were interviewed as soon after admission as feasible, usually by the third day. Clinicians' diagnoses and revisions were culled from the records and compared with patients' HOS scores. The HOS discriminated quite well between non-psychotic psychiatric patients and persons from the general population (16). Moreover, in the general population HOS scores increased as the person's assigned risk factor scores increased. Some with physical illness had high HOS scores, prompting these investigators to ask to what extent physical problems and psychiatric simptoms were associated.

In our major survey, 466 of the 1645 respondents (28.3%) scored in the possible or probable "caseness" range on the HOS.

As shown in Table 6-5, the major sociodemographic associations revealed by the respondents' HOS scores were:

1) a curvilinear relationship between age and caseness range;
2) significantly more blacks than whites, females than males, and black females than other race-sex groups had caseness scores;
3) a strong inverse relationship between SES and percentages in the caseness range;
4) unusually high percentages of the separated or widowed had caseness scores.

Almost equal percentages of the 1645 respondents were in the SPI category (28.1%) and in the HOS caseness range (28.3%). But the two groups did not necessarily contain the same respondents. The overall SPI-HOS correlation was 0.58. It varied considerably with the different SPI scales: psychopathology-HOS (0.74); impairment of functioning-HOS (0.66); interpersonal distress-HOS (0.47). Such correlations met our expectations. The psychopathology scale contained many more specific indicators of mental and behavioral symptomatology, e.g., paranoia and hallucinations, than did the HOS. We think that the Bell Global Psychopathology Scale identifies those at high risk for psychoses, specific neurotic patterns, and alcoholism, whereas the HOS detects primarily respondents with anxiety, depression, and psychophysiological

TABLE 6-5

Scores on HOS by sociodemographic variables.

Sociodemographics	N	Mean ± s.d.	Sig.	% Caseness (30+)
TOTAL	1645	27.5±5.6	—	28.3
Age:				
16-22	270	27.1±4.9		25.6
23-29	315	25.9±4.3	F (4,1638) = 20.17	16.5
30-44	411	26.6±5.6	p<.0005	23.8
45-59	332	28.5±5.9		34.9
60+	315	29.2±6.2		41.3
Sex:				
Male	736	26.7±5.5	t (1643) = 4.81	21.6
Female	909	28.0±5.5	p<.0005	33.8
Race:				
White	1267	27.0±5.3	t (1631) = 5.84	25.4
Black	366	29.0±6.3	p<.0005	39.3
Race-Sex:				
White Male	574	26.2±5.0		18.1
White Female	693	27.7±5.4	F (3,1629) = 19.35	31.5
Black Male	153	28.7±7.0	p<.0005	35.9
Black Female	213	29.1±5.7		41.8
SES:				
Lower	212	31.5±6.4		54.2
Lower-Middle	379	28.7±6.3		37.2
Middle	479	26.7±4.6	F (4,1640) = 55.79	25.0
Upper-Middle	351	25.9±4.5	p<.0005	16.8
High	224	25.5±4.0		13.8
Marital Status:				
Single	295	27.1±4.9		24.7
Married	1009	26.8±5.4		25.1
Widowed	170	30.0±5.8	F (4,1640) = 19.50	45.3
Separated	69	30.8±7.2	p<.0005	49.3
Divorced	102	27.9±5.6		28.4
Geographic Origin:				
Alachua	451	28.2±5.7		33.0
Other Florida	469	27.1±5.6	F (3,1641) = 6.91	26.4
Deep South	213	28.2±5.8	p<.0005	32.4
Elsewhere	512	26.8±5.2		24.2

symptomatology. The HOS barely taps impairment of functioning and has no items related to interpersonal distress.

The SPI-HOS correlations were better than 0.60 for blacks and for respondents in the age groups 30-44 or 60+. But the correlations were < 0.51 for respondents aged 23-29 and 45-59, and for those in the upper-middle and the top SES quintiles.

The major sociodemographic differences pertained to age and SES. Fewer respondents aged 60+ were in the SPI category than in the HOS caseness range, and the significant inverse relationship between SPI and SES was somewhat less pronounced than that for HOS caseness scores and SES: A slightly smaller percentage of lower SES respondents and a slightly larger percentage of upper SES respondents were in the SPI category than in the HOS caseness range.

An epidemiologic assessment of mental health and illness in the general population is not complete unless the frequency and distribution of other types of illnesses—psychosomatic and physical—are also examined because the concurrence of mental and physical illnesses is so common. We think that our concept of SPI is limited more strictly to risk for psychiatric disorder than measures used by other investigators. In the next chapter we will present data on the frequency and distribution of reported psychosomatic distress and physical illness and their concurrence with SPI. Thus, we will be able to identify a "Social Psychiatric Impairment Only" group, a group that is at high risk for mental disorder only, not mental disorder compounded with psychosomatic and/or physical ailments.

REFERENCES

1. Langner, T. S., and Michael, S. T., *Life Stress and Mental Health, Thomas A. C. Rennie Series in Social Psychiatry, Volume II, The Midtown Manhattan Study.* New York: The Free Press of Glencoe, Division of Macmillan Company, 1963.
2. Ibid.
3. *Florida Health Study Program.* Gainesville, Fla.: College of Medicine, University of Florida, 1969, 60.
4. Dohrenwend, B. S., and Dohrenwend, B. P., *Social Status and Psychological Disorder: A Causal Inquiry.* New York: John Wiley and Sons, 1969.
5. Warheit, G. J., Holzer, C. E., III, Bell, R. A., and Arey, S. A., "Sex, Marital Status, and Mental Health: A Reappraisal," *Social Forces,* Vol. 44, No. 2, December 1976, 459-470.
6. Gurin, G., Veroff, J., and Feld, S., *Americans View Their Mental Health.* New York: Basic Books, 1960.
7. Gove, W. R., "The Relationship Between Sex Roles. Marital Status, and Mental Illness," *Social Forces,* Vol. 51, September 1972, 34-44.
8. See Reference 5.
9. See Reference 4.

10. KOHN, M. L., "The Interaction of Social Class and Other Factors in the Etiology of Schizophrenia," *American Journal of Psychiatry,* Vol. 133, 1976, 177-180.
11. MACMILLAN, A. M., "The Health Opinion Survey: Technique for Estimating Prevalence of Psychoneurotic and Related Types of Disorder in Communities," *Psychological Reports,* Southern Universities Press, 1957, 325-339.
12. Ibid.
13. SPIRO, H., SIASSI, I., and CROCETTI, G. M., "What Gets Surveyed in a Psychiatric Survey?" *Journal of Nervous and Mental Disorders,* Vol. 154, 1972, 105-114.
14. TOUSIGNANT, M. et al., "Some Considerations Concerning the Validity and Use of the Health Opinion Survey," *Journal of Health and Social Behavior,* Vol. 15, 1974, 241-252.
15. LEIGHTON, A. H., LAMBO, T. A., HUGHES, C. C., LEIGHTON, D. C., MURPHY, J. M., and MACKLIN, D. B., *Psychiatric Disorder Among the Yoruba,* Ithaca, N.Y.: Cornell University Press, 1963.
16. KULDAU, J. M., WARHEIT, G. J., and HOLZER, C. E., III, "Health Opinion Survey Valid for Needs Assessment." Unpublished paper.

7

Concurrence of Psychosomatic Distress and Physical Illness

One of the major criticisms of community surveys of mental disorder is that the group reported as mentally ill includes a number of persons who are suffering primarily from psychosomatic or physical illness. In their critique of the scales used to measure mental disorders in the general population, Crandell and Dohrenwend point out that some of the scales do not distinguish between mental and physical illness precisely, and, as a consequence, the results may have been misleading (1). The global psychopathology scales used in the Stirling County Study (the Health Opinion Survey (HOS)) and Midtown Manhattan Study (Langner's 22-Item Symptom scale) contain many psychophysiologic items that could be indicative of either mental or physical illness, for example, questions about rapid heartbeat, hands and feet sweating, or dizziness (2, 3). Thus, it is possible that many persons with psychosomatic and/or physical illnesses were included in the mental disorder category, inflating the percentages reported as suffering from mental illness. Both the Stirling County and Midtown Manhattan Studies reported high mental illness or impairment rates; only about one-fourth to one-third of the samples were asymptomatic (4, 5).

We attempted to delineate the social psychiatric impairment (SPI) group—those we considered to be at high risk for mental disorders—and also to measure those with reported psychosomatic distress and physical illness. Our 33-item Bell Global Psychopathology Scale contained only five items (loss of appetite, sleep difficulties, hallucinations, and two involving difficulties with memory) that possibly could be indicators of psychosomatic distress or physical illness as well as mental disorder. Our interview instrument contained a separate psychosomatic illness inventory; thus, we could evaluate the extent and types of psychosomatic distress and concurrence with SPI in our sample of the general population. It also contained a separate physical illness inventory and questions about utilization of services; consequently, we could assess different types of reported distress and later compare health care needs with utilization of services.

Part I—Psychosomatic Distress

In Western societies more patients seek general medical care for psychosomatic disorders—bodily complaints thought to be caused, at least in part, by psychological and social factors—than for all other kinds of illnesses. Von Mering and Earley maintain that one-third of all patients suffer from such "undifferentiated health aberrations"—admixtures of psychic, somatic, and social distress that often become ways of life (6). Moreover, modern technological medicine is unable to provide care for many of these "problem" patients.

We asked each of our respondents about the occurrence during the past year of 10 psychophysiologic symptoms or conditions: headaches, indigestion, constipation, nervous stomach, stomachaches, diarrhea, hypertension, asthma, ulcer (peptic), and colitis.* About 40% reported headaches; 20% to 35% various gastrointestinal symptoms (indigestion, stomachache, nervous stomach, or constipation); 15% diarrhea or hypertension; and about 2% to 3% peptic ulcer, asthma, or colitis. The large percentages reporting these symptoms or conditions support the contention that we are a psychosomatically-oriented society.

The Psychosomatic Group

To delineate the psychosomatic group, we included only respondents reporting that their psychosomatic symptoms or conditions had occurred "regularly" during the preceding year and omitted those who reported occurrence to be "occasionally." Over one-fourth of the total sample reported at least one of the symptoms or conditions "regularly"; 9.3% reported two or more. The percentage with at least one psychosomatic complaint "regularly" (26.1%) was much smaller than the approximately 60% reported in the Stirling County and Midtown Manhattan studies as having psychophysiologic symptom patterns (7, 8).

* A large proportion of respondents (35.4%) reported weight problems. Because we did not probe for the frequency and severity of "trouble gaining or losing weight," we did not include these persons in the psychosomatically-ill group.

Sociodemographic Characteristics of the Psychosomatic Group

Comparing the 429 respondents who reported at least one of the psychosomatic symptoms or conditions "regularly" with the 1216 who reported none "regularly" revealed significant group differences. The psychosomatic group was composed of higher proportions of older than younger and of female than male respondents. We found no significant black-white differences in the prevalence of reported psychosomatic distress. Race-sex differences were related primarily to sex; but the proportion of black females was much greater than expected. Large proportions with psychosomatic distress were in the low and lower-middle SES quintiles. This finding explodes the myth that psychosomatic illness is mainly a middle-class affliction. And as we shall see, when concurrent mental and physical conditions were excluded, psychosomatic distress was not significantly associated with any SES category, indicating that it was not a specific social class affliction. Higher proportions of the widowed, divorced, and particularly the separated respondents were in the psychosomatic group than the married or the single. A larger than expected proportion of Alachua natives were in the psychosomatic group compared to those from Other Florida, the Deep South, or Elsewhere.

Predictors

A multiple regression equation using only sociodemographic variables showed that being older, female, in low SES, and separated were significantly related to reported psychosomatic distress. However, these four variables explained only 4.2% of the variance.

Concurrence of SPI and Psychosomatic Distress

We examined the SPI and psychosomatic groups to determine the extent to which they overlapped. This analysis showed that 42.8% of those in the SPI group reported psychosomatic distress as well, and that 46.2% of those in the psychosomatic group also were in the SPI category. Thus, almost one-half of the persons in either the social psychiatric impairment or psychosomatic group had concurrent conditions. Later in this chapter we shall look at the concurrence of reported physical illnesses with SPI and psychosomatic distress.

Somatization

Thirty years ago, James L. Halliday reported that between 1900 and 1939 certain psychosomatic disorders had increased rapidly in Great

Britain (9). He predicted that these disorders that are produced by multiple etiologic factors, "a synergy of causes," would continue to become more common. In his opinion, changes in child-rearing practices accompanying the development of highly-specialized technological societies would be conducive to the emergence of the obsessive character type prone to react psychophysiologically to stressors.

Halliday proposed an ontogenetic theory of psychosomatic illness grounded on the "progressive unfolding of a 'life' in historical time in accordance with the orderly mode of development characteristic of its species" (10). He related changes in the social and emotional climate in Great Britain between the 1870s and 1930s to changes in the frequency of various illnesses. For example, in the Victorian Era, children were not repressed until the age of five or six (the Oedipal period); then they were admonished to be "seen and not heard." Hysteria was an exceedingly common neurosis. But, during the 1930s, the psychology of child-rearing dictated socialization at the age of two or three (the anal period). This conditioning turned out to be conducive to obsessional neuroses and physiologic dysfunctions.

Clinically, many patients obtaining psychiatric care complain of bodily distress as well as some degree of mental anguish. Psychiatric theory holds that mental mechanisms are the first line of defense. When confronted with stressful situations, an individual utilizes previously successful coping strategies or attempts to develop new ones. However, when these are ineffective or when the person has limited resources or options, defenses such as denial or projection are used extensively; often somatization occurs, generally accompanied by some degree of regression. Thus, somatization is seen as a primitive defense. In contemporary society, bodily complaints legitimatize the sickness role, allowing for diminished responsibilities, gratification of dependency needs, and other elements of secondary gain as well as medical care.

We found that indicators of SPI and psychosomatic distress overlapped considerably. How one responds to stressors—psychically, psychosomatically, or in both ways—is the result of complex factors which include learning in childhood, previous experience, types and numbers of stressors, and the availability of mediating resources.

To evaluate the concurrence of various types of distress as completely as possible, we must also take into account the presence or absence of more strictly "physical" illnesses. Part II of this chapter deals with reported physical illness and our evaluation of its concurrence with SPI and psychosomatic distress in the sample.

Part II—Physical Illness

As another part of the medical systems review, we asked each respondent about the occurrence during the preceding year of 14 physical complaints or illnesses related to: skin, bones and joints, eyes, ears, nose, throat, back, chest, heart, anemia, diabetes, genitourinary tract, and "female problems." Respondents who gave affirmative answers were also questioned about the frequency of occurrence—"occasionally?" or "regularly?".

About 30% reported having trouble during the preceding year with the bones and joints, eyes, or back; about 15% reported having symptoms associated with the throat, skin, "female problems," or the genitourinary tract; and from 8 to 13% reported trouble with their ears, nose, chest, heart, or with anemia. About 5% indicated that they had diabetes or gall bladder disease.

The Physically-Ill Group

To delineate the physically-ill group we tabulated only the responses of those reporting physical complaints or illnesses "regularly," omitting those who replied "occasionally." Of the 1645 respondents, 39.0% reported at least one of the complaints or illnesses "regularly"; 16.7% reported two or more.

Sociodemographic Characteristics of the Physically-Ill Group

We compared the 641 respondents reporting one or more physical illnesses "regularly" during the preceding year with the remaining 1004 reporting none "regularly" and found the following differences. The physically-ill group was composed of proportionately more older than younger and more female than male respondents. The prevalence of reported physical illness was somewhat, but not significantly, greater among blacks than whites. Significantly lower proportions of white males than of those in other race-sex groups reported physical illness. Higher proportions of low and lower-middle SES than upper SES quintile persons, and of the widowed or separated than the single, married, or divorced reported physical illness. Geographic origin—having grown up in Alachua County, Other Florida, the Deep South, or Elsewhere—was not significantly associated with reported physical illness.

Predictors

A multiple regression equation using only sociodemographic variables showed that physical illness was related to being: 1) older rather than younger, 2) female rather than male, 3) white rather than black,* 4) in lower SES, and 5) widowed. These five explained 10.5% of the variance.

Concurrence of SPI with Physical Illness

We examined the SPI and physically-ill groups to determine the extent to which they overlapped. This analysis showed that 58.1% of those in the SPI category reported physical illness as well, and that 41.9% of those in the physically-ill group also were in the SPI category. Thus the concurrence of mental and physical distress was very high.

Part III—Concurrence of SPI with Psychosomatic and Physical Illness

Although the concurrence of mental and physical illness has been noted by psychoanalysts, clinical psychiatrists, and epidemiologists, it is a relatively neglected topic. In his 1916 case study, "Disease or Patho-neurosis," Ferenczi postulated that relationships between neurosis and somatic illness could be attributed to a withdrawal of libido from inter-personal relationships and external events, and its consequent redirection toward both diseased organs and the ego (11). Karl Menninger has emphasized that the ego's involvement in physical illness is one of its major homeostatic functions (12).

A number of controlled studies of psychiatric and medical inpatients and outpatients and samples from the general population carried out by Lovett Doust, Brodman and his colleagues, and Matarazzo et al. showed consistently that patients with psychiatric illnesses also tended to have more medical illnesses than did the others (13-15). From their prospective studies of illness in relatively healthy populations, Hinkle and Wolff concluded: "Those people who had the greatest number of bodily illnesses, regardless of their nature and regardless of their etiology,

* This apparent contradiction to the previous discussion results from multicollinearity. This phenomenon occurs when some predictors are highly intercorrelated. The high correlation between race and SES has the effect of converting a very slightly positive correlation (0.04) to a very slightly negative one (—0.07).

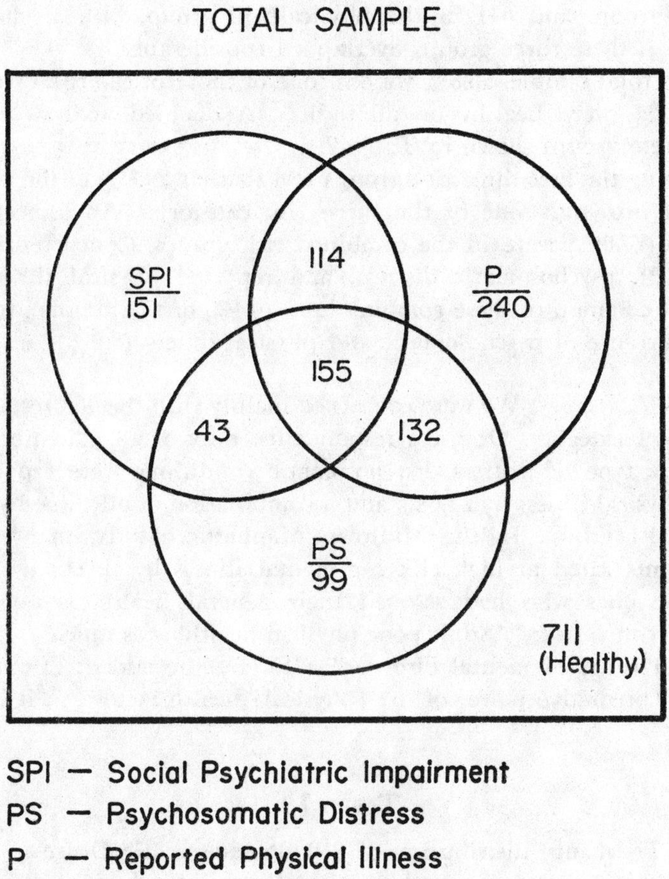

FIGURE 7-1. Extent of overlap among SPI, Psychosomatic Distress, and Physical Illness in the total sample.

were the ones who experienced the greater number of disturbances of mood, thought, and behavior" (16). Although we could not tabulate the number and types of illness episodes over time as Hinkle and Wolff have done, our findings support their statement.

Findings on Concurrence of SPI with Psychosomatic and Physical Illness

We analyzed the three groups to determine the extent of concurrence. Of the 1645 respondents, 463 were in the SPI group, 429 in the psychosomatic group, and 641 in the physically-ill group, but, as shown in Figure 7-1, these three groups overlapped considerably.

Of the total sample, 56.8% were in one or more of the risk categories; only 43.2% were healthy on all indices. A detailed analysis revealed the discrete groups shown in Table 7-1.

Summing the first three risk groups reveals that 29.8% of the respondents fell into only one of the three risk categories. An almost equal number (27.0%) were in the combined risk groups. Concurrence of all three—SPI, psychosomatic distress, and reported physical illness—was the most common of these combinations (9.4% of the sample), followed by concurrence of psychosomatic and physical illness (8.0%).

The SPI category: We were concerned mainly with the 463 respondents in the SPI category. Of these respondents, only 32.6% did not report any other type of distress. Psychosomatic conditions were reported by 9.3%, physical illness by 24.6%, and a combination of all three by 33.5% of the SPI group. In the Midtown Manhattan Study, many of the respondents rated at high risk for mental illness by psychiatrists were the same ones who had assessed their general health as poor (17). Langner concluded: " 'Adult poor physical health' is as much a symptom as it is a cause of mental disorder" (18). But he added: "Despite the excellent predictive power of the [physical] health factor . . . it is meth-

TABLE 7-1

Frequency distribution of SPI, Psychosomatic Distress, and reported Physical Illness groups.

Risk Group	Respondents N	Respondents %
Social Psychiatric Impairment Only	151	9.2
Psychosomatic Only	99	6.0
Physical Only	240	14.6
Social Psychiatric Impairment and Psychosomatic	43	2.6
Social Psychiatric Impairment and Physical Illness	114	6.9
Psychosomatic and Physical Illness	132	8.0
Social Psychiatric Impairment, Psychosomatic, and Physical Illness	155	9.4
Healthy on all Indices	711	43.2
TOTAL	1645	100.0

odologically 'impure' because it is a part of the original Mental Health Rating (I) and hopelessly intertwined with the psychophysiological symptoms given a great deal of weight in the psychiatrists' rating procedure" (19).

Psychosomatic and Physical Illnesses as Predictors of SPI

We found that the reported psychosomatic conditions and physical illnesses were significant predictors of SPI. However, a multivariate analysis showed that the reported psychosomatic and physical illnesses explained only 11.3% of the variance in the SPI ratings. We had made a serious effort to insure that our assessment of SPI was not confounded methodologically by symptoms of "purely" psychosomatic or physical disorders. Therefore, we think that the 11.3% of the variance in the SPI ratings can be attributed to the concurrence of mental and physical distress.

SOCIODEMOGRAPHIC CHARACTERISTICS OF THE GROUPS

As shown in Table 7-2, the various groups differed demographically. The younger respondents tended to cluster in the SPI Only group. In contrast, those in the oldest age group tended to report Physical Illness in combination with Psychosomatic Distress, and many were in the SPI category as well. Disproportionately more females than males reported either Psychosomatic Distress or the combination of Physical Illness, Psychosomatic Distress, and being in the SPI category. Disproportionately more blacks than expected were in two or more of the combined groups. A higher than expected proportion of white females, however, was in the Psychosomatic Only group, whereas black females were significantly over-represented in the combined illnesses category.

We found a strong association between lower SES and concurrent conditions of mental and physical health. The formerly married—particularly the separated and widowed—showed evidence of pervasive mental and physical distress. Significantly large proportions of them reported concurrent conditions. Repeatedly, we found that the separated were at very high risk for the conditions we were considering. Many were lower SES black females. We conjecture that they are a marginal group. They lack status or, at best, are in a stressful transitional status. Although the widowed had more defined statuses, many of them lacked support systems, were older and thus, vulnerable.

TABLE 7-2

SPI, Psychosomatic Distress, and Physical Illness combinations by sociodemographic characteristics*

SOCIODEMOGRAPHIC CHARACTERISTICS	SPI Only	PS Only	Phys. Only	SPI + PS	SPI + Phys.	PS + Phys.	SPI, PS, Phys.	Healthy on All
AGE:								
16-22	◆							
23-29								
30-44								◆
45-59								
60+						◆	◆	
SEX:								
Male								◆
Female							◆	
RACE:								
White								
Black					◆		◆	
RACE-SEX:								
White Male								◆
White Female		◆						
Black Male								
Black Female							◆	
SES:								
Lower					◆		◆	
Lower-Middle							◆	
Middle								
Upper-Middle								◆
High								◆
MARITAL STATUS:								
Single								
Married								
Widowed					◆	◆	◆	
Separated				◆			◆	
Divorced								
GEOGRAPHIC ORIGIN:								
Alachua		◆					◆	
Other Florida								
Deep South								
Elsewhere								

* ◆ = significantly greater than expected
SPI = Social Psychiatric Impairment
PS = Psychomatic Distress
Phys. = Physical Illness

Geographic Origin

Our next task was to look at possible relationships between the geographic locale in which the respondents had grown up and the various risk groups. Disproportionately large proportions of those who had grown up in Alachua County were in the Psychosomatic Only and the triple combination—SPI, Psychosomatic, and Physical-Illness—groups. Many respondents from Alachua County and to some extent those from the Deep South were marginal groups, occupying lower positions in the social structure than the respondents from Other Florida or Elsewhere. Disproportionately large percentages of Alachuans and those from the Deep South were black, in the two lower SES quintiles, separated, widowed, or divorced—groups that we hypothesized would be at high risk for emotional distress.

Healthy on All Indices

A profile of the respondents who were healthy on all indices revealed that they were relatively advantaged. They were in the 30-44 age group, white males, and, most significantly in the upper-middle and high SES groups.

SUMMARY AND CONCLUSIONS

A summary of our findings shows that:

1. Of the total sample, 56.8% were in one or more of the risk categories for social psychiatric impairment, psychosomatic distress, or physical illnesses; only 43.2% were healthy on all indices.
2. Of the total sample, 28.1% were in the SPI category (28.3% in the HOS caseness range). However, only about one-third of those in the SPI category (32.6%) did not report concurrent psychosomatic and/or physical illness—just 9.2% of the total sample were in the SPI Only category.
3. The concurrence of various types of distress—SPI, psychosomatic, and physical—was found to be extensive. Of the total sample, only 29.8% were in just one of the risk groups; 27.0% were in two or more. Concurrent conditions were found significantly more often in the older respondents, the blacks, those in the low and lower-middle SES quintiles, and the separated or widowed than other sociodemographic groups. The relationships among concurrent conditions, older age, and indicators of deprivation and marginality—lower SES, being, separated, or widowed—point to the multiple, pervasive distress of these persons. This finding

lends weight to the social causation hypothesis: when conditions of life are stressful and resources limited, illnesses are more common. Elements of psychiatric theory which postulate that somatization occurs because mental mechanisms are inadequate appear to have only limited validity. Our findings can be explained more completely by social psychological concepts that consider material, interpersonal, and other resources as having greater influences on health or illness than intrapsychic and other highly personal dynamics.

4. A disproportionately large number of those in the combined illness groups were females. Many of these women reporting concurrent illnesses were older, in low SES, widowed, or separated. We think that they lacked status in a rapidly changing society in which ready adaptability and keeping pace with the rate of social change are requisites for access to material resources and, thus, success. A number of these women can be viewed as victims of culture lag, bereft of protective cultural patterns and often lacking social support systems considered by Gerald Caplan and others to be vital for the maintenance of an individual's psychological and physiological integrity (20).
5. Our results have implications for both epidemiologists and health planners. The high rate of concurrence indicates that merely assessing risk for mental disorders without considering psychosomatic and physical disorders is an incomplete epidemiologic approach to the problem of mental illness. Not only are mental and physical illnesses often confounded but, also, we do not know which condition is primary. Undoubtedly, a number of the respondents in the SPI category had symptoms of emotional distress as a reaction to physical illness. This topic, emotional reactions to physical illness, has been described by Bartemeier as one of the "silent areas in medical practice" (21). Furthermore, the extensive concurrence of mental and physical conditions indicates that the majority of those at high risk for mental disorders are in need of continuing medical care.

NEED FOR HEALTH CARE

Measuring need for health care becomes more meaningful when we compare needs with the utilization of services. Alachua County had an adequate health care system: a large number of physicians, surgeons, nurses, and other professionals. Patients were referred from a primary radius of 75 miles and a secondary one of 150 miles to the University or Veterans Administration Hospital and clinics. These services were complemented by a well-staffed community hospital, an active Public Health Service, and a few doctors practicing in rural areas.

The mental health services were more abundant than in most counties in Florida. Four psychiatrists and a number of psychologists and social workers were in private practice in Gainesville. The Department of Psychiatry at the University was staffed with 16 psychiatrists (some of whom were in private practice on a part-time basis) and an equal number of psychiatric residents.

Comparing need with utilization of services is basic evaluation research—one of the uses of epidemiology. We think such evaluations can supply guidelines for improving mental health care services. Obviously, it will be some time before there are a sufficient number of mental health professionals to care for the many persons reported to be at risk for mental illness—28.1% of our sample, and even higher percentages in other major studies. In Chapter 8, we will examine the utilization of mental and physical health care services by our respondents.

REFERENCES

1. CRANDELL, D. L., and DOHRENWEND, B. P., "Some Relations Among Psychiatric Symptoms, Organic Illness, and Social Class." *American Journal of Psychiatry,* Vol. 123, 1967, 1527-1538.
2. MACMILLAN, A. M., "The Health Opinion Survey: Technique for Estimating Prevalence of Psychoneurotic and Related Types of Disorder in Communities," *Psychological Reports,* Monograph Supplement 7, Southern Universities Press, 1957, 325-339.
3. LANGNER, T. S., and MICHAEL, S. T., *Life Stress and Mental Health. Vol. II of the Midtown Manhattan Study, T.A.C. Rennie Series in Social Psychiatry.* New York: The Free Press of Glencoe, 1963.
4. LEIGHTON, D. C., HARDING, J. S., MACKLIN, D. G., MACMILLAN, A. M., and LEIGHTON, A. H., *The Character of Danger.* New York: Basic Books, Inc., 1963.
5. See Reference 3.
6. VON MERING, O., and EARLEY, L. W., "Major Changes in the Western Medical Environment." *Archives of General Psychiatry,* Vol. 13, 1965, 195-201.
7. See Reference 4.
8. See Reference 3.
9. HALLIDAY, J. L., *Psychosocial Medicine: A Study of the Sick Society.* New York: W. W. Norton, 1948, 164.
10. Ibid., p. 89.
11. FERENCZI, S., "Disease or Pathoneurosis." In: *Theory and the Technique of Psychoanalysis.* New York: Basic Books, Inc., 1952, 78-89.
12. MENNINGER, K. A., "Psychological Aspects of the Organism Under Stress: Part I: The Homeostatic Regulatory Function of the Ego." *Journal of the American Psychoanalysis Association,* Vol. 2, 1954, 67.
13. LOVETT DOUST, J. W., "Psychiatric Aspects of Somatic Immunity: Differential Evidence of Physical Disease in Histories of Psychiatric Patients." *British Journal of Social Medicine,* Vol. 6, 1952, 49.
14. BRODMAN, K., ERDMANN, A., LORGE, GERSHENSON, and WOLFF, "The Cornell Medical Index Health Questionnaire, III. The Evaluation of Emotional Disturbances." *Journal of Clinical Psychology,* Vol. 8, 1952, 119-124.

15. Matarazzo, R. G., Matarazzo, J. D., and Saslow, G., "The Relationship Between Medical and Psychiatric Symptoms." *Journal of Abnormal Social Psychology,* Vol. 62, 1961, 55-61.
16. Hinkle, L. E., and Wolff, H. G., "Health and the Social Environment: Experimental Investigation." In: A. Leighton, J. Clausen, and R. Wilson (Eds.), *Explorations in Social Psychiatry*. New York: Basic Books, Inc., 1957, 115.
17. See Reference 3.
18. Ibid., p. 267.
19. Ibid., p. 299.
20. Caplan, G., *Social Support Systems and Community Mental Health: Lectures on Concept Development.* New York: Behavioral Publications, 1974.
21. Bartemeier, L. H., "Psychiatric Aspects of Medical Practice. Emotional Reactions to Illness." *Maryland Medical Journal,* Vol. 10, May 1961, 240.

8

Health Needs and Utilization of Services

In this chapter, we shall examine our respondents' utilization of mental and physical health services and then compare their need with utilization. Thus, we will be describing a basic first step in *evaluation research.*

There is a pressing need for evaluation because mental health programs consume a large portion of the funds expended for mental health care as well as the energies of professionals, allied mental health workers, and volunteers. More specific reasons for carrying out evaluation research are: 1) both private and public facilities and services must gauge scientifically the effectiveness of their programs in order to modify them or launch new ones tailored to meet the changing and variable needs of the population, and 2) the disciplines involved in mental health care require information obtained by evaluation research to keep their educational and service endeavors creative and timely; otherwise, health care workers of the future may be locked into ideas and stereotypes of the past and present.

The urgency for evaluation research was expressed by the American Psychiatric Association in the report of a Task Force in 1971, by the American Psychological Association in its 1971 Report of the Task Force on Issues in Community Psychology and Preventive Mental Health, and by the Nader Report on Community Mental Health Centers (CMHCs) (1-3).

Such research involves the collection of information that can be used for policy decisions after it has been systematically developed, quantified, and critically appraised. Of necessity, this eventually entails value judgments which should be made as objectively as possible, but which are undoubtedly influenced by the biases of investigators, workers, administrators, and/or policy makers. When evaluation research follows scientific principles, the results can be tested for validity and reliability and compared with other findings and hypothetical or established standards. And, to enrich the significance of evaluation research, the findings can be used for theory building. Evaluation research, therefore, involves quantification, comparison, theory building, and value judgments; its ultimate purpose is pragmatic—to enhance the delivery of mental health services.

Our first step in evaluation was to develop a typology of needers and utilizers. A *needer* was defined as one who was found to be in any of the single or combined Social Psychiatric Impairment (SPI), psychosomatic, or physical illness categories. Responses to items in the interview schedule concerning visits to physicians, hospitals, the county health department, chiropractors, and clinics during the last year were developed into a physical health utilization scale. Visits to psychiatrists, the Community Mental Health Center, psychologists, social workers and faith healers were put into a mental health utilization scale.

UTILIZATION OF HEALTH CARE SERVICES

Of the 1645 respondents, 1392 (84.6%) reported using a physical health care facility during the past year; 253 respondents (15.4%) had not utilized any physical health care facilities. The data reveal that the highest utilization of physical health care was among the young, female, those in the middle or upper SES, or single respondents. In contrast, those who significantly underutilized the physical health care system were the elderly, those in the lower SES, or the separated.

Of the total sample, 184 respondents (11.2%) reported utilization of the mental health services; 1461 (88.8%) reported no utilization. It should be noted that the percentage reported as receiving mental health services may be inflated because it includes those who gave affirmative answers to the item asking about having visited a social worker. Some of the social workers were counseling their clients but, in many instances, the social workers' activities were directed primarily toward securing welfare or other benefits for those who needed them. It was impossible for us to define these services more precisely and to attempt to do so might have been unrealistic; many Community Mental Health Centers throughout the nation are now comprehensive care centers that supply both mental health and welfare services to their clients.

Only 45 of the 1645 respondents reported seeing a psychiatrist during the preceding year, 35 saw a psychologist, 32 visited a Community Mental Health Worker, and 32 utilized faith healers.

Examination of the sociodemographic characteristics of the mental health service utilizers and nonutilizers showed that both the young and the elderly were significantly high utilizers of mental health services. Moreover, large proportions of females, the blacks, those in the lowest SES quintile, or the separated utilized the mental health care system.

An analysis of the utilization of both physical and mental health care services revealed that 10.0% of the sample were dual system utilizers; 74.7% were utilizers of the physical health care system only, 1.2% utilizers of the mental health care system only, and 14.2% did not utilize any services.

SPI AND UTILIZATION OF HEALTH SERVICES

The overwhelming majority, 88.8%, of the respondents in the SPI category utilized the physical health care system. Interestingly, as groups, the utilizers and the nonutilizers did not have different sociodemographic characteristics.

Of the 463 respondents in the SPI category, 108 (23.3%) were utilizers of the mental health system whereas 355 (76.7%) were not. Other surveys report similarly low levels of utilization of mental health care services by needers.

Although a relatively small percentage of those in the SPI category utilized the mental health care system, more than 80% had used the physical health care system, indicating that the primary care physician was performing a significant role in the delivery of mental health care, probably a greater one than has been recognized. Furthermore, 92.1% of those who were taking psychotropic medications were physical health care utilizers, whereas only 20.3% of those taking psychotropic medications were mental health care utilizers. Thus, we found significantly high needs for services among persons identified as mental health needers, although only 1.2% were solely mental health care users.

RELIABILITY AND VALIDITY

Reliability

Data obtained from interviews with respondents about their health are always subject to questions of reliability and validity. For example, the National Health Survey of 1967 found that the differences between reports of chronic conditions on interview and information on medical records were a function of the seriousness of the condition, i.e., serious illnesses were reported more consistently than minor ones. Furthermore, the percentage of unreported conditions increased from 30.4% of those who rated their health as poor to 60.4% of those who rated their health as excellent (4).

We conducted reliability and validity checks by processing a random sample of 231 of our respondents at the Multiphasic Screening Center in Gainesville in 1971, four to twelve months after they had been interviewed in their homes. We included items from the original interview in the intake interview at the Screening Center to measure test-retest reliability.

There was almost total reliability on demographic data, e.g., 96.3% agreement for marital status and 92.2% for age. We found a wider range of variability between Time-1:Time-2 responses on reports of surgical procedures: from a high of 99.5% agreement for thyroidectomies to a low of 90.8% agreement for gynecological surgery. The percentage of agreement on a number of selected symptoms varied more. High agreement between Time-1:Time-2 responses was found for physical symptomatology, e.g., loss of appetite (96.4%), and gall bladder trouble (93.9%). However, there were much lower percentages of agreement for diffuse symptoms, e.g., nervousness (70.8%), and for affective states, e.g., hopelessness (75.0%). The lowest percentage of agreement (65.8%) was found for the question about whether the respondent had physical or health problems at present. An analysis of the reliability of sociodemographic groups' Time-1:Time-2 responses revealed surprisingly little variation by race, sex, age, income, etc. Furthermore, the length of time between Time-1 and Time-2 (four to twelve months) was not a significant factor in the reliability of response.

Validity

The multiphasic screening also provided a validity check. The differences between self-report of five selected conditions compared to clinical laboratory findings were: 1) hypertension: —9.4%; 2) glaucoma: 11.3%; 3) heart disease: 2.2%; 4) deafness: 9.6% and 5) lung disease: 0.6%. For all conditions except hypertension, higher percentages of the respondents were found to have abnormal laboratory results than they reported by history. The discrepancies were 11% or less. In view of the fact that multiphasic testing casts a wide net—it selects a high percentage of false positives—these findings are evidence of the validity of self-report in this study. Adequacy of treatment for the condition is another factor producing discrepancies, e.g., the smaller percentages found to have elevated blood pressure than reported on history might be attributable in part to successful treatment.

Higher proportions of blacks than whites had abnormal test findings, e.g., tonometry: blacks 29.6%, whites 18.7%; high blood pressure: blacks 36.1%, whites 15.1%. Also, higher percentages of blacks than whites underreported health conditions, e.g., hearing difficulties: blacks 36.8%, whites 20.4%. Sex differences were found between self-reports and the results of EKGs and chest X-rays; males tended to underreport (EKG by 9.6% and X-ray by 8.2%), whereas females tended to overreport (EKG by 4.1% and X-ray by 5.5%). Respondents aged 60+ underreported hearing problems by 39% and conditions found on chest X-rays by 31.3%. Such findings on the validity check indicate that underreporting of health conditions was more common than overreporting, particularly among blacks, males, and the elderly.

SUMMARY OF FINDINGS ON NEED AND UTILIZATION

First, the data obtained by the survey seem to have an acceptable level of reliability and validity; therefore, we think that an individual's report of his physical and/or mental health can be used to assess health needs.

Second, certain groups within the general population had much higher levels of health care *need* than others. In particular, the blacks, the elderly, and the economically deprived respondents reported significantly more physical and mental health care needs than did their counterparts.

Third, self-report can be used to determine whether different population subgroups have different rates of *utilization.* Surprisingly, we found that the younger respondents utilized physical and mental health care services to a greater extent than any other age group, even the elderly. Predictably, however, as SES level rose, utilization of services increased.

Fourth, there was a tendency for males to underreport and to underutilize services. Although females tended to overreported and overutilize services, as a group, they did not make the excessive demands on the services which some popular mythology suggests.

Fifth, we found a striking difference in utilization according to type of health service. Although the overwhelming majority of our respondents had made at least one visit to a professional for physical care within the year, less than 10% reported visits to mental health care agencies or to professionals. Many of the respondents who reported mental health need did not seek mental health care. It appears that either mental health care services were still relatively unavailable (or not visible) within our community, or that many of the respondents sought treatment from their physicians for mental as well as physical complaints. It is likely that both conclusions are partially correct. Although the County Mental Health Clinic had been in existence since 1965 in Alachua County, the Community Mental Health Center did not open until late in 1971. A limited survey of practicing physicians in the County in 1969 indicated that about 30% of their patients were being treated primarily for emotional or psychophysiologic problems.

Sixth, we found that reported satisfaction with health care was related to perceived health status. Believing that one was either in poor physical or in poor mental health was a major factor related to an individual's satisfaction with the amount of care received. When health was seen as poor, fewer respondents thought that they received enough health care. But, regardless of the state of their health, more blacks and the poor than their counterparts tended to report dissatisfaction with the amount of care received.

IMPLICATIONS

The findings have implications for educators as well as for health planners. Medical students, regardless of future specialty, should be receiving extensive instruction about and experience in working with patients with emotional distress, not just the seriously psychiatrically ill in the university hospitals and other tertiary care settings. It is essential that the family practitioner be equipped with the skills necessary to deal with the large numbers of people with emotional distress. If people are not using mental health services for reasons that may be attitudinal, e.g., the stigma attached to mental illness, or if they do not understand that their symptoms may be indicators of mental illness, they are likely to use familiar channels, i.e., go to the family doctor for care regardless of the nature of their illness. Primary care physicians, by virtue of contact with patients and their families, are in an ideal position to detect patients at risk for mental disorders. Therefore, medical education should include a much greater emphasis on the primary physician's training for dealing with "social psychiatric disorders" in the general population.

Current efforts to support community mental health centers that are in financial difficulties require that we find accurate methods for needs assessment. Such assessments may help determine whether massive amounts of money should be used to rejuvenate the Community Mental Health Movement or, on the other hand, to support more traditional medical care with an endorsed role for the family physician. Obviously, primary physicians were caring for both physical and mental health care needers at the time our study was conducted.

CONCLUSIONS

The results illustrate some of the types of information a human service agency can obtain by assessing needs and utilization of services as part of its evaluation research program. Epidemiologic methods are necessary because they have been developed to study patterns of illness and delivery of health services in groups within an ecologic setting. Also, epidemiologic studies can provide us with an understanding of the impediments to receiving mental health care—the economic, geographic, cultural, and psychological barriers.

As we have seen, a field survey of the general population in a catchment area can identify high-risk groups, differentiate between need and demand, and delineate target groups and locales for mental health care priorities. For example, the blacks, as a group, and particularly the elderly respondents in our study were found to have the highest levels of mental health need and the lowest utilization of existing services. With such data, a human service agency can gear its programs to meet the needs of blacks or the elderly. For example, it might be necessary to hire more black mental health workers, provide transportation and/or mobile units, or initiate measures to combat the loneliness and isolation of senior citizens. An agency that allocated a disproportionate share of funds for the publicized problems of the young might be remiss in meeting the less apparent needs of the elderly, who, all too often, reside outside the spotlight of public concern.

Although mental health epidemiology is in an early stage of development, it can make *pragmatic, methodologic,* and *substantive* contributions to evaluation research. The *pragmatic* are the data on needs and utilization patterns that can be used for program development and therapeutic interventions. The *methodologic* deal with the development of instruments for assessing need, with how to count in a way that assures the data are not misleading, and with strategies for testing the findings and using the results. The *substantive* contributions pertain to one of Morris' "uses of epidemiology"—completing the clinical picture in depth as well as in breadth (5). Assessment of need in the general population reveals how many complain of mental or behavioral disorder, who they are, and where they are located geographically and socially.

And by uncovering subacute, borderline, or mild cases, the clinical picture gains depth. Such information is vital at this time because we cannot define mental health and illness precisely and because the body of knowledge in psychiatry and psychology has been derived primarily from observations of highly selected populations—mainly patients in state hospitals, the middle class in Western society who could afford outpatient therapies, and student groups who have been research subjects.

Eventually, epidemiologic studies may shed some light on etiology, particularly when follow-up investigations show what happens to people over time. For example, why does the subacute case develop a full-blown distress syndrome; or, why does the symptomatic person not later become impaired, with or without treatment? Knowledge about etiology may lead to preventive action, the long-range objective of epidemiology. Bloom emphasizes, "The research base of primary prevention is rooted in the science and methods of epidemiology" (6).

REFERENCES

1. "Research Aspects of Community Mental Health Centers: Report of the American Psychiatric Association Task Force." *American Journal of Psychiatry*, Vol. 127, July 1971, 993-1000.
2. GLIDEWELL, J. C. (Ed.), *Issues in Community Psychology and Preventive Mental Health: Division 27 of the American Psychological Association Task Force on Community Mental Health*. New York: Behavioral Publications, Inc., 1971.
3. CHU, F. D., and TROTTER, S,. *The Madness Establishment: Ralph Nader's Study Group Report on the National Institute of Mental Health*. New York: Grossman Publishers, 1974, 105-120.
4. Interview Data on Chronic Conditions Compared with Information Derived from Medical Records. Series 2, Number 23, National Center for Health Statistics. Washington, D.C.: U.S. Department of Health, Education, and Welfare, May 1967.
5. MORRIS, J. N., *Uses of Epidemiology*, 2nd Edition. Baltimore: Williams and Wilkins, 1964.
6. BLOOM, B., "Strategies for the Prevention of Mental Disorders." In: Glidewell, J. C. (Ed.). See Reference 2, 1-20.

9

Perception of Social Change and Social Psychiatric Impairment (SPI)

SOCIAL CHANGE

During the 1950s and 1960s, indicators of social change, such as urbanization, increased income, and educational achievements, showed that social and culture change was occurring more rapidly in the South than elsewhere in the United States (1). But such large-scale indices only inform us about what is happening to humanity in the aggregate and the community at large. They do not supply information about groups' and individuals' different perceptions of the changes and their feelings about them. What change means to a person is highly subjective. Years ago, the great American sociologist, W. I. Thomas asserted that an individual's "definition of the situation" influences perception of events and circumstances and determines their personal meaning (2). The same event may be disastrous for one person and advantageous for another. Moreover, at one period in life a person may "define" an event as calamitous but at another time as propitious. In this chapter, we shall examine the respondents' reported perceptions of and concerns about social change processes and how these were associated with social psychiatric impairment (SPI) ratings.

Impact of Change

Social and cultural changes have repercussions on institutions, groups, and individuals. These effects involve gains and losses, entail adjustments and adaptations, and require behavioral responses directly related to health and illness. Our institutions—legal, educational, religious, or marital—are compelled to adjust to change, or to become obsolete. For groups as well as individuals, social and cultural changes not only disrupt developed patterns which serve as protective and expressive functions but, concurrently, may perpetuate injustice and deprivation. For individuals, the rapidity of our current rate of change increases the general problem of adaptation—how to achieve a more perfect fit between the human being and the environment which is no longer a natural one but, instead, is mainly social and technological.

Some concepts of how social change produces mental and behavioral disorders focus on the altered role-expectations and functions, the consequent disorientation, and the shifting values and norms that accompany change. For example, Fried proposes that the specific effects of change on the individual result more from the changed expectations people have of one another with respect to any form of interaction than from institutional changes (3).

As early as 1949, Margaret Mead discussed the implications of rapid culture change for personality development (4). She emphasized the disorienting effects of rapid change; just its rapidity makes it difficult for the individual to utilize previous experience as a guide for daily living, disrupts coherent sequences of behavior, and deprives one of the capacity to view the future as reasonably predictable—all of which can result in anxiety, personal disorientation, and social and cultural confusion. Furthermore, succeeding generations display the effects of having been reared by people who were subjected to the stressors of rapid change. She states:

> Fragmented types of development may occur as the growing child patterns his conscience on some member of the older generation, and shapes his ideal of himself upon the expressed day dreams of some other member who belongs to a different generation or possibly to both a different generation and a different original culture. Serious distortions occur when the mechanisms of inter-generation behavior, whatever that may be, break down (5).

Effects on Mores and Customs

About 30 years ago, the prominent Southern sociologist, Howard Odum, pointed out that the rate of social change was so great that mores and folkways had been supplanted by technicways (6). Folkways are the habits of the individual and the customs of the group which have been developed over long periods of time to meet their needs and, thus, in a sense, represent the store of folk wisdom. On the other hand, technicways are the individual's habits and the group's customs which arise to meet needs in the modern, technological world. In contrast to folkways, technicways have no tradition; moreover, they are evanescent. Odum explains: "They arise quickly from specific, definite, observable pressures and needs, and their survival or success depends upon their quick adoption and usage" (7). Since technicways change roles (consider, for example, the widespread effect of the development of "the pill" on men as well as women), transcend folkways, and supplant mores, Odum maintains that they can accelerate the tempo of societal evolution and that they are integral aspects of much of the dilemmas, confusion, and chaos present in our civilization.

A case vignette: Some effects of these changes, particularly from folkways to technicways, are illustrated by the following:

> A 53-year old, married woman was referred for psychiatric consultation because of severe backaches. She exhibited many symptoms typical of depression—crying, wringing of hands, slowed speech, and sadness, occasionally punctuated by oblique, hostile references to her husband. This patient, who seemed to be having a grief reaction, stated that her symptoms had begun gradually about two years ago. For more than 30 years, she and her husband had lived on a large, prosperous farm located near a rapidly-growing city. They had lived simple lives, rising at dawn, fitting their daily routine to the crop cycle and the demands of their livestock, and attending a rural evangelical church. But in the last decade the city had expanded, surrounding their farm and multiplying land values immensely. They sold part of their farm for a huge profit to entrepreneurs who had constructed a large shopping center. Her husband realized that he could make more money building apartments and homes on the balance of their property than by farming it. Their entire life style changed; they built a modern home and left the farmhouse which had been in the family for generations.
>
> She said that in former years she had often made picnic lunches which the two of them had shared while he was tending the crops, but that now she waits at home from 11 to 3 o'clock each day so that she can have a few minutes with him when he comes in between business meetings for a "quick bite." Both of them feel out of place in their new business and social worlds, but her husband stays busy, involved with contractors and other businessmen. She feels that their way of life has disappeared and that all of her supports have been knocked out from under her. She is no longer comfortable attending farm meetings since she and her husband are now business people rather than farmers. They no longer attend their church because they are disturbed by the minister's derogatory allusions to wealth and monetary gain, an anathema to the fundamentalist religion.

This housewife is a casualty of the technological era, grieving over a lost way of life and unprepared to enter a new one. Her depressive reaction is one of the consequences.

Scientific Studies of Social Change

Social and cultural determinists were the first to engage in scientific studies of social change and behavior. In the 1830s, the Belgian astronomer and statistician, Quetelet, applied the statistical method used by Gauss and others in the physical sciences to the study of human characteristics. Quetelet's "social physics" involved actuarial studies of crime; he stated that: "Society includes within itself the germs of all the crimes committed. . . . It is the social state, in some measure, which prepares these crimes, and the criminal is merely the instrument to execute them" (8). Harris notes that when Quetelet concluded that there were sociocultural uniformities in suicide, he anticipated Durkheim's work by almost 60 years.

A cultural determinist and proponent of the "organic" life of societies, Emile Durkheim attributed the social changes occurring in Western society to increased specialization, competition, and the breakdown of collective sentiments necessary for the mechanical solidarity of simpler, pretechnological societies. His classic study, written in the 1890s, showed a relationship between suicide and the growing anomie characteristic of modern, highly-technical societies (9). We should note that Durkheim believed that cohesion within a society—social order—is dependent mainly upon shared sentiments, that the personality is transformed by the cultural milieu, and that there is an emotional basis for both culture and behavior (10).

In a recent study of social change and mental illness, Brenner found that for more than a century—1840 to 1960—higher hospitalization rates among middle- and lower-social class persons in New York State were significantly related to recessions (11). But almost all studies of social change and mental illness are subject to the ecological fallacy (described by Robinson in 1950) that aggregate data have the same type of validity as data obtained from individuals (12).

THE FLORIDA HEALTH STUDY

In an effort to avoid this methodologic problem—to evaluate the possible relationships between social change processes and mental health risk at the level of the individual, not the aggregate—we asked our respondents about their perceptions of the following in the community:

1. Racial unrest
2. Crowding in the schools
3. Outsiders moving in
4. Traffic problems
5. More industries moving in
6. Pollution of lakes/streams
7. Increased crime/violence
8. Young people using drugs
9. No voice in community affairs
10. People aren't as friendly as they used to be
11. Faster pace of living and pressure
12. Young people leaving the community
13. Fewer jobs in town/area
14. More people on welfare

Our respondents had the options of replying "Yes" (it is occurring), "No" (it is not occurring), or "Don't Know" (it may be occurring but I am not aware of it). Each respondent who answered "Yes" to an item was then asked whether it upset him or her "Very Much," "Some," or "Not at all." Thus, we obtained responses about both perception of social changes and the degree of concern about them at the individual level. Subsequently, we compared the SPI and the Not-Impaired groups' responses.

Perception of Social Change Processes

Our respondents' perceptions of the social change items are shown in Table 9-1.

Substantial percentages of the respondents reported perceptions of the changes we studied. At least in some instances, the respondents' perceptions of these social change processes were not just subjective impressions. For example, according to the 1973 Uniform Crime Reports issued by the Federal Bureau of Investigation, both the raw figures and rates per 100,000 had increased significantly during the years of our study. "Being upset about *increased crime*," a manifest concern expressed by 60% of our sample, can only be judged as reality-based in view of the 34.8% increase in murder, the 54.8% increase in rape, and the 39.2% increase in robbery between 1968 and 1973 (13).

TABLE 9-1

Percentages of total sample reporting perception of social changes in the community.*

Social Change	Perception of Change (%)	Change Not Perceived (%)	Don't Know (%)
Young Using Drugs	74.1	14.2	10.7
Crowded Schools	70.6	15.1	13.6
Racial Unrest	68.8	26.1	4.6
Crime Rising	68.3	23.4	7.5
Faster Pace and Pressure	64.5	29.5	4.8
More Traffic	62.1	34.9	2.5
Pollution	60.9	27.4	11.0
Outsiders Moving In	56.0	35.4	7.8
More People on Welfare	53.3	12.4	31.0
Fewer Jobs	42.1	38.1	18.8
People Unfriendly	38.2	56.8	4.1
No Voice in Community	35.5	52.2	10.9
Young People Leaving	35.3	49.5	13.6
More Industry	30.2	55.4	13.4

* Total number of respondents is 1,645. On some items there was an additional category of "Did Not Respond."

Concern about Social Change Processes

Table 9-2 shows that the percentages of respondents reporting that they were upset by the social change processes varied widely. Not only did substantial numbers of the respondents report perception of the changes occurring in Alachua County, but 50 to 60% of all 1645 respondents were upset by five of them. These five—*use of drugs, increased crime, racial unrest, crowding in schools,* and *pollution*—encompass a wide range of societal problems that accompany social change.

Sociodemographic Relationships

Analyses of the responses according to age, sex, race, socioeconomic status (SES), and marital status revealed the following trends.

Age: Generally, the percentages of respondents reporting a sense of concern about the social processes decreased with advancing age. Of those who discerned the social changes, about two-thirds of those aged 16-29 were upset about *crime* or *drugs* whereas only one-half of those

TABLE 9-2

Percentages of respondents perceiving changes and upset or not upset about them.*

Social Change	Total Sample Perceiving Change (%)	Respondents Perceiving Changes Who Were Upset (%)	Respondents Perceiving Changes Who Were Not Upset (%)
Crime Rising	68.3	88.4	11.6
Young Using Drugs	74.1	83.8	16.2
Pollution	60.9	82.8	17.2
Racial Unrest	68.8	77.3	22.7
Crowded Schools	70.6	73.4	26.6
More Traffic	62.1	65.3	34.7
More People on Welfare	53.3	64.0	36.0
Fewer Jobs	42.1	60.8	39.2
Unfriendly People	38.2	56.0	44.0
Faster Pace and Pressure	64.5	54.6	45.4
No Voice in Community	35.5	54.6	45.4
Young People Leaving	35.3	25.5	74.5
Outsiders Moving In	56.0	12.7	87.3
More Industry	30.2	17.1	82.9

* Total number of respondents is 1,645. On some items there was an additional category of "Did Not Respond."

aged 60+ reported concern about these. One exception to this age trend was that a somewhat higher proportion of the older (42%) than younger (35%) reported that they thought *people were more unfriendly.* However, only about 20% of both groups were upset about this sense of unfriendliness in the people about them. Another exception was that a higher proportion of the middle-aged respondents (72%) perceived that there was a *faster pace and pressure* in life than did those in either the younger or older aged groups.

Sex: The differences in responses between the sexes were small, but slightly higher percentages of men than women tended to report that they perceived the changes. One exception was that 65% of the women, compared to 55% of the men, reported feeling there was a *faster pace and pressure* in daily living. Almost equal percentages of men and women reported concern about the social changes.

Race: Proportionately more whites than blacks reported perception of the changes. Among those who reported feeling the changes, higher percentages of whites than blacks reported that they were upset by them. For example, concern about *racial unrest* was reported by 64% of the whites in contrast to only 23% of the blacks. On the *crowded schools* issue, which practically convulsed the community during the early 1970s, the racial differences were smaller; 75% of the whites perceived *crowding* in the schools compared to 55% of the blacks. Of those reporting perception of *crowded schools,* 76% of the whites and 61% of the blacks reported being upset by it. Although somewhat more of the whites than blacks reported that there was *more pressure in daily living* and that they were upset about it, these differences between the races were not large. There were two exceptions to the general racial trends. Relatively more blacks (47%) than whites (36%) reported that *people were more unfriendly* but only 19% of those blacks and 22% of those whites were upset about it. Also, higher proportions of blacks (54%) than whites (39%) reported that there were fewer jobs available and more of the blacks (31%) than the whites (24%) were upset about it.

The smaller percentages of blacks than whites reporting perception of and concern about most of the social change processes that were related both to community issues and to personal well-being can be looked upon as evidence of the enduring effects of the caste system. The two exceptions also support this conjecture. As an inferior caste, the blacks were not supposed to be involved in community affairs but rather to be concerned only with how they related to other persons and with earning a living.

SES: On six items—*drugs, crime, racial unrest, crowded schools, traffic problems,* or *pollution*—more of the higher than the lower SES respondents reported that they both perceived and were concerned about the changes. For example, of those reporting perception of *racial unrest, crime,* or *drugs,* about 75% of the upper SES respondents also were upset about them, in contrast to only 20 to 30% of those in the lowest SES group.

We found no consistent relationships between SES and being upset about: *no voice in the community, people more unfriendly, faster pace and pressure, fewer jobs,* or *more people on welfare.* On some of these items, slightly higher percentages of respondents in the middle SES groups reported both perceiving and being concerned about the changes than did either the lower or upper SES groups.

The much larger percentages of the higher than the lower SES respondents expressing concern about the obvious community problems is consistent with Marxian and other social action theorists' views on the psychology of deprivation. Furthermore, finding that a larger proportion in the lower SES group were unconcerned about *no voice in the community* or *fewer jobs* indicates anomie and, to some extent, apathy.

Marital Status: Much larger percentages of the single and married than the widowed, separated, or divorced respondents felt that 10 of the social change processes were upsetting. They were particularly concerned about *crime, drugs, pollution, racial unrest, crowding in the schools, more people on welfare, people less friendly, faster pace and pressure, no voice in the community,* or *outsiders moving in.*

In Summary: Those who reported both a perception of and concern about the social changes tended to be: 1) younger than age 44, 2) white males and females, 3) in the middle or higher SES brackets, and/or 4) either single or married.

RELATIONSHIPS WITH SOCIAL PSYCHIATRIC IMPAIRMENT (SPI)

We compared the SPI group's responses to the questions about social change processes with the responses of the not-impaired. Generally, as large a percentage of respondents in the SPI category as in the not-impaired discerned the social changes. This finding surprised us. We had anticipated that in accord with Freudian concepts of the economic distribution of libido, a lower proportion of those in the SPI group would report perception of the changes, i.e., that their symptomatology would absorb the energy required for perception of the broad social changes.

In a preliminary study of perceptions of social change processes and scores on a depression scale, we had found that those with the highest depression scores often gave "Don't Know" replies to questions about the more remote, impersonal social change items. Not perceiving societal problems may have been indicative of the apathy integral to the depressive condition. This is consistent with concepts of depression as a psychobiologic reaction characterized by a turning inward of the emotions and a lack of interest in external events and other persons. The SPI group contained many individuals with various types of symptomatology, not just depression, which we would conjecture to be the reason we found them, as a group, to be more perceptive of what was going on in the world about them (14).

Significantly more respondents in the SPI category than the Not-Impaired group reported that they were "upset very much" about nine of the 14 social changes: *more traffic, young people leaving, outsiders moving in, more people on welfare, racial unrest, people more unfriendly, fewer jobs available, no voice in community affairs,* and *faster pace and pressure* in everyday living. Most of these nine tended to have a greater interpersonal and personal quality than the five on which there were no group differences. Those more impersonal five were: *rising crime, use of drugs, pollution, crowded schools,* and *industry moving in.*

Many in the SPI group were distressed by changes that would disrupt accustomed life styles, alter the character of the community life, and demand adjustments. In a general discussion of the impact of social change on mental health, Louis Miller points out that the effects of change have four manifestations (15).

1. Rapid change is felt acutely by children and youth, many of whom respond by adopting new behavioral patterns, e.g., the increased use of drugs.
2. Rapid change influences adult functioning as illustrated by the case vignette presented earlier in this chapter.
3. Social change is accompanied by altered forms of psychopathology. For example, in the developing nations, depression and suicide are now reported much more commonly than in the past. In the technological societies, the classic psychiatric syndromes are diagnosed much less often than they were just two decades ago. "Borderline" is the diagnosis used to encompass a wide number and variety of mixed neurotic-psychotic symptoms, particularly intertwined affective and cognitive disorders. Furthermore, some degree of paranoid symptomatology is now a conspicuous feature seen in many mental patients with various types of drug-induced, affective, schizophrenic, or "borderline" disorders.
4. Rapid social change also influences the type of treatment received by the mentally ill, e.g., the developing nations are constructing large mental hospitals while the Western nations are deinstitutionalizing the mentally ill.

In a recent review of social change and mental disorder, H.B.M. Murphy concludes that social change is too complex a variable for scientific study of its relationship to mental health and illness at our current level of conceptualization and with the limitations of our methodology (16). In our study, we could not attempt to determine causal relationships between social change and risk for mental disorder as measured by SPI. Moreover, interpreting reactions to social processes is complicated because the behaviors involved in the processes, such as increased use of drugs and crime, may be either the results of mental disorders or maladaptive responses to more fundamental social problems such as deprivation. Commission of a crime, for example, may represent the individual's willingness to resort to aggression as a result of frustration or may be a miscarried coping response.

Although studies of social change and mental health are complicated and often inexact, Alexander Leighton and his colleagues found in their study of the Yoruba that rapid social change had a differential impact on various segments of that Nigerian society (17). They divided 15 villages into four categories: 1) traditional-integrated, 2) traditional-disintegrated, 3) changing-integrated, and 4) changing-disintegrated. They found that the mental health risk was higher in the disintegrated than the integrated villages, but was much lower than expected in the changing-disintegrated. In the disintegrated communities undergoing changes, social change was having a salutary effect. Thus, it appears that when conditions of life are harsh, adverse, and deleterious, social change can be beneficial.

Invention and technology, the ingredients of social change and culture lag, yield demonstrable benefits for some. We think that in our study those groups with low percentages in the SPI category were in phase with the rate of change. But high percentages of those who were in the SPI category—not benefitting from the changes because they were unprepared, left in the wake, or disoriented by them—appear to be out of phase with the rate of change.

Inability to keep pace with the rate of social change leaves one in a residual, marginal group—at high risk for mental illness. Also, exceeding the rate of change—attempting to be in the vanguard—can be deleterious. Ogburn's theory of culture lag set forth such views (18). He maintained that continuing social maladaptation occurs during periods of rapid social change, when material culture (technology) proceeds at a faster rate of change than adaptive culture (beliefs, role prescriptions, and institutions).

As discussed in Chapter 2, racial attitudes have changed significantly during the last few decades. In particular, the majority of our respondents endorsed either "assimilation" or "acceptance"; only small percentages were classified as "accommodators" or "avoiders." We looked at the percentages of those in the SPI category in the four attitudinal groups. The percentages in the SPI category who were "assimilators," "acceptors," or "accommodators" varied only slightly, from 25.1% to 29.8%, but of the "avoiders," 36.1% were in the SPI category. The total analysis barely reached statistical significance ($p = .04$).

REFERENCES

1. McKinney, J. G., and Bourque, L. B., "The Changing South: National Incorporation of a Region." *American Sociological Review,* Vol. 36, No. 3, June 1971, 399-412.
2. Thomas, W. I., *The Polish Peasant in Europe and America,* with F. Zananeicki, 5 vols. Chicago: University of Chicago Press, 1918-1920.
3. Fried, M., "Effects of Social Change on Mental Health." In: B. Bergen, and C. S. Thomas (Eds.), *Issues and Problems in Social Psychiatry.* Springfield, Ill.: Charles C Thomas, 1966.
4. Mead, M., "The Implications of Culture Change for Personality Development." In: D. G. Harind (Ed.), *Personal Character and Cultural Milieu,* Revised Edition. Syracuse, N.Y.: Syracuse University Press, 1949, 549-563.
5. Ibid., 557.
6. Odum, H. W., *Understanding Society: The Principles of Dynamic Sociology.* New York: Macmillan Co., 1947.
7. Ibid.
8. Harris, M., *The Rise of Anthropological Theory.* New York: Thomas Y. Crowell Co., 1968, 74.
9. Durkheim, E., *Suicide: A Study in Sociology.* J. A. Spaulding and G. Simpson (trans.), G. Simpson (Ed.). Glencoe, Ill.: Free Press of Glencoe, 1951.
10. Hatch, E., *Theories of Man and Culture.* New York: Columbia University Press, 1973, 162-213.
11. Brenner, M. H., *Mental Illness and the Economy.* Cambridge, Mass.: Harvard University Press, 1973, 36 and 123-126.
12. Robinson, W. S., "Ecological Correlations and the Behavior of Individuals." *American Sociological Review,* Vol. 15, 1950, 351-357.
13. *World Almanac and Book of Facts, 1975.* New York: Newspaper Enterprise Association, Inc., 1975, 966.
14. Schwab, J. J., "Perception of Social Change and Depressive Symptomatology" In: J. H. Masserman and J. J. Schwab (Eds.), *Social Psychiatry,* Vol. I. New York: Grune and Stratton, Inc., 1974.
15. Miller, L., Personal communication.
16. Murphy, H. B. M., "Migration and the Major Mental Disorders: A Reappraisal." In: Zwingman, C., and Pfister-Ammende, M., *Uprooting and After. . . .* New York: Springer-Verlag New York Inc., 1973, 204-220.
17. Leighton, A. H., Lambo, T. A., Hughes, C. C., Leighton, D. C., Murphy, J. M., and Macklin, D. B., *Psychiatric Disorder Among the Yoruba.* Ithaca, N.Y.: Cornell University Press, 1963, 203-240.
18. Ogburn, W., *On Culture and Social Change.* Selected papers edited with an Introduction by O. D. Duncan. Chicago: Chicago University Press, 1964, 101.

10

Aspirations, Social Mobility, and Geographic Mobility

In the preceding chapters we have looked at the prevalence and concurrence of SPI, psychosomatic distress, and physical illness according to the classic epidemiologic criteria—time, place, and person—that supply necessary, objective data about the condition (s) being studied. For example, in the early 1970s *(time)*, in Alachua County *(place)*, a significantly high proportion of the separated respondents *(person)* was found to be at risk for mental illness as measured by SPI. These criteria and the sociodemographic characteristics of the population enable the researcher to ascertain basic associations between the condition (s) and those at risk. But, when possible, the researcher should supplement these findings with analyses of other variables that may show, for example, associations between risk and more subjective or more complex factors than age, sex, etc.

In this chapter we shall examine possible associations between SPI and three such variables: 1) aspirations and achievements as perceived by the respondents; 2) intergenerational social mobility; and 3) geographic mobility. We selected self perceptions of aspirations and achievements because they have been found to be associated with risk for mental disorder. They are subjective and to a limited extent indicate ego strengths. Social and geographic mobility have been found to be variably and inconsistently related to risk for mental illness. We chose to study them because Alachua County, like many other areas in the Southeast, had been undergoing rapid social change. The social order had been disrupted by sweeping political, economic, and institutional changes and by the influx of newcomers.

Part I—Aspirations and Achievements

Clinically, either unrealistically high or very low levels of aspiration are observed in many patients seeking psychiatric care. In 1967, Kleiner and Parker reviewed the relationships among "goal-striving, social status, and mental disorder" (1). They suggested that goal-striving behavior, particularly mobility orientation, which they defined as "the discrepancy between achievement and aspiration" and its relation to mental illness, offers a unifying construct for understanding some of the complex interactions between social variables and mental disorders (2). The research they reviewed indicated that achievement-related behavior may be either a cause or an effect of mental disorder and that there may be vast differences between an individual's expected and desired goals. Expected goals may be more realistic than desired goals, but the former may represent a defensive if not painful compromise. Kleiner and Parker viewed goal-striving behavior as a possibly significant intervening variable between social processes on the one hand and mental health or illness on the other.

THE CANTRIL SELF-ANCHORING STRIVING SCALE

We used the Cantril Self-Anchoring Striving Scale to assess each respondent's view of where he or she stood on the "ladder of life" in the past, in the present, and in the anticipated future (3). This scale is an ingenious two-part instrument that can be used to appraise an individual's concept of self in relation to life. In the first section, the respondents are asked to list their wishes and hopes about the future and then their fears and worries about it. As mentioned in Chapter 3, the most common wishes and hopes expressed by our respondents were for an improved standard of living, a happy family life, and good health. The most commonly expressed fears and worries about the future were substandard living conditions, sickness in the family, and personal illness.

The second part of the scale is a more projective test. The respondent is shown a ladder and told, "Here is a picture of a ladder. Suppose the top of the ladder represents the best possible life for you. Where on the ladder do you feel you stand at the present time?" (See Figure 10-1.) Then the respondent is asked to mark where he or she stood on the Ladder five years ago and will stand five years in the future (4).

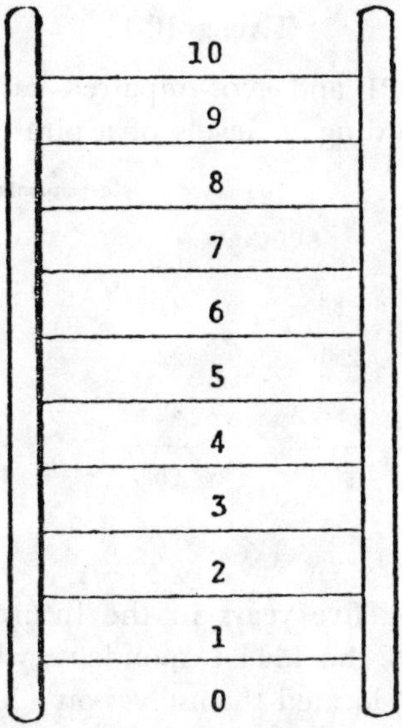

FIGURE 10-1. Cantril's Ladder. Source: The Pattern of Human Concerns by Hadley Cantril. Copyright 1965 by Rutgers, The State University. Reprinted by permission of the Rutgers University Press.

In discussing the Ladder, Cantril stated that:

> Too often a researcher who studies different aspects of human behavior will confuse the level of experience with which he is dealing and begin to think that the abstractions he has created are the reality when, in fact, they are several steps removed from the ongoing process of experience itself. . . . Since abstractions are brought about and communicated by the nouns or adjectives man himself has devised, they often provide a static rather than a moving picture, leaving out the genesis or process-of-becoming, with its irreversible sequence, which seems to be a major characterization of personal, social, and political life. . . . I have tried to understand people in their own terms (6).

LEVELS OF ASPIRATION AND SPI

Unrealistically high aspirations may be stressful and conducive to the development of mental disorder when an individual strives toward goals beyond his reach, or they may be indications of mental illness. On the other hand, unrealistically low levels of aspiration may reflect lack of motivation or be symptomatic of mental disorders, e.g., depression. We used the differences between our respondents' positions on the Ladder

TABLE 10-1

Percentages in SPI and Not-Impaired categories grouped according to levels of aspiration.

Level of Aspiration	SPI Category (N)	SPI Category (%)	Not-Impaired Category (N)	Not-Impaired Category (%)
Low	35	41.2	50	58.8
Moderate	250	22.1	879	77.9
High	98	42.6	132	57.4
TOTAL	383	26.5	1061	73.5

at the present time and five years in the future as an index of their levels of aspiration.* Of the 1444 respondents who completed all three Ladders, only 85 (5.9%) located themselves on a lower rung in the future than in the present (low aspiration group).** In contrast, 230 (15.9%) located themselves higher in the future than one standard deviation above the mean rise for the total sample (high aspiration group). Table 10-1 shows the percentages of respondents in the SPI and Not-Impaired categories grouped according to the differences between their present and future positions on the Ladder.

Significantly larger percentages of both the low- and high-aspiration groups were in the SPI category than persons whose expectations of the future were for only a moderate rise in their position in life. We think that our findings from this study of a general population support clinicians' observations about patients' levels of aspiration and mental disorder.

Positions on Cantril's Ladder

Figure 10-2 shows the means for our respondents' positions on the Ladder five years prior to the survey, at the time of the study, and five

* For purposes of this discussion, "present" is considered to be the time at which the respondents were tested, "past" is considered to be five years previous to "present," and "future" is considered to be five years hence.

** Of the total sample of 1645 respondents, 201 did not complete all three Ladders for a number of reasons, e.g., some of the elderly did not think they would be alive five years in the future; or, since the Ladder was placed at the end of the two-hour interview, some degree of fatigue may have been responsible for incomplete results.

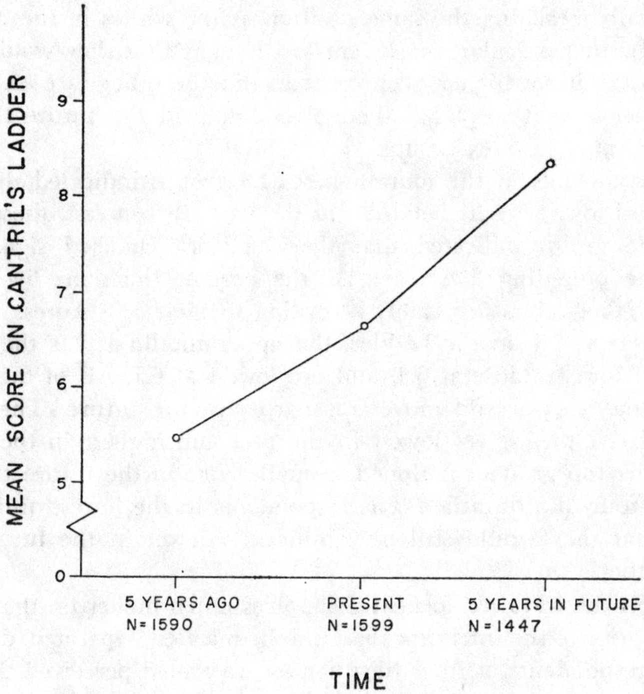

FIGURE 10-2. Mean score on Cantril's Ladder by "past," "present," and "future."

years in the future. The mean for our total sample rose sharply between the past and the present and even more sharply for the future.

Sociodemographic Factors

The older respondents placed themselves at a higher position on the Ladder at the present time than did the younger. But those under the age of 45 indicated that they had moved farther up the Ladder during the preceding five years than did the older respondents and also that they would move even farther upward during the next five years. Females' mean scores for the past, the present, and the future were at slightly higher levels than the males' mean scores.

The blacks located themselves significantly lower than did the whites five years ago (blacks, 5.0, whites, 5.7) and in the present (blacks, 6.0, whites, 6.9). Thus, the blacks perceived that they had been and still were in a low position in the social order. But they viewed the future optimistically, reaching the same position as the whites in the next five years (8.4). In particular, black females thought that they would climb sharply, attaining a higher position than did the other race-sex groups. Black males, however, placed themselves lower in the future than did any of the other race-sex groups.

The respondents in the four highest SES groups indicated that their present positions were higher than in the past. In contrast, those in the lowest SES group indicated that they had not changed significantly during the preceding five years. At the present time, the five groups positioned themselves accurately according to their SES scores. The top quintile was at 7.4 on the Ladder, the upper-middle at 7.0, the middle at 6.8, the lower-middle at 6.4, and the lowest at 6.1. All of the groups thought that they would move up sharply in the future. The upper-middle placed themselves lowest in the past and highest in the future, whereas the top group envisioned a smaller rise in the future than did the other four SES quintiles. The respondents in the lowest quintile indicated that they would still be significantly lower in the future than did the others.

Although the widowed located themselves much higher on the Ladder five years prior to the interview than did the married, separated, divorced, or single respondents, neither they nor the separated perceived that they had in fact moved upward during the past five years. Moreover, the widowed expected that they would climb only to the 7.9 level in the future; the other marital status groups believed that they would move farther upward.

Figure 10-3 shows where the respondents (grouped by geographic origin) positioned themselves on the Ladder. The Alachuans placed themselves at a significantly lower position both five years ago and at present than did those from Other Florida, the Deep South, or Elsewhere. Also, the Alachuans located themselves slightly lower in the future than did the other groups.

Comparison of SPI and Not-Impaired Groups

We compared the positions of the respondents in the SPI category with those of the Not-Impaired group at the three times. As shown in Figure 10-4, those in the SPI category had significantly lower positions on the Ladder five years ago than did those in the Not-Impaired group. Further analyses showed that respondents in the SPI category aged 23-29 and 45+, the white females, those in the lower-middle and middle SES quintiles, and those from the Deep South and Elsewhere, positioned

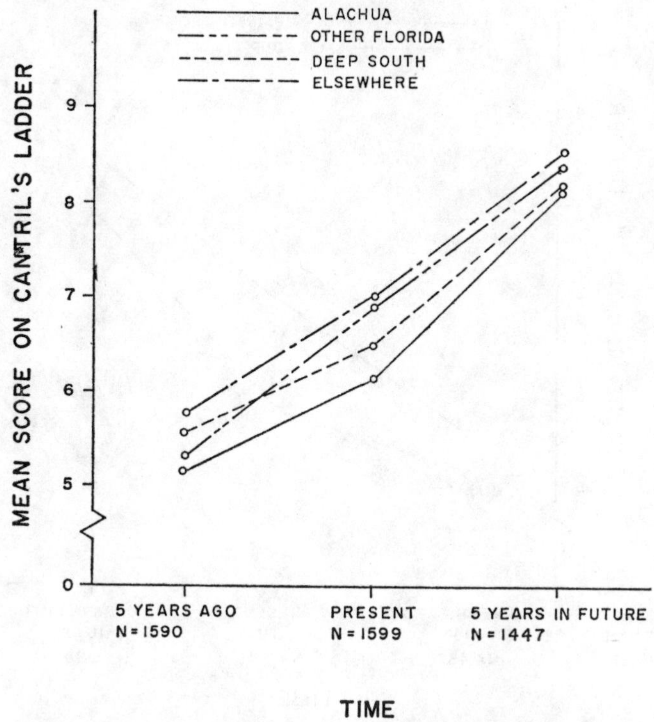

FIGURE 10-3. Mean scores on Cantril's Ladder, "five" years ago, "present," and "five years in the future" by geographic origin.

themselves much lower five years ago than did their counterparts in the Not-Impaired group.

Also, the respondents in the SPI category consistently located themselves at significantly lower positions on the Ladder at the present time than did those in the Not-Impaired group. Those in the SPI category who located themselves very low at present were the blacks, the lower-middle SES group, and the separated.

Respondents in both the SPI and Not-Impaired categories indicated that they would move upward sharply during the next five years. (See Figure 10-4). In the SPI category, the younger respondents and those in the upper-middle SES quintile expected that they would attain particularly high positions in the future. In contrast, those in the SPI category aged 45-59 and the black males did not believe that they would move as far upward as did those in the other groups.

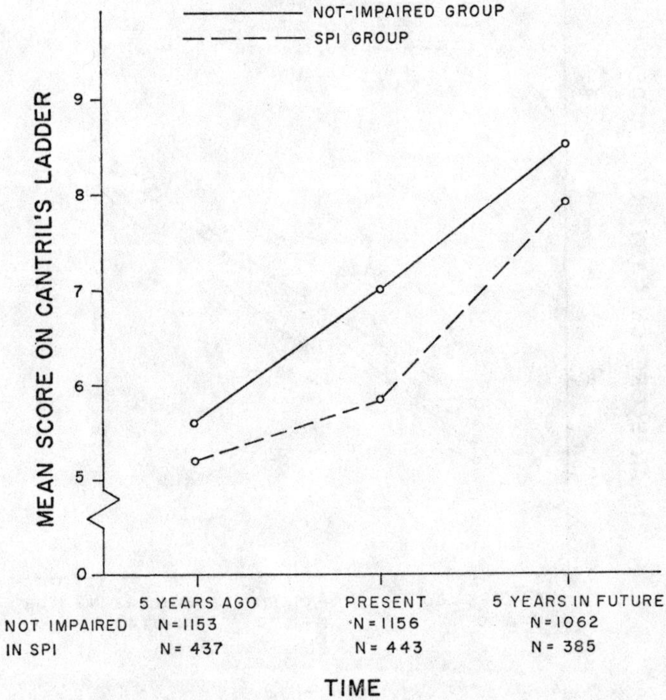

FIGURE 10-4. Mean scores on Cantril's Ladder, "five" years ago, "present," and "five years in the future" by SPI and Not-Impaired groups.

CONCLUSIONS

We found a highly significant relationship between SPI and self-perception of a low position in the social order, as indicated by location on Cantril's Ladder—in the past, at present, and in the future. The mental anguish, diminished function, and interpersonal distress indicative of SPI are associated with a view of one's self as being relatively low on the "ladder of life." The consistency and significance of the differences between the SPI and the Not-Impaired groups are remarkable. However, we should recall that a disproportionately large number of the respondents in the SPI category were in the lower SES groups—groups which placed themselves much lower on the Ladder in the present and usually in the past than did those in the higher SES groups. Although lower SES respondents in both the SPI and the Not-Impaired groups projected a sharp rise in the future, the rise was not to as high a level as that projected by respondents in the upper SES quintiles.

Part II—Social Mobility and SPI*

America has billed itself as the land of opportunity. From the time of the Pilgrims who came seeking religious freedom through succeeding waves of immigrants who were searching for more rewarding lives, Americans have regarded their country as the place where talent and the willingness to work are the only necessary requisites for success.

Much of the nation's progress, however, has been made at the expense, and often the oppression, of various groups. Westward expansion, ennobled by tales of our pioneering forebears, was marred by the unjust treatment of the American Indians. The Industrial Revolution, which stimulated modernization and economic growth, was accompanied by widespread abuses of workers and their families. Although women "made the wilderness a home" and worked and died on the frontier, they have been denied equal opportunity for status and prestige. The "golden age" of the South, beginning in 1793 with Eli Whitney's cotton gin, depended on the exploitation of slaves.

This apparent contradiction between the dream of opportunity and the reality of inequity led to the development of two explanations of those who were "unsuccessful." Social Darwinists argued that the less fortunate lacked the necessary abilities to succeed and thus were responsible for their own inferior condition. Women were considered to be weaker than men, and blacks were viewed as incapable of civilized behavior. Others blamed the social system and attempted to change it. Abraham Flexner's reform of medical education, Jane Addams' Hull House, and the establishment of labor unions are examples of the efforts of individuals and groups to correct the social imbalances they perceived.

While the entire nation has been subject to the forces of social change, the character and social structure of the South have been transformed by the Civil Rights movement as well (see Chapter 2). Social changes in Alachua County during the 1960s and 1970s were taking place on three levels. First were changes reflecting national trends toward greater urbanization, mass education, and sexual equality (7, 8). Second were regional changes stemming from the impact of desegregation. Third was a large increase in the County's population produced by in-migration

* This part was written by Elizabeth Lin.

from other parts of Florida, the nearby Southern states, and especially, from the North (9). As a result, the County contained many mobile persons—students and newcomers—as well as native Alachuans, many of whom were poor and black.

In view of the rapid rate of social change, we had an excellent opportunity to study social mobility and the hypothesized relationships between it and risk for mental illness.

MEASURES OF SOCIAL MOBILITY

Social mobility is the movement of individuals between hierarchically arranged social positions (10). Movement toward the top of the hierarchical ladder is defined as upward and movement toward the bottom as downward. Individuals who maintain their original positions are categorized as non-mobile.

The hierarchical arrangement of social positions can be defined by use of a single index, such as education or occupation, or by using more complex indices, such as socioeconomic status (SES). To evaluate social mobility, we chose education and occupation as two reasonably valid indices of social status that would permit comparisons with other studies.

Movement up or down the social scale can be measured in a number of ways. *Intra*generational mobility compares an individual's present or highest position with a previous one. The most commonly used method measures *inter*generational mobility—the individual's position is compared with that of a member of the previous generation (usually a male with his father or with his father-in-law) (11). We chose to measure *inter*generational mobility for two reasons. First, a comparison of generations seemed the best approach for tapping social changes. Second, intergenerational mobility and risk for mental illness have been studied in both the general population and mental patients; thus, we could compare our findings with those of others.

Social Mobility and Female Status

Until recently, most researchers have examined only the statuses of males and have paid little attention to female statuses. Problems are definitional and methodological; for example, men who do not work are considered unemployed whereas women without jobs are considered first and foremost to be homemakers. Moreover, when actively employed, women usually receive lower wages which often are regarded as supplementary family income. Also, they are more likely than men to work part-time, and the jobs they take may lack advancement opportunities (12).

As a result, conventional indices of social status, e.g. occupation and income, are difficult to apply to women. Researchers therefore often evaluate women by their husbands' statuses and, in effect, appraise their social positions by how they marry rather than by their education or talents. Furthermore, intergenerational comparisons between the social positions of men and their fathers have *prima facie* validity that comparisons between women and their fathers lack. Comparisons between mothers and daughters are even more problematic. Housewives cannot be compared with working women, and even women in the same occupation cannot be compared accurately if they are of different generations. In the past, a housewife may have held a different status than her modern-day daughter who views herself as a "home administrator."

A study of social mobility in the general population, therefore, faces two questions. First, can the same definitions of social position be used for men and women? Second, can mobility, however defined, be *equated* for males and females? In a study of male and female household heads, Ayella and Williamson suggest that separate models for the sexes are needed and conclude that "the socioeconomic success of women is more fixed by background, education, and occupational factors, and is less a function of individual ability than is the case for men" (13).

On the other hand, support for use of a single model is provided by DeJong et al., who found little difference between male and female intergenerational mobility, and by McClendon, who recently reported that although occupational structures differ for the sexes, the attainment of occupational status is not significantly different (14, 15). There is no simple answer to these questions, and, as will be discussed in the methodology section, we were compelled to devise a complex method for measuring female social mobility.

Social Mobility and Age

Another problem with the study of intergenerational mobility is the influence of age. For example, how accurately can an older man with a lower occupation than his father's be compared with a young man whose entry-level job is also lower than his father's? Both are downwardly mobile, but the older man is nearing the end of his career while the young man is just starting his. Some researchers have solved this problem by sampling only older, well-established men, a strategy which we used partially.

SOCIAL MOBILITY AND MENTAL DISORDER

Sorokin, basing his arguments in part on Durkheim's *Suicide,* suggested that social mobility produces both biological and social stress. He thought that the greater versatility and adaptability needed by the mobile person increase ". . . the activity of the nervous system . . . [causing] a permanent mental strain" (16). Furthermore, both social and geographic mobility reduce opportunities for creating and maintaining lasting social ties. The mobile person can readily become psychosocially isolated and subject to "anomie," hypothesized by Durkheim as being conducive to suicide (17).

However, both theorists and researchers have two different views about relationships between social mobility and risk for mental illness. The first is that mental illness is a determinant of social mobility. For example, Dunham et al. conclude that "it is the nature of the disease that determines the class position of the schizophrenic, at least by the measure of occupation and education, and that it is not the class position that influences the nature of the disease" (18).

The second viewpoint is that the stresses inherent in social mobility contribute to mental illness. In the Midtown Manhattan Study, Srole and Langner reported that a larger proportion of the downwardly mobile were rated as "probable psychotic" than of the non-mobile and upwardly mobile; individuals in the latter two categories were more likely to be rated "probable neurotic," suggesting that the particular stress patterns associated with upward and downward mobility were accompanied by different symptom configurations (19). Although our results do not conclusively support either point of view, they do show significant relationships between social mobility and risk for mental illness in a general population.

*Methodology**

We assigned each respondent and his/her father both educational and occupational scores.** Educational scores were based on the number of years of schooling, and occupational scores were based on the occupational ranking developed by Nam, et al. (20).

Intergenerational mobility, for the male respondents, was measured by

* Readers interested in further details of either the methodology or results sections should contact Elizabeth Lin, Department of Psychiatry and Behavioral Sciences, University of Louisville, Louisville, KY 40232.

** Scores were used in collapsed forms in some of our analyses.

subtracting the father's score from the respondent's.* For the female respondents, we had a choice among three intergenerational comparisons: 1) women with their mothers, 2) women with their fathers, and 3) their husbands with their fathers. Because of the methodological problems in comparing housewives with women working outside the home and in assessing the impact of changing women's roles, the mother-daughter comparison was rejected. Of the two remaining choices (father-daughter and father-husband), neither was completely satisfactory by itself. The father-daughter measure ignored the possible influence of a husband's status on his wife, and the father-husband measure excluded all the non-married women. Consequently, for both educational and occupational mobility for women, we used *both* methods whenever possible.

For our entire sample, we computed three sets of *educational mobility measures:*

1. *Male respondents* were compared with their fathers.
2. *Female respondents* were compared with their fathers.
3. *Husbands of female respondents* were compared with the women's fathers.

No score was computed for full or part-time students unless they were better educated than their fathers (or fathers-in-law) since currently non-mobile or downward scores might not reflect accurately their ultimate educational mobility.

We computed five sets of *occupational mobility measures:*

1. *Male respondents* were compared with their fathers.
2. *Married housewives' husbands* were compared with the housewives' fathers.
3. *Married working women* were compared with their fathers.
4. *Husbands of these working women* were compared with the women's fathers.
5. *Non-married working women* were compared with their fathers.

Non-married housewives and full-time students were omitted. Retired, disabled, and unemployed respondents were included only when we had information about their previous employment.

Respondents were divided into three categories for both educational and occupational mobility: 1) upwardly mobile, 2) non-mobile, and 3) downwardly mobile.

* Scores were in uncollapsed form for the computation of intergenerational measures.

EDUCATIONAL AND OCCUPATIONAL PROFILES

Education

Table 10-2 shows the mean educational levels of our respondents and their fathers.* Two trends are apparent. First, with the exception of the youngest age group, both men and women were better educated than their fathers.** Second, the mean educational level of both the respondents and their fathers had risen steadily during this century, corresponding to similar changes taking place nationally.

The mean educational levels of males and females were not significantly different for respondents over age 45. However, males under the age of 45 had significantly higher mean educational levels than their female counterparts. Thus, all but the youngest respondents were generally better educated than their fathers, and the educational level of males exceeded that of females in each age group born after 1927.

Occupation

Respondents' and their fathers' mean occupational scores are presented in Table 10-3. Male respondents in all but the youngest age group had higher scores than their fathers*** (similar to the educational comparisons). In contrast, married women's mean occupational scores were not significantly different from their fathers', and the younger non-married women had significantly *lower* occupational mean scores than their fathers.

The most striking feature of the educational and occupational profiles is the intergenerational difference between men and women. With the exception of the younger males (16-22 and 23-29 years old), male respondents were better educated than their fathers and had achieved higher occupational statuses. Women were also better educated than their fathers; however, their occupational statuses were either no different from their fathers' (married working women) or significantly lower (non-married working women).

---

* Results for this and the Occupational section are for male and female respondents only. Husbands of female respondents showed a pattern similar to male respondents.

** The deviation of the youngest respondents from the basic rising linear trend is also apparent in the occupational profiles and indicates that many of these respondents have either not yet completed their education or are just starting their careers.

*** Although the general trend for male respondents was an increase in mean occupational scores over time, further analyses showed that 63% of those in the lower-middle occupational quintile were non-mobile.

TABLE 10-2

Mean education scores of respondents and respondents' fathers by age groups.

	MEAN EDUCATION SCORES		
MALE RESPONDENTS:	Respondents	Fathers	Sig.
Total (N = 736)	5.50	4.80	$p < .0005$
Age Groups			
16-22	5.80	6.00	n.s.
23-29	6.60	5.15	$p < .0005$
30-44	5.75	4.37	$p < .0005$
45-59	5.23	4.09	$p < .0005$
60+	3.89	3.52	n.s.
FEMALE RESPONDENTS:			
Total (N = 905)	5.08	4.57	$p < .0005$
Age Groups			
16-22	5.43	5.60	$p < .0005$
23-29	5.93	5.30	n.s.
30-44	5.27	4.22	$p < .005$
45-59	4.80	3.83	$p < .0005$
60+	4.12	3.38	$p < .005$

Interpretations

The rise in the mean occupational scores of the male respondents paralleled the nationwide shift from rural to urban occupations. Only 6.2% of the male respondents were farmers in contrast to 31.8% of their fathers. This shift from agriculture to other occupations was pronounced in the three oldest male groups. It has implications for the two youngest male groups; they may achieve only slightly higher occupational statuses than their fathers as the balance between rural and non-rural occupations stabilizes. Thus, unless drastic changes occur in the occupational structure, statuses of fathers and sons may eventually show little difference. Similarly, we predict a leveling-off of the rising trend in education because of the increased time, effort, and money which higher education demands.

TABLE 10-3

Mean occupation scores of respondents and respondents' fathers by age groups.

	MEAN OCCUPATION SCORES		
MALE RESPONDENTS:	Respondents	Fathers	Sig.
Total (N = 542)	58.15	53.39	p < .001
Age Groups			
16-22	46.05	69.84	p < .0005
23-29	66.34	60.57	n.s.
30-44	61.67	49.04	p < .0005
45-59	58.12	45.04	p < .0005
60+	49.03	41.56	p < .025
MARRIED WORKING WOMEN:			
Total (N = 235)	48.43	50.62	n.s.
Age Groups			
16-22	46.78	58.94	n.s.
23-29	57.44	62.84	n.s.
30-44	45.78	43.77	n.s.
45-59	44.44	43.72	n.s.
60+	39.75	45.10	n.s.
NON-MARRIED WORKING WOMEN:			
Total (N = 222)	37.30	46.28	p < .0005
Age Groups			
16-22	37.96	53.26	p < .025
23-29	41.72	57.52	p < .025
30-44	37.79	47.70	n.s.
45-59	40.52	43.28	n.s.
60+	32.03	39.72	n.s.

TABLE 10-4

Educational mobility by significant sociodemographic variables.

	SOCIODEMOGRAPHIC VARIABLES				
	Age	Race	SES	Marital Status	Geographic Origin
Upwardly mobile					
Male respondents	30-44	n.s.	upper levels	n.s.	Other Florida, Elsewhere
Female respondents	n.s.	n.s.	all SES	n.s.	n.s.
Female respondents' Husbands	30-44	white	upper levels	(——)	n.s.
Non-mobile					
Male respondents	60+	n.s.	lower levels	n.s.	Deep South, Alachua
Female respondents	n.s.	n.s.	——	n.s.	n.s.
Female respondents' Husbands	60+	black	lower levels	(——)	n.s.
Downwardly mobile					
Male respondents	60+	n.s.	——	n.s.	Alachua
Female respondents	n.s.	n.s.	——	n.s.	n.s.
Female respondents' Husbands	60+	black	——	(——)	n.s.

Notes: n.s. = not significant
—— = no significant pattern
(——) = not relevant

TABLE 10-5

Occupational mobility by significant sociodemographic variables.

SOCIODEMOGRAPHIC VARIABLES

	Age	Race	SES	Marital Status	Geographic Origin
Upwardly mobile					
Male respondents	n.s.	white	upper levels	married	n.s.
Housewives' husbands	n.s.	white	upper levels	(——)	n.s.
Working wives	n.s.	——	upper levels	(——)	Other Florida, Elsewhere
Work. wives' husbs.	n.s.	white	upper levels	(——)	n.s.
Non-mar. females	n.s.	white	upper levels	single	n.s.
Non-mobile					
Male respondents	n.s.	black	all SES	separated	n.s.
Housewives' husbands	n.s.	black	all but High	(——)	n.s.
Working wives	n.s.	white	all but Low	(——)	Elsewhere
Work. wives' husbs.	n.s.	black	all SES	(——)	n.s.
Non-mar. females	n.s.	white	all but High	widowed	n.s.
Downwardly mobile					
Male respondents	n.s.	black	lower levels	divorced	n.s.
Housewives' husbands	n.s.	black	Lower-Middle	(——)	n.s.
Working wives	n.s.	black	lower levels	(——)	Deep South, Alachua
Work. wives' husbs.	n.s.	——	——	(——)	n.s.
Non-mar. females	n.s.	black	lower levels	separated	n.s.

Notes: n.s. = not significant
—— = no significant pattern
(——) = not relevant

Differences between married working women's and non-married working women's patterns are shown by three additional findings. Working wives had a significantly higher mean education level than non-married working women ($p < .0005$). Also, many of the working wives (75%+) had working husbands. McClendon suggests that such women can opt to stay out of the labor market and are thus in a position to refuse lower-status or poorer-paying jobs (21). In contrast, non-married women—the single, separated, widowed, or divorced—who may have to provide for a family are probably compelled to accept whatever jobs are available. Finally, significantly more of the non-married women were native Alachuans. Possibly, Alachua County women had different attitudes than other women toward occupational achievement, or, as is more likely, they may have been too handicapped to move and start a new life elsewhere.

The sharply different educational and occupational patterns of our male and female respondents suggest that if social mobility is related to mental health, it should be differentially associated with sex. Furthermore, for women, marital status should be an important factor in this relationship since married and non-married working women have different intergenerational occupational patterns.

SOCIAL MOBILITY AND SOCIODEMOGRAPHIC VARIABLES

The sociodemographic characteristics of upwardly mobile, non-mobile, and downwardly mobile respondents (age 30 and older) are shown in Tables 10-4 and 10-5.*

Educational Mobility

Over 65% of the male respondents, the female respondents, and the female respondents' husbands were upwardly mobile. Both the male and female respondents, as groups, contained about the same proportion of non-mobile and downwardly mobile individuals. However, comparing female respondents and their husbands showed that whereas women tended to be less educated than their fathers, their husbands tended to match or exceed their fathers' educational levels ($p < .005$).

---

* Because of the methodological problems discussed earlier in this chapter, we focused on respondents who were 30 years of age or older for the analyses presented in this and the succeeding sections of Part II. Analyses were also done for the entire sample and are available upon request.

Occupational Mobility

About 45 to 54% of the five groups—male respondents, husbands of housewives, working wives, husbands of working wives, and non-married working women—were occupationally non-mobile. Comparisons among these groups showed that the upwardly mobile were most likely to be male respondents and that the downwardly mobile tended to be non-married working women ($p < .0005$). Working married women were more likely to have lower job levels than their fathers did, while their husbands tended to have the same or higher job levels ($p < .0005$).

Summary of Findings on Social Mobility

Our key findings were:

1. Educational levels have been rising over the past century for the majority of the respondents and husbands of female respondents.
2. The mobility patterns associated with occupational indices were more complex. Roughly one-half of respondents and husbands of respondents were non-mobile; but the remainder showed differing patterns of upward and downward occupational mobility depending on the sex of the individual.
3. Men appeared to be more upwardly mobile than women, both educationally and occupationally.
4. SES was strongly and positively related to both educational and occupational mobility. This finding was anticipated since education and occupation are two of the three components of SES.
5. Race was significantly related to occupational mobility but not to educational mobility; whites tended to be upwardly mobile while blacks tended to be downwardly mobile occupationally.
6. Age was significantly related to educational mobility (but not occupational mobility) for all groups but female respondents; early middle-aged male respondents and husbands of female respondents were likely to be upwardly educated while those who were older (60+) tended to be non-mobile or downwardly mobile.
7. There were some significant associations between geographic origin and social mobility. Male respondents who were upwardly mobile educationally tended to be Other Floridians or from Elsewhere. In contrast, males who were downwardly mobile educationally tended to be native Alachuans. The same pattern held true for working wives whose husbands were upwardly or downwardly mobile occupationally.

Thus, SES, sex, race, and to some extent, age were significantly related to the social mobility of the respondents (30 years old and older) and would be expected to be associated with any relationship between mobility and mental health. Of particular interest were the discrepant educational and occupational patterns for women and for blacks. Both groups have made educational advances but not similar progress in the occupational field; thus, they are more likely to be status inconsistent. This inconsistency may be a factor associated with their higher risk for SPI.

SOCIAL MOBILITY AND SOCIAL PSYCHIATRIC IMPAIRMENT (SPI)

If intergenerational mobility and mental illness are associated, then what is the nature of this relationship? Is an individual's mental health related to the difference between one's status and one's father's status or is it related to how much an individual moves compared with how much other people in his or her status group are moving? We attempted to answer these questions, first, by comparing intergenerational mobility scores with risk for SPI, and then, by examining the relationship between mobility and SPI for individuals within each SES level.

Relationships between social mobility and Health Opinion Survey (HOS) scores were also analyzed to allow comparison with studies which have used this scale both nationally and transculturally. To round out the results we also compared social mobility with the number of reported physical illnesses. We examined possible relationships between mobility and reported psychosomatic distress to test the widely held hypothesis that upward mobility with its attendant stressors is related to psychosomatic disorders.

SUMMARY AND IMPLICATIONS

A summary of the significant relationships between social mobility and the health-illness variables is presented in Table 10-6. Our major findings were:

1. In general, downward social mobility was significantly related to SPI, HOS caseness scores, psychosomatic distress, and physical illness. For males, only downward occupational mobility was statistically significant, whereas for females, downward mobility on both educational and occupational indices was significant.
2. For married women, both their husbands' educational and occupational downward mobility were significant correlates of risk

for mental disorder (as measured by SPI and by HOS caseness scores) and of a number of physical illnesses. For women in general, their own downward educational mobility was significantly associated with risk for mental illness (as measured by SPI) and physical illnesses, while their own occupational mobility was not.

3. Within SES levels, the striking finding for men was that *upward* mobility—educational and occupational—was related to impaired functioning among upper-middle SES males. Since the largest proportion of extremely upwardly mobile men (i.e. upward by 40 points or more) was in this SES level, the relationship may reflect the effects of extreme mobility or the crossing of the blue-collar/white-collar class line.
4. Within SES levels, the upper-middle SES women who were better educated than their fathers tended to score high on the Impairment of Functioning scale. However, the most frequent associations were between a woman's risk for mental disorder or other type of impairment and her *husband's* mobility scores. These associations were found for married women at every SES level. There was, however, no consistent pattern between either the kind of husband's mobility (educational or occupational) or its direction (upward or downward) and any risk measure.
5. For non-married working women, there were no significant associations between social mobility and any of the health-illness variables, even within SES levels.

Our major finding for male respondents was that downward occupational mobility was associated with risk as measured by all the health-illness variables. We also found that, for upper-middle SES males, upward mobility was significantly associated with impairment of functioning. Our results are consistent with other's reports of positive relationships between downward mobility and risk for mental illness *and* also with those which show associations between upward mobility and mental disorder. Also consistent with other studies is our finding that upwardly and downwardly mobile individuals are subject to different risk patterns. We suggest that the effects of downward mobility are direct and tangible—the individual makes less money, may live in poorer quality housing, and is forced to pay closer attention to insuring his/her physical survival. On the other hand, the stressors attendant on upward mobility may be more subtle, stemming from interactions with a specific reference group. Although upwardly mobile individuals usually can provide adequately for physical comforts, they may have to learn new ways of

TABLE 10-6

Respondents (age 30+) at risk by educational and occupational mobility.

	MEASURES OF RISK						
EDUCATION:	Px	Fx	Ix	SPI	HOS	Psycho-somatic	Physical Illness
Upwardly mobile	—	—	—	—	—	—	—
Non-mobile	—	—	—	—	—	—	—
Downwardly mobile							
Male respondents	—	—	—	—	—	—	—
Female respondents	—	X	—	X	—	—	X
Female respondents (husbands' mobility)	X	—	X	X	—	—	X
OCCUPATION:							
Upwardly mobile	—	—	—	—	—	—	—
Non-mobile	—	—	—	—	—	—	—
Downwardly mobile							
Male respondents	—	X	—	X	X	X	X
Housewives (husbands' mobility)	—	—	—	—	—	—	X
Working wives	—	—	—	—	—	—	—
Working wives (husbands' mobility)	X	—	X	X	X	—	X
Non-married working females	—	—	—	—	—	—	—

X = significant association
— = no significant association

communicating or new sets of values in order to enjoy the fruits of their achievements without the anguish of illness.

Our results for the female respondents cannot be compared directly with those from other community studies because most social mobility research has included only males. In general, our findings suggest that the women in our sample participated in a different status system than their male counterparts. For the men, the critical mobility index was their own occupation. For the women, however, the critical indices were their own *education* and their *husbands' occupation.* Our study did not provide data which could untangle how the differences among a woman's own achievements, her father's, and her husband's were related to her well-being. In terms of risk for SPI, however, the results indicated that husbands' statuses and mobility patterns were associated with women's level of risk.

Part III—Geographic Mobility

Migration has been a prominent feature of life in the middle part of the 20th century. Startling advances in transportation, the horrors of war, and the desire for change have conjoined to increase the movement of peoples. America, in particular, has been known to be a land in which people moved about.

MIGRATION AND MENTAL ILLNESS

Researchers have been interested in possible relationships between migration and mental illness for years. In his famous 1855 *Report on Insanity and Idiocy in Massachusetts,* Edward Jarvis noted that the proportion of "foreign insane" among the population was higher (1:368) than the proportion of "native insane" (1:445) (22). He added: "The most observable fact among the foreign lunatics is that they have a very great preponderance of paupers" (23). Ødegaard's classic study in the 1930s showed that Norwegian immigrants to Minnesota had higher mental illness rates than control groups (24). He attributed the extremely higher rates of arteriosclerotic and senile conditions among the immigrants to the environmental "strains" of immigrant life and the relative absence of protective social systems. But he thought that the immigrants' much higher schizophrenia rates were attributable to constitutional factors; often social difficulties or incipient psychosis provided the impetuses for emigration.

Studies Conducted since World War II

Studies conducted since World War II, however, report inconsistent results about associations between migration and mental illness. Malzberg found that a disproportionately large number of Negro in-migrants had been admitted to public mental hospitals in New York State during the 1920s and 1930s (25). In 1958, Hollingshead and Redlich reported that mental illness rates for the foreign born in New Haven were *not* significantly higher than the rates for the native born (26). Lazarus and his colleagues reported in 1963 that migrants from elsewhere in the United States to New York, Ohio, and California had higher mental illness rates than non-migrants (27). The Midtown Manhattan Study, however, found that migrants from small cities had much lower rates for mental disorders than native New Yorkers (28).

H. B. M. Murphy and others emphasize that, as Ødegaard concluded, persons with incipient mental disorders who may be having difficulties adjusting to life at home tend to migrate; also the hardships of migration are stressful, possibly conducive to mental disorder (29). Murphy asserts that, as a unitary variable, migration has not been found to be directly related to increased mental illness; it is one of several factors such as age, SES, and culture conflict that combine to be associated with higher rates of mental disorder.

MIGRATION AND SPI

As discussed in Chapter 3, in the early 1970s, Alachua County was peopled with in-migrants. The University attracted students and others from all parts of the State and the nation. For years, groups from the nearby Deep South had been moving into the County; in fact, it was initially settled mainly by Georgians and Carolinians. And accompanying the social changes following World War II, many Northerners and Mid-Westerners moved into Alachua County as well as into other parts of Florida. Thus, we had an excellent opportunity to study the relationship between migration and mental health risk. The geographic origins of our sample and the percentages in the SPI category are shown in Table 10-7.*

We compared the length of time those in the SPI and the Not-Impaired categories had lived in Alachua County. We hypothesized that higher percentages of those who had been in the County a very short time—about one year or less—than those who were more settled would be in the SPI category. But, we found no significant relationships between the length of time our respondents had lived in the County and being in the SPI or Not-Impaired group, although significantly more of those from the Deep South and the Alachuans were in the SPI category. But as Murphy has noted, geographic mobility is only one of several factors that, in combination, are associated with higher rates of mental

* We categorized our respondents geographically by their responses to the item: "Where did you live while you were growing up?"

TABLE 10-7

Geographic origin of respondents and percentages in the SPI category*

Geographic Origin	All Respondents N	(%)	In SPI Category Geographic Origin Group N	(%)
Alachua County	451	27.4	150	33.3
Other Florida	469	28.5	111	23.7
Deep South	213	12.9	78	36.6
Elsewhere	512	31.1	124	24.2
TOTAL	1645	100.0	463	28.1

* In our sample there were 52 respondents, 3.2%, who had been raised outside the United States; they have been included in the Elsewhere category.

TABLE 10-8

Socioeconomic status (SES) as three strata.

SES Strata	Raw SES Score	Respondents (N)	(%)
Low	(0-32)	417	25.3
Middle	(33-66)	810	49.2
High	(67-99)	418	25.4
TOTAL		1645	100.0

TABLE 10-9

SES distribution of the respondents by geographic origin.

Geographic Origin	SES STRATA Low (%)	Middle (%)	High (%)
Alachua	41.7	46.6	11.8
Other Florida	19.8	55.0	25.2
Deep South	35.2	41.3	23.5
Elsewhere	11.9	49.6	38.5
TOTAL	25.3	49.2	25.4

disorder. Because we found repeatedly that low SES was strongly related to SPI, we conducted further analyses controlling for SES. We proceeded to divide our random sample into three strata according to their SES scores. (See Table 10-8.)

Geographic Origin Groups According to SES

Each of the three SES groups was classified according to the four geographic categories. As shown in Table 10-9 the percentages of respondents in the geographic groups differed greatly in the low and the high SES strata but not in the middle one.

The SES distribution for the Alachuans was skewed; many were in the low stratum whereas few were in the high. The distribution for the Other Florida respondents resembled a normal curve, and the distribution for the Deep South was more evenly divided than that of the other three areas. In contrast, the distribution for those from Elsewhere was skewed in the opposite direction from that of the Alachuans. Few were in the low SES stratum and a relatively large percentage was in the high.

Geographic Origin, SES, and SPI

This partitioning of the sample enabled us to examine the associations between two social factors—SES and geographic mobility—and risk for mental illness as measured by the percentages of respondents in the SPI category. Table 10-10 shows the percentages in the SPI category in the various groups.

TABLE 10-10

Percentages of the respondents in the SPI category in SES and geographic groups.

	SES STRATA			
Geographic Origin	Low (%)	Middle (%)	High (%)	Total (%)
Alachua County	45.7	25.2	20.8	33.3
Other Florida	39.8	19.8	19.5	23.7
Deep South	61.3	28.4	14.0	36.6
Elsewhere	45.9	22.8	19.3	24.2
TOTAL	47.2	23.1	18.9	28.1

The most striking finding was the significantly higher percentages of low than middle or high SES respondents in the SPI category, regardless of geographic origin ($p < .001$). In some of the geographic groups, there were disproportionately more low than middle or high SES respondents in the SPI category (see Figure 10-5). Some differences in the percentages within and between the middle and high SES groups—when divided according to geographic origin—can be observed, but these are relatively small compared to the great difference between the low and the middle SES strata. Furthermore, within the three SES groups, the percentages in the SPI category varied to a much greater extent among the four geographic groupings in the low SES stratum (about 15-20%) than in the middle SES (about 7-8%) or the high SES stratum (6-7%).

Analysis of Variance

We conducted a two-way analysis of variance to determine the significance of SES, geographic mobility, and the interactions between them for the percentages in the SPI category in the 12 groups. The percentages in the SPI category within the low SES-geographic groups differed significantly ($p < .025$); in particular, a large percentage of those in the SPI category were from the Deep South. (See Figures 10-5.)

We were surprised at the lack of significant differences in the percentages in the SPI category among the geographic groups in the middle and upper SES strata in view of the fact that 38.5% of the respondents from Elsewhere were in the high SES stratum in contrast to 11.8% of those from Alachua (Table 10-9). Repeatedly, we found that high SES was associated with lower risk as indicated by percentage in the SPI category.

Inspection of the 12 SES-geographic origin groups' percentages in the SPI category (Table 10-10) shows that within SES strata, low SES respondents from the Deep South were a very high-risk group. But, those from the Deep South who were in the high SES stratum had an especially small percentage in the SPI category.

Groups at High Risk for Mental Disorder

When we began the study of the County, we hypothesized that certain groups would be at high risk for mental disorder, that the accelerated rate of social change and the disruption of the social order would place at risk not only the poor, but also those whose positions in the social order were declining. As discussed in Chapter 3, some hypothesized to

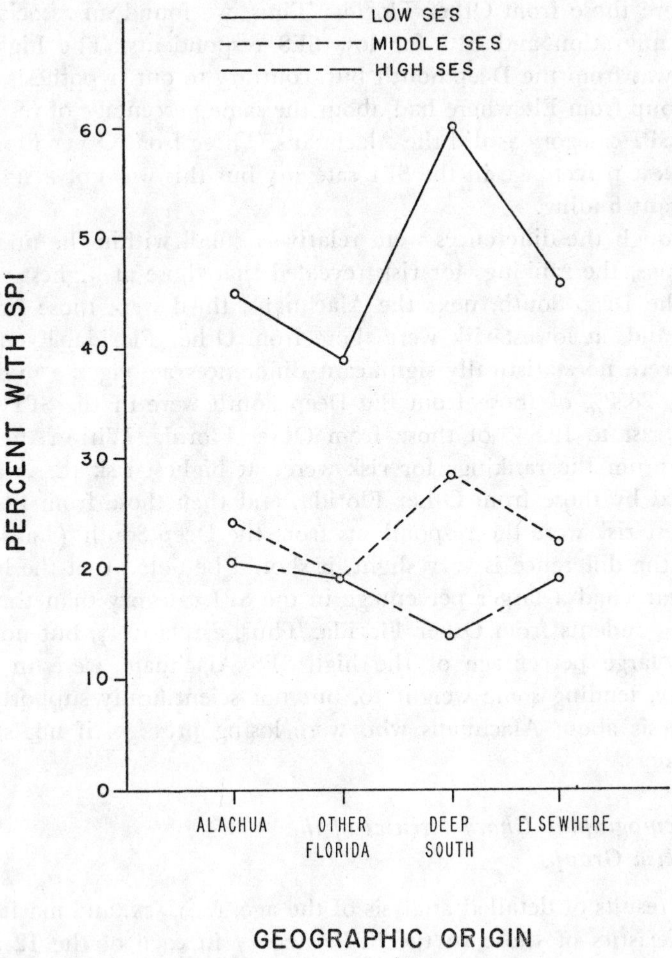

FIGURE 10-5. Percentage of respondents in the SPI category controlling for SES.

be at high risk were: 1) the poor and the blacks who had lived in the County all of their lives, 2) Alachuans who had lost prestige or "status" to the better-educated, technologically-oriented "newcomers," and 3) other marginal groups who had migrated into the County.

Within the low SES stratum, the geographic groups were ranked for risk according to their percentages in the SPI category. As shown in Table 10-10, respondents from the Deep South were at highest risk. Next were those from Elsewhere, followed by the Alachuans. At lowest risk were those from Other Florida. Thus, we found an association between migration and SPI for low SES respondents. The highest risk group was from the Deep South but, contrary to our hypothesis, the low SES group from Elsewhere had about the same percentage of respondents in the SPI category as did the Alachuans. Those from Other Florida had the lowest percentage in the SPI category but this was not a statistically significant finding.

Although the differences were relatively small within the middle SES groupings, the rankings for risk revealed that those at highest risk were from the Deep South, next the Alachuans, third were those from Elsewhere and, at lowest risk were those from Other Florida. Even though there were no statistically significant differences among the middle SES groups, 28.4% of those from the Deep South were in the SPI category in contrast to 19.8% of those from Other Florida. Within the highest SES stratum the rankings for risk were: at highest risk the Alachuans, followed by those from Other Florida, and then those from Elsewhere; at lowest risk were the respondents from the Deep South (Table 10-10). While the difference is very slight, it should be noted that the high SES Alachuans had a larger percentage in the SPI category than the middle SES respondents from Other Florida. Thus, a relatively, but not significantly, large percentage of the high SES Alachuans were in the SPI category, lending some weight to, but not scientifically supporting, our hypothesis about Alachuans who were losing prestige, if not status, to newcomers.

Sociodemographic Characteristics of the High-Risk Groups

The results of detailed analysis of the age, race, sex, and marital status characteristics of those in the SPI category in each of the 12 SES-geographic origin groups revealed very few significant relationships. Among middle-SES persons from Elsewhere, the divorced were at especially high risk. Among high-SES respondents from the Deep South, those aged 45-59 also were at high risk. Low socioeconomic status was the most consistent predictor of high risk for SPI (see Figure 10-5).

Comparisons of the 12 SES-Geographic Groups' HOS Scores and Percentages in the SPI Category

Because our major hypotheses centered on mobility and its possible association with SPI in the County that appeared to be in a state of social flux, we also looked at the various groups' Health Opinion Survey (HOS) scores. We wanted to compare rankings for SPI with rankings according to the HOS caseness scores and also to supply data that other investigators could use for purposes of comparison. The overall differences between those in the SPI category and those with HOS caseness scores were small. We found that 28.1% were in the SPI category and 28.3% were in the HOS caseness range. The main differences between the SPI and HOS caseness groups were related to age and SES. In the total sample, more persons aged 60+ had HOS caseness scores (41.3%) than were in the SPI category (33.0%). Also, the inverse relationship between SES and HOS caseness scores was slightly more pronounced than it was for SES and SPI.*

Groups' Rankings According to HOS Caseness Scores

In the lowest SES grouping, those at highest risk according to percentages with HOS caseness scores were: first, those from the Deep South (58.7%); next, those from Elsewhere (52.5%); third, Other Floridians (51.6%); and last, the native Alachuans (46.8%). The percentages varied less than those for SPI—about 12% in contrast to 21%.

In the middle SES grouping, the percentages with HOS caseness scores varied in a narrow range, only from 20.5% to 25.7%. Ranked for risk according to percentages in the HOS caseness range, the Alachuans were first, those from Elsewhere second, those from the Deep South third, and those from Other Florida were fourth.

In the high SES grouping, the differences in the percentages with HOS caseness scores were greater (about 10%) than for SPI (about 7%). The high SES-geographic groups' rankings for risk according to percentages with HOS caseness scores were: first, those from Other Florida (19.5%); next, those from Elsewhere (16.2%); third, native Alachuans (13.2%); and last, the Deep South (10.0%).

Generally, the rankings according to percentages with HOS caseness scores were very close to the rankings according to percentages in the SPI categories. But within the high SES stratum, there was a wider spread in the HOS caseness scores. Also, smaller percentages of high SES respondents, both from the Deep South and from Alachua County, had HOS caseness scores than their counterparts in the SPI category.

---

* In the low, middle, and high SES groups, percentages with HOS caseness scores were 50.8, 23.1, and 16.0%; in the SPI category they were 47.4, 23.1, and 18.9% respectively.

CONCLUSIONS

Our findings point to several conclusions about migration and risk for mental disorder. Risk was higher for low SES migrants, especially from the Deep South and also from Elsewhere, than for low-SES native Alachuans or for low-SES Other Floridians. The poorer, less educated, and unskilled persons who had migrated appeared to be at higher risk for mental illness than those with similar sociodemographic characteristics who were natives. Although we do not know the direction of this association between risk and migration—whether those at risk may have tended to migrate or those who migrated became at risk—the low SES respondents who remained in familiar surroundings may have had greater opportunities for coping and some social support systems. Also, they may have developed patterns of living that the migrants lacked. Those who had moved into the County from the Deep South were the highest risk group; many of them were black, and as a group they were unskilled and probably ill-prepared for migration.

Risk for those in the middle and high SES strata was not associated with migration. In fact, as measured by both SPI and HOS caseness scores, the high SES respondents from the Deep South were the lowest risk group. We speculate that they were well-educated, talented Southerners who were able to move into a rapidly changing County and either achieve or maintain status with its perquisites. The history of the Southeast reveals that many of the so-called "better families" have far-flung social and economic networks in the region. For years, they have occupied the highest position in the social order and dominated the political and economic life in the Southern states. They are at home in the area, can capitalize on their abilities, and have extensive social support systems.

Our rankings according to SPI, but not according to HOS scores, showed that the high SES native Alachuans were a group that was at relatively higher risk than other groups in the middle and high SES strata. We had hypothesized that the Alachuans were losing status and that concomitantly more of them would tend to show evidence of emotional distress than those in the other high SES-geographic groups. We think that SPI identified this group with emotional distress that was not identified by the HOS because SPI assesses alcoholism, interpersonal distress, and other indicators of risk for mental disorder not tapped by HOS.

Part IV—Social Order and Mental Health

Whether the changing social structure and character of life in the County during the 1960s was associated with differing degrees of risk for mental illness for various groups was one of the major reasons for conducting this study. We had hypothesized that the rapid rate of social change and the accompanying disruption of the established social order would be associated differentially with risk in various groups. Although we studied only one county, it was typical of many in the Southeast; perhaps our findings might have some meaning and utility in other parts of the nation that were experiencing social dislocations and were in "transition."

We were particularly interested in the native Alachuans; in 1970 they constituted less than one-third of the County's population. We hypothesized that many of them would show evidence of high risk for mental illness. The results indicate that a disproportionately large percentage of them were in the low SES stratum and that a disproportionately small percentage were in the high SES stratum. Furthermore, measures of intergenerational social mobility revealed that significantly more of the Alachuans (with several exceptions in certain subgroups) were either non-mobile or downwardly mobile educationally and occupationally than were the respondents from Other Florida, the Deep South, or Elsewhere in the nation. And on Cantril's Ladder, the Alachuans located themselves at significantly lower positions both five years "in the past" and especially at present than did the respondents in the other three geographic origin groups. The objective findings revealed by the analyses of both SES and social mobility were paralleled by the Alachuan's subjective perceptions—they ranked themselves lower on the "ladder of life" than did the other groups.

The Alachuans' lower positions in the social order were associated with symptoms of emotional distress. On the Bell Global Psychopathology Scale, the Alachuans had the highest mean score and over 20% scored in the high-risk range. On the symptom pattern subscales, the Alachuans scored relatively high on anxiety, depression, phobias, depersonalization, and paranoia; in contrast, respondents from Elsewhere had low mean scores. On other measures, such as the psychosomatic inventory (singly or in combination with SPI and physical illness) those who had grown up in Alachua County were a much higher risk group than the respondents from Other Florida, the Deep South, or Elsewhere. With only one exception, therefore, the findings support our hypotheses about the

Alachuans' loss of status and concomitant risk for—and symptoms of—mental disorder. The exception, discussed in Part III of this chapter, was that a larger proportion of the low SES in-migrants from the Deep South were at risk for SPI than any of the other groups. We conclude that there were associations between changing status in the social order and varying degrees of risk for mental illness.

There are no answers to the age-old questions—formulated by Plato and discussed at length by Emil Grotjahn, the Father of Social Pathology, in 1923—that are at the heart of the matter: To what extent does the quality of life in the community determine its inhabitants' well-being? Or, to what extent do the inhabitants shape the character of the community? Our findings, like those of other social psychiatrists and researchers, indicate that the quality of the social environment is related to individuals' and groups' varying degrees of risk for mental illness. Although we know little about the exact nature of that relationship, we think that emotional well-being is dependent largely on the dignity and humaneness of community life and on the material and cultural benefits that are shared commensally.

REFERENCES

1. KLEINER, R. J., and PARKER, S., "Goal Striving, Social Status, and Mental Disorder: A Research Review." In: S. K. Weinberg (Ed.), *The Sociology of Mental Disorders.* Chicago: Aldine, 1967, 55-66.
2. Ibid., 55.
3. CANTRIL, H., *The Pattern of Human Concerns.* New Brunswick, N.J.: Rutgers University Press, 1965.
4. *Florida Health Study Program.* Gainesville, Fla.: College of Medicine, University of Florida, 1969.
5. See Reference 3, 22.
6. Ibid., 7.
7. LESLIE, G. R., LARSON, R. F., and GORMAN, B. L., *Order and Change.* New York: Oxford University Press, 1973, 384.
8. *1960 Census of Population, Vol. 1.* Washington, D.C.: U.S. Bureau of the Census, 1960, 386 and *1970 Census of Population, Vol. 1.* Washington, D.C.: U.S. Bureau of the Census, 1970, 208.
9. BUREAU OF ECONOMIC AND BUSINESS RESEARCH. COLLEGE OF BUSINESS ADMINISTRATION, UNIVERSITY OF FLORIDA, *Florida Statistical Abstract, 1972.* Gainesville, Fla.: University of Florida Press, 1972, 49-53.
10. LIPSET, S. N., and BENDIX, R., *Social Mobility in Industrial Society.* Berkeley, Calif.: University of California Press, 1959, 1-2.
11. BLAU, P. M., and DUNCAN, O. D., *The American Occupational Structure.* New York: John Wiley and Sons, Inc., 1967.
12. See Reference 8, 1960, 487; 1970, 679.
13. AYELLA, M. E., and WILLIAMSON, J. B., "The Social Mobility of Women: A Causal Model of Socioeconomic Success," *The Sociological Quarterly,* Vol. 17, No. 4, Autumn, 1976, 534.

14. DeJong, P. Y., Brawer, M. J., and Robin, S. S., "Patterns of Female Intergenerational Occupational Mobility: A Comparison with Male Patterns of Intergenerational Occupational Mobility," *American Sociological Review*, Vol. 36, December 1971, 1033-1042.
15. McClendon, McK. J., "The Occupational Status Attainment Processes of Males and Females," *American Sociological Review*, Vol. 41, February, 1976, 52-64.
16. Sorokin, P. A., *Social and Cultural Mobility*. London: The Free Press of Glencoe, Collier-Macmillan Limited, 1959, 510.
17. Durkheim, E., Cited in Reference 16, 524.
18. Dunham, H. W., Phillips, P., and Srinivasan, "A Research Note on Diagnosed Mental Illness and Social Class," *American Sociological Review*, Vol. 31, No. 2, April 1966, 226.
19. Srole, L., and Langner, S. T., "Socioeconomic Status Groups: Their Mental Health Composition." In: S. K. Weinberg (Ed.), *The Sociology of Mental Disorders*. Chicago: Aldine, 1967, 33-47.
20. Nam, C. B., LaRocque, J., Powers, M. G., and Holmberg, H., "Occupational Status Scores: Stability and Change," *American Statistical Association, Proceedings of the Social Statistics Section*, 1975, 570-575.
21. See Reference 15, 60.
22. Jarvis, E., *Insanity and Idiocy in Massachusetts: Report of the Commission on Lunacy, 1855*. Cambridge, Mass.: Harvard University Press, 1971, 59.
23. Ibid., 60.
24. Ødegaard, Ø., *Emigration and Insanity: A Study of Mental Disease Among the Norwegianborn Population of Minnesota*. Copenhagen: Levin and Munksgaards Publishers, 1932.
25. Malzberg, B., "Mental Disease Among American Negroes: A Statistical Analysis." In: O. Klineberg (Ed.), *Characteristics of the American Negro*. New York: Harper and Brothers, 1944, 371-399.
26. Hollingshead, A. B., and Redlich, F. C. *Social Class and Mental Illness: A Community Study*. New York: John Wiley and Sons, Inc., 1958.
27. Lazarus, J., Locke, B. Z., and Thomas, D. S., "Migration Differentials in Mental Disease," *Milbank Memorial Fund Quarterly*, Vol. 41, 1963, 25-42.
28. Srole, L., Langner, T. S., Opler, M. K., and Rennie, T. A. C., *Mental Health in the Metropolis, Vol. 1 of the Midtown Manhattan Study*. New York: McGraw-Hill Book Company, Inc., 1962, 267.
29. Murphy, H. B. M., "Migration and the Major Mental Disorders: A Reappraisal." In: M. B. Kantor (Ed.), *Mobility and Mental Health*. Springfield, Ill.: Charles C Thomas Publisher, 1965, 5-29.

11

The Follow-Up Study*

In 1973 we conducted a three-year follow-up study of about one-third of our original sample. Our major goal was to determine our respondents' mental health statuses at the two points in time and ascertain possible factors associated with any changes. We were particularly interested in whether the follow-up study would show, for example, that:

1. Many in the high-risk groups such as the low SES respondents from the Deep South had continued to exhibit symptoms and other indicators of emotional distress;
2. The successes achieved by the tumultuous battles for desegregation were reflected by an improvement in the mental health status of the blacks;
3. Fewer of the young people would report symptoms of emotional distress now that the Vietnam conflict was ending.

USE OF THE HEALTH OPINION SURVEY (HOS) AND PAYKEL LIFE EVENTS INVENTORY

Because we had funds for only about 500 interviews, we used a stratified random sampling procedure to insure that all of the subgroups in the original population were included in the follow-up. Also, we shortened the interview instrument moderately and employed the widely used, intensively standardized Health Opinion Survey (HOS) to assess risk for mental disorder rather than the more elaborate set of scales in the SPI measure (1). The HOS scores could be compared with those obtained by other researchers conducting community studies of mental health and illness in various parts of the world.

We added the 61-item Paykel Life Events Inventory to learn what had

---

* Written in collaboration with Charles E. Holzer, III, Ph.D.

happened to our respondents during the previous three years (2). This inventory consists of a list of events that are considered to be stressful because they require some degree of social readjustment. It covers a wide range of occurrences such as a death in the family, major illness for self or family member (s), and changes in marital status, e.g., divorce. Paykel developed scores for the "degree of upset" entailed by life events; for example, the death of a child was given an upset rating of 19.3, menopause, 11.0, pregnancy of wife, 5.7 (3). Furthermore, Paykel and his co-workers classified the events as either exits from or entrances into the social field. They found, for example, that depression was significantly associated with a greater number of exits.

THE PANEL

The original sample turned out to have been highly mobile during the three years that had transpired. To obtain 517 follow-up interviews, we had to search for 1183 of the original 1645 respondents. Obviously, the respondents would be three years older. There were relatively few young respondents; many of the college students who had not been permanent residents had left the County. Also, we had slightly higher percentages of females and blacks in the follow-up sample than in our original. About 60 of the respondents had died; a disproportionate number of these were elderly males.

Health Opinion Survey (HOS) Scores

In 1970, the mean HOS score for the total sample (N = 1645) was 27.5 (S.D. 5.6); 28.3% had scored in the possible or probable caseness range. In 1970, those who later composed the follow-up sample had a mean HOS score of 27.6 (S.D. 5.6), almost the same as that of the original total sample. But a slightly larger percentage (30.0%) of the follow-up sample (the *panel*) had had scores in the caseness range in 1970 than the total original sample. Table 11-1 shows the HOS scores for the panel in 1970 and 1973.

Sociodemographic Comparisons

The panel's scores and the percentages in the caseness range did not differ significantly between 1970 and 1973. Sociodemographic comparisons showed that significantly more middle-aged respondents, aged 45-59, had scores in the caseness range in 1973 than in 1970. A slightly higher percentage of those aged 60+ were in the caseness range in 1973

TABLE 11-1

1970 and 1973 HOS scores for respondents in the panel.

Year	Mean Score	Normal Range (%)	Caseness Range (%)	Sig.
1970	27.6	70.0	30.0	t (516) = 1.86
1973	28.0	68.9	31.1	*n.s.*

than in 1970. Contrary to our expectations, many more blacks, regardless of sex, had scores in the caseness range in 1973 than in 1970. Also, a disproportionately larger number of those in the lowest SES quintile and the widowed or separated had scores in the caseness range in 1973 than in 1970. The groups that tended to have lower percentages of respondents in the caseness range in 1973 than in 1970 were whites, those in the middle and highest SES quintiles, and the divorced. The groups that tended to have almost the same percentages scoring in the caseness range in 1973 as in 1970 were those under the age of 23, those aged 30-44, the white males, those in the lower- and upper-middle SES quintiles, and the single or the married.

Some questions were partially answered. The health status of the blacks, as a group, had not improved with the changes accompanying desegregation. Instead, in 1973, many more blacks had HOS caseness scores than in 1970. This finding can be interpreted by the following speculations. Perhaps three years is too short a period of time in which to expect changes in health status to accompany political changes. Or possibly the "trauma" of the struggle for civil rights might still be counterbalancing the benefits. We think that the effects of the caste system endured; many of the blacks still held only the lowest paying jobs and lived in substandard housing. Desegregation had brought few material benefits as yet to most of the blacks, particularly the older ones. Furthermore, many of the younger, talented, better-educated blacks were moving to metropolitan areas in Florida, Georgia (Atlanta), and the Northeast, leaving behind a residual group. We had conjectured that with the ending of the Vietnam conflict fewer young persons would report emotional distress in 1973 than in 1970. However, almost equal percentages of those in the age groups under 22, 23-29, and 30-44 had HOS caseness scores in 1973 and 1970. Thus, the health statuses of the younger respondents had not changed.

Predictors

Multiple regression equations showed that the most significant predictor of 1973 HOS scores was the respondents' 1970 HOS scores. As Holzer has reported, the 1970 scores alone explained 53.4% of the variance in the 1973 scores (4). This implies an unusually high degree of stability—most of those who were symptomatic in 1970 continued to be so and most who were asymptomatic in 1970 remained so in 1973. Thus, for over 80% of the follow-up sample, the level of symptomatology had not changed between 1970 and 1973.

The 18.6% who had experienced changes in their health statuses are the most important group. As we shall see, those whose scores had changed from the normal to the caseness range provided us with information about the incidence, not just the prevalence, of risk for mental disorder. And those who moved in the opposite direction provided us with information about remission. The epidemiology of mental illness is in an embryonic stage and, in particular, has not developed to the level that there is more than skeletal knowledge about incidence and remission.

Relationship Among Life Events, Social Class and HOS Scores

As we anticipated, more of the low than high SES respondents in 1970 tended as a group to have elevated HOS scores on the follow-up. However, SES accounted for only 2.7% of the changes in the scores. Of the 61 Paykel Life Events, only nine were significantly related to changes in HOS caseness scores from 1970 to 1973. These were: major illness, extramarital affair, financial difficulty, negative changes in work conditions, serious argument with non-resident family members, unemployment for at least one month, increased arguments with spouse, a wanted pregnancy, and the marriage of a child. We were surprised that the life events that had occurred explained only 2.1% of the changes between the 1970 and the 1973 scores.*

Holzer found a three-way relationship among life events, SES, and

* The percentages of the respondents experiencing some of the events during the three-year period were: major illness—15.7%; extramarital affair (partner)—2.8%; financial difficulty—9.5%; negative changes in work conditions—11.3%, serious argument with non-resident family member—3.9%.

HOS scores. When he scaled the life events from 0 (none) to 200 (many), the strength of the association between high scores on the Life Events Scale and an increase in the HOS scores was inversely related to SES (5). For example, a Life Events score of 200 was associated with a more than nine-point increase in the HOS score of the respondents in the lowest SES quintile, a seven-point increase for those in the lower-middle, a five-point increase in the middle, a three-point increase in the upper-middle, and only one point in the top SES quintile (6).

A relationship among life events, social class, and mental symptomatology has been observed by other researchers and is subject to a number of different interpretations. Rogler and Hollingshead found that lower social class persons sustained more stressful events than did those in higher statuses (7). Moreover, those in the lower social strata have fewer resources for coping with adverse events and for buffering their impact. Thus, the often reported higher prevalence of mental illness in lower social class groups can be attributed in part both to the more frequent occurrence of life events requiring social readjustment and to such groups' more limited resources for coping.

An alternative view is that the greater prevalence of mental illness in lower social class groups is a by-product of the many intricate social selection processes that account for social mobility and stratification. For example, it is thought that some in the lower social strata have drifted down the social ladder as a result of prior mental illness (8). Or, perhaps some marginal persons and others voluntarily seek the greater degree of isolation and freedom from the strictures of middle-class life found in less demanding social environments. Furthermore, many of the life events may be manifestations of mental illness rather than just stressors that require social readjustment. For example, the loss of a job can be caused by poor work performance; a divorce can be the result of serious interpersonal frictions. Either event can be produced by anxiety or depression.

Holzer's finding that the Life Events accounted for only 2.1% of the changes in the respondents' HOS scores between 1970 and 1973 diminishes their possible etiologic significance. Also, HOS scores were predictive of Life Events scores: those with higher HOS scores in 1970 tended to have higher Life Events scores in 1973 than the respondents with lower HOS scores in 1970. This finding suggests that "a reciprocal influence [was] taking place between life events and symptomatology over time" (9). Consequently, we cannot draw conclusions about cause and effect relationships between life events and HOS scores in our study.

CHANGES IN RISK

Changes in HOS Scores 1970-1973

An analysis of the panel's 1970 and 1973 HOS scores showed that we had four health status groups. Those who had:

1. Scores in the normal range at both times (stayed at low risk—311 respondents, 60.2%).
2. Scores in the caseness range at both times (stayed at high risk—110 respondents, 21.3%).
3. Changed from normal to caseness range (incidence—51 respondents, 9.9%).
4. Changed from caseness to normal range between 1970 and 1973 (remission—45 respondents, 8.7%).

Incidence of Risk

These findings from the follow-up study gave us an opportunity to look at incidence of risk for mental illness. Almost all community studies of mental disorder measure prevalence only. To measure incidence—the rate of occurrence over a period of time—one must have data on the population at least at two points in time. The most important investigation of the incidence of mental illness in the general population is the Lundby Study begun by Essen-Möller in 1947 and then conducted on the same population by Hagnell in 1957 (10). On the basis of impairment ratings, Hagnell reported that the crude ten-year incidence rate for developing a mental illness was 11.3% for men and 20.4% for women. He concluded that "the estimated cumulative risk for all mental illness up till the age of 60 is 43% for men and 73% for women" (11).

Leo Srole has carried out a 20-year follow-up of the Midtown Manhattan Study started in 1954 (12). Srole and his colleagues were able to locate and interview 695 of their original 1660 respondents. They found that the prevalence of serious impairment had risen only 2.2% between 1954 and 1974, but only about 40% of the panel had the same mental health status at both times. The 20-year incidence of "less favorable mental health" was about 22% (13).

In our study, the three-year "incidence risk" for mental illness as measured by a change in HOS scores from the normal to the caseness range was 14.1%. Figure 11-1 shows the numbers and percentages of

1970 HOS SCORES	1973 HOS SCORES: Normal	1973 HOS SCORES: Caseness Range	
Normal	A 311 (60.2%)	B 51 (9.9%)	(N=362) (70.0%)
Caseness Range	C 45 (8.7%)	D 110 (21.3%)	(N=155) (30.0%)
TOTAL	(N=356) (68.9%)	(N=161) (31.1%)	(N=517) (100.0%)

FIGURE 11-1. HOS scores 1970 and 1973.

the respondents in the four health status groups classified according to their 1970 and 1973 scores.

The percentage of the total sample that had moved from normal to caseness was 9.9%. The incidence rate is 51 divided by 362, shown in Figure 11-1 as Box B divided by Box A plus B, since by definition incidence refers to those who were not in the caseness range at an earlier point in time.

Remission Rate

As measured by a change in HOS scores from the caseness to the normal range, the three-year "remission rate" was 29.0%, shown in Figure 11-1 as Box C divided by Box C plus D. (The remission rate is usually higher than the incidence rate because the denominator—those who were in the caseness range at an earlier point in time—is much smaller than the denominator used in the incidence rate.)

Inspection of Table 11-2 shows that the sociodemographic characteristics of the incidence and remission groups differ in some ways. Although the χ^2 tests generally were non-significant, higher percentages of those who had moved from normal to caseness range than those who had moved in the opposite direction were the older respondents, blacks, those in the low SES quintile, or the widowed or separated. More of

TABLE 11-2

1970 and 1973 HOS caseness categories by sociodemographic characteristics.

Sociodemographic Characteristics	N	Not Case '70 or '73 (%)	Not Case '70 Case '73 "Incidence" (%)	Case '70 Not '73 "Remission" (%)	Case '70 and '73 (%)
Age:					
16-22	26	65.4	7.7	7.7	19.2
23-29	68	75.0	8.8	10.3	5.9
30-44	150	71.3	6.7	6.7	15.3
45-49	140	51.4	12.9	9.3	26.4
60+	133	48.1	11.3	9.8	30.8
Sex:					
Male	211	67.8	9.5	7.6	15.2
Female	306	54.9	10.1	9.5	25.5
Race:					
White	378	64.3	8.5	10.3	16.9
Black	137	48.2	13.9	4.4	33.6
Race-Sex:					
White Male	157	73.9	8.3	9.6	8.3
White Female	221	57.5	8.6	10.9	23.1
Black Male	52	48.1	13.5	1.9	36.5
Black Female	85	48.2	14.1	5.9	31.8
SES:					
Low	84	29.8	15.5	4.8	50.0
Lower-Middle	115	52.2	10.4	8.7	28.7
Middle	135	66.7	8.9	11.1	13.3
Upper-Middle	90	73.3	8.9	6.7	11.1
High	93	75.3	6.5	10.8	7.5
Marital Status:					
Single	46	63.0	8.7	8.7	19.6
Married	353	64.9	9.3	8.8	17.0
Widowed	67	41.8	13.4	9.0	35.8
Separated	20	40.0	15.0	—	45.0
Divorced	31	54.8	6.5	12.9	25.8
TOTAL	517	60.2	9.9	8.7	21.3

those who had moved from caseness in 1970 to the normal range in 1973 were in the top SES quintile or divorced than were in the other sociodemographic groups (Table 11-2).

Changes in Symptom Patterns

From 1970 to 1973 some changes in symptom patterns occurred as shown by the percentages of the respondents scoring higher than one standard deviation above the mean on the subscales designed to measure the neurotic conditions, more serious mental disturbances, and alcoholism (Table 11-3).

As shown in Table 11-3, significantly fewer of the respondents scored in the high-risk range for depression in 1973 than had done so in 1970. Significantly more scored in the high-risk range on hallucinations in 1973 than in 1970.

One of the "uses of epidemiology" is to complete the clinical picture (14). As discussed in Chapter 5 clinicians are concerned about symptoms of depersonalization—for example, whether they are indicative of a serious neurosis or presage increasingly severe emotional difficulties. Of the panel, 42 respondents had scored in the high-risk range on depersonalization but not on the more serious symptom pattern subscales in 1970. In 1973, 11 of them (26.2%) still had high scores only on depersonalization; seven of them (16.7%) had high scores on depersonalization and other serious symptom subscales, seven of them (16.7%) had scores in the normal range on depersonalization but high scores on more serious symptom pattern subscales (memory difficulties, paranoia, or hallucinations), and 17 respondents (40.5%) did not have high scores on depersonalization or the other three subscales. Thus, about two-fifths had either improved or had less serious mental symptoms.

Changes on the Psychosomatic Inventory

There were no significant differences in the percentages reporting psychosomatic distress in 1970 and 1973 (28.0% and 29.2% respectively). The three-year incidence rate for developing a psychosomatic complaint was 15.1%. The remission rate was 34.5%. Incidence rates for a few selected symptoms and disorders are shown in Table 11-4.

Changes on the Physical Illness Inventory

A somewhat higher percentage of the panel (52.0%) reported physical illnesses in 1973 than had done so in 1970 (41.2%). The three-year

TABLE 11-3

Percentages scoring high on Psychopathology subscales in 1970 and 1973 and incidence and remission rates.

Subscale	High* in 1970 (%)	High in 1973 (%)	Incidence Rate (%)	Remission Rate (%)
Neurotic Conditions:				
Anxiety	7.9	10.6	7.4	51.2
Depression	9.7	6.2	3.6	70.0
Obsessive-Compulsiveness	13.0	10.6	7.3	67.2
More Serious Mental Disturbances				
Memory Difficulties	22.6	19.9	13.8	59.0
Paranoia	8.5	7.4	4.2	59.1
Depersonalization	18.2	17.2	10.6	53.2
Hallucinations	8.7	14.3	11.0	51.1
Alcoholism	5.8	4.6	2.7	63.3

* Scoring higher than one standard deviation above the mean.

TABLE 11-4

Three-year incidence rates for selected psychosomatic ailments.

Symptom or Disorder	Incidence Rate (%)
Hypertension	5.1
Headaches	2.6
Asthma	—
Constipation	3.3
Colitis	—
Peptic Ulcer	1.8
Indigestion	2.5

incidence rate for 14 physical illnesses studied was 38.8%. The increase over three years is to be expected because the respondents were older.

The three-year incidence rate for selected physical illnesses is shown in Table 11-5. It should be noted that 29.1% of those who had reported physical illnesses in 1970 were in an improved health status in 1973.

Geographic Origin

We found no significant changes in the percentages scoring in the caseness range on the HOS, 1970-1973, in the four geographic groups. As shown in Table 11-6, higher percentages of those who had grown up in the Deep South or in Alachua County scored in the caseness range in 1973 than in 1970. About an equal percentage of those from Other Florida and a smaller percentage of those from Elsewhere had scores in the caseness range in 1973 than in 1970.

An analysis of variance showed that there were no statistically significant differences among the mean HOS scores in 1973 across the four geographic groups.

These groups' incidence and remission rates 1970-1973 are shown in Table 11-7. Inspection of the geographic groups' incidence and remission rates showed that the three-year incidence rate was higher for those from the Deep South than for respondents in the three other geographic groups.

Geographic Origin, SES, and HOS Scores

To evaluate health trends further, we classified the respondents in the four geographic groups into three SES strata. Repeatedly we had found that low SES was strongly related to higher risk for mental disorders. The results of the geographic origin-SES analysis are shown in Table 11-8.

Larger percentages of low, middle, and high SES respondents from the Deep South were in the caseness range in 1973 than in 1970. Also, somewhat larger percentages of both high and low SES Alachuans were in the caseness range in 1973 than in 1970. But only about the same percentage of the low SES respondents from Other Florida were in the caseness range both in 1973 and 1970. And smaller percentages of low SES respondents from Elsewhere were in the caseness range in 1973 than in 1970. Thus, the mental health risk for those from the Deep South—regardless of SES—had increased. The analysis of variance showed that lower SES, within each of the four groups, was significantly associated with caseness. Low SES respondents, regardless of geographic origin, had

TABLE 11-5

Three-year incidence rates for selected physical illnesses.

Affected Part	Incidence Rate (%)
Eyes	12.5
Ears	5.9
Gall Bladder	1.6
Heart	3.3
Back	4.9
Kidneys and Bladder	3.8
Skin	4.2
Specific Illnesses	
Arthritis	17.9
Diabetes	2.6

TABLE 11-6

Percentages scoring in the HOS caseness range by geographic origin, 1970-1973.

Geographic Group	N	Percentage in Caseness Range 1970	1973
Alachua	176	30.7	35.2
Other Florida	135	28.9	29.6
Deep South	59	37.3	45.8
Elsewhere	147	27.2	21.8

TABLE 11-7

"Incidence" and "remission" rates by geographic origin, 1970-1973.

Geographic Origin	"Incidence Rate" (%)	"Remission Rate" (%)
Alachua County	14.8	18.5
Other Florida	13.5	30.8
Deep South	21.6	13.6
Elsewhere	11.2	50.0

TABLE 11-8

Percentages in HOS caseness range by geographic origin and SES, 1970-1973.

	N	CASENESS 1970 %	1973 %
Alachua	176	30.7	35.2
Low	76	42.1	52.6
Middle	74	25.7	24.3
High	26	11.5	15.4
Other Florida	135	28.9	29.6
Low	39	51.3	53.8
Middle	62	19.4	24.2
High	34	20.6	11.8
Deep South	59	37.3	45.8
Low	21	71.4	81.0
Middle	22	27.3	36.4
High	16	6.3	12.5
Elsewhere	147	27.2	21.8
Low	18	55.6	44.4
Middle	59	23.7	23.7
High	70	22.9	14.3
Total	517	30.0	31.1

higher mean HOS scores than those who were in the middle or high SES strata. As shown in Figure 11-2 the mean HOS scores of those from the Deep South varied from the low to the high SES groups to a greater extent than did those in the three other geographic groups.

Possible Factors Associated with Changing Health Status

We looked for factors that might be associated with changes in the panel's 1970-1973 HOS scores. We used the schema described by Masserman—the human being's Ur-needs—to guide our search (15). He classified the Ur-needs as:

1. The *biological*—needs for food, shelter, and physical well-being.
2. The *social*—needs for the company of one's fellow human beings.
3. The *spiritual* or *philosophic*—need for a faith or metaphysic that gives meaning to everyday existence.

From our interview instrument, therefore, we selected items pertaining to physical well being, social support systems, and religion that might

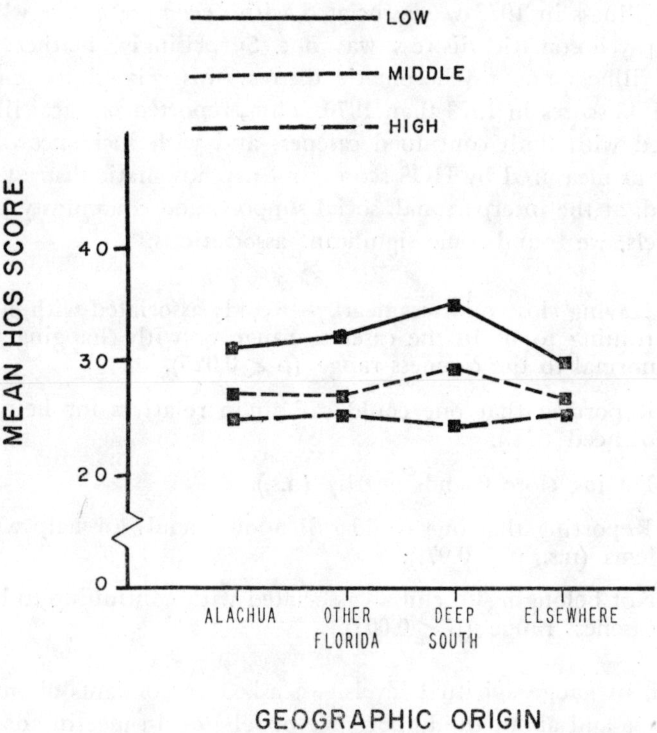

FIGURE 11-2. Mean 1973 HOS score of panel by geographic origin, controlling for socioeconomic status (SES).

be associated with the mental health risk of those who: 1) were at low mental health risk both in 1970 and 1973 as indicated by their HOS scores; 2) had continued to be at high risk; 3) had changed from low to high risk (incidence group); and 4) had changed from high to low risk (remission group).

Our Findings

First, as anticipated, we found that being in the high-risk range on either the psychosomatic or physical illness inventory in 1973 was significantly associated with being in the HOS caseness range both in 1973 and in 1970. Conversely, being in low risk on the psychosomatic or physical illness inventories in 1973 was significantly associated with being in the normal range on HOS scores at both times. However, reported physical illness in 1973 was associated with *becoming a case* whereas reported psychosomatic distress was not. Surprisingly, neither reported physical illness nor psychosomatic distress was related to remission—lower HOS scores in 1973 than 1970. Thus, reported physical illness was associated with both continued caseness and with incidence of mental disorder as measured by HOS scores, but psychosomatic distress was not.

Second, at the interpersonal, social support, and community participation levels, we found some significant associations:*

1. Having close relatives nearby—weakly associated with either continuing to be in the caseness range or with changing from the normal to the caseness range ($p < 0.025$).
2. Reporting that one could call upon relatives for help in time of need (n.s.).
3. Having close friends nearby (n.s.).
4. Reporting that one could call upon friends for help with problems (n.s., $p = 0.971$).
5. Not belonging to clubs—associated with continuing to be in the caseness range ($p < 0.001$).

Third, to gauge spiritual levels, we asked respondents about church attendance and about the importance of religion in meeting daily problems. Oddly, attending church was associated with not scoring in the caseness range in 1970 or 1973, and also with moving from the normal to the caseness range. Believing that religion was "very" important in meeting daily problems was associated weakly with being in the caseness range both in 1970 and 1973 and also with moving from normal to caseness.

Our finding that physical illness was related to both continuing risk for mental disorder and to incidence, as measured by HOS scores, assesses indirectly the relationship between biological needs and emotional well-being. Repeatedly, we have found that low SES was significantly related to risk for either mental or physical illness and to the concurrence of the two. Possibly it is the important intervening variable. The poor in Alachua County suffered from obvious deprivations associated with poverty and these deprivations produce disease. Historically, the vitamin

* Both 1970 and 1973 data were available on close relatives living nearby, friends living nearby, and friends to call upon, but only 1970 data were available for calling on relatives for help, belonging to clubs, etc.

deficiency disease, pellagra, was much more prevalent in the South than in other parts of our nation and we should note that early studies of it were prompted by the finding that many patients in the State mental hospitals in the South in the 1900-1920 era had pellagra. The satisfaction of biological needs, requisite for satisfaction of physical and mental well-being, is dependent upon an adequate standard of living.

Some of the seemingly paradoxical findings, especially those pertaining to support systems (friends and relatives) and religion can be explained in part by the social structure of the County. As we have seen, disproportionately large percentages of those in the incidence group were from the Deep South or Alachuans. Many were elderly, poor, black, widowed, or separated. Although they were in close contact with relatives and friends, the relatives and friends often were in marginal statuses and could provide little more than solace when called upon for help. These groups occupied a low position in the social order in Alachua County in the early 1970s. But relatively larger percentages of the "Southerners" and the Alachuans in the upper SES bracket were in the caseness range in 1973 than in 1970 compared with those from Other Florida or Elsewhere. We conjecture that the disruption of the long-established social order accompanying the rapid social change was stressful even for those in the upper SES. Their formerly preeminent positions were being lost to the newcomers who were securing the preferred occupations and engaged in expanding business activities.

Aspirations

We looked at the four mental health status groups' aspirations as measured in 1973 by self-perception of positions on Cantril's Ladder at present, five years ago, and five years in the future (16). There were no significant differences between any of the four mental health status groups' locations on the Ladder at present or in the future in 1973 and the total original sample's positions in 1970. Furthermore, the panel's sociodemographic subgroups—age, sex, race, SES, etc.—placed themselves on the Ladder at almost the same positions in the past, at present, and in the future in 1973 as did those subgroups in 1970. Even though three years had elapsed, the much higher positions envisioned in 1970 for the future had not materialized; the self-perceived locations at present (in 1973) were remarkably similar to the locations for the present in 1970—not the optimistic 1970-1975 projections to much higher positions.

Significantly many of those whose scores on the aspiration index (difference between future and present positions on the Ladder) were greater than one standard deviation above the mean were in the caseness range both in 1970 and in 1973, and many of those who positioned themselves lower in the future than at present had moved from normal to caseness range. Thus, having exceedingly high expectations of the future was associated with continued caseness scores and having low expectations of the future was associated with incidence. The first finding supports clinical impressions that some patients reveal unrealistically high aspirations. Finding that very low aspirations were associated with incidence may indicate that these respondents were depressed or feeling relatively hopeless about themselves for other reasons.

Factors Associated with Incidence

The factors we found to be associated with incidence were older age, being black, low SES, being widowed or separated, reported physical illness, and either unrealistically high or low appraisals of one's present status and position in life five years from the present. Compared to the other health status groups, those who were in the normal range in 1970 but in caseness range in 1973 utilized friends and relatives as social support systems to a slightly greater extent. Believing that religion is important in meeting daily problems and church attendance also were associated with incidence.

Spontaneous Remission

Beiser cited a few reports that associated spontaneous remission with higher SES, the availability of social support systems, and participation in community activities (17). We found that being in the age group 23-29, a white male, in upper SES, or married, along with the realistic (close to the average) views of one's achievements and hopes for the future, were the only factors significantly associated with remission, with one exception—having grown up in Other Florida or Elsewhere. The availability of social support systems as measured by nearness to relatives and having friends was not associated with remission. But, participation in community activities as measured by club membership was significantly related to remission.

Implications

The results of the follow-up study have numerous implications. Probably the most important is Holzer's finding that the respondents' 1970 health statuses were the most significant predictors of their 1973 statuses.

This has somber implications. Most of those who were at risk for mental disorder at one time remained in that precarious condition three years later and, conversely, most of those who were not at risk at the earlier time were not at risk later, implying pessimistically that emotional distress is characterized by its chronicity or recurrence.

It appears as if we dealt mainly with two very different groups of respondents—those who continued to be at high risk and those who continued to be at low risk. Other studies of mental disorder showing that genetic factors have etiologic significance are persistent, disquieting facts that cannot be dismissed. But we should not accept such thoughts without question and concern.

Social factors associated with risk for mental disorder, the focus of this study, cannot be gainsaid. The people of this world may be divided into two groups in many ways, according to health and illness, according to constitutional strength or weakness, but also according to affluence and poverty—sufficiency and deprivation. Lower SES was related not only to risk for mental disorder but also reciprocally to the occurrence of life events requiring social readjustment that tax the human being. So long as inequities endure, proponents of genetic or constitutional theories of mental illness are compelled to weigh them—to recall that Aristotle defined the human being as a political animal.

REFERENCES

1. MACMILLAN, A. M., "The Health Opinion Survey: Technique for Estimating Prevalence of Psychoneurotic and Related Types of Disorder in Communities," *Psychological Reports,* Monograph Supplement 7, Southern Universities Press, 1957, 325-339.
2. PAYKEL, E. S., MYERS, J. K., DIENELT, M. N., KLERMAN, G. L., LINDENTHAL, J. J., and PEPPER, M. P., "Life Events and Depression," *Archives of General Psychiatry,* Vol. 21, December 1969, 753-760.
3. HOLZER, C. E., III, *The Impact of Life Events on Psychiatric Symptomatology.* Doctoral Dissertation, University of Florida, Gainesville, Fla., 1977, 37-39.
4. Ibid., 81.
5. Ibid., 78, 83, and 118.
6. Ibid., 85.
7. ROGLER, L. H., and HOLLINGSHEAD, A. B., *Trapped: Families and Schizophrenia.* New York: John Wiley & Sons, 1965.
8. MYERSON, A., "Review, Mental Disorders in Urban Areas," *American Journal of Psychiatry,* 96, 1940, 995-997.
9. See Reference 3, 131.
10. ESSEN-MÖLLER, E., "Individual Traits and Morbidity in a Swedish Rural Population," *Acta Psychiat. et Neurol. Scand., Suppl. 100.* Copenhagen: Enjar Munksgaard, 1956.
11. HAGNELL, O., *A Prospective Study of the Incidence of Mental Disorder.* Lund, Sweden: Scandinavian University Books, 1966.

12. Srole, L., 'Measurement and Classification in Socio-Psychiatric Epidemiology: Midtown Manhattan Study (1954) and Midtown Manhattan Restudy (1974)," *Journal of Health and Social Behavior,* Vol. 16, June 1975, 347-364.
13. Ibid.
14. Morris, J. N., *Uses of Epidemiology,* 2nd Edition. Baltimore: Williams and Wilkins, 1964.
15. Masserman, J. H., *The Practice of Dynamic Psychiatry.* Philadelphia: W. B. Saunders Co., 1955.
16. Cantril, H., *The Pattern of Human Concerns.* New Brunswick, N.J.: Rutgers University Press, 1965.
17. Beiser, M., "Psychiatric Epidemiology." In: A. N. Armand, Jr. (Ed.), *The Harvard Guide to Modern Psychiatry.* Cambridge, Mass.: The Belknap Press of Harvard University Press, 1978, 617.

12

Summary and Implications

T. S. Eliot asked, "Where is the wisdom we have lost in knowledge?/ Where is the knowledge we have lost in information?" (1). Most community studies of mental illness, such as our study of social order and mental health, yield so many data that the investigators usually are compelled to compress them and then skim the surface to present the major findings. In this chapter, we shall list the salient results, discuss them briefly, and point out a few of their implications.

PREVALENCE OF RISK FOR MENTAL DISORDER

We found in our random community sample that the prevalence of risk for mental disorder in the County was about 28% as assessed by two different measures. Based on our model of Social Psychiatric Impairment (SPI), 28.1% were in the high-risk range for mental disorder; on the standardized Health Opinion Survey (HOS), a remarkably similar percentage (28.3%) had scores in the possible or probable caseness range. This 28% is considerably lower than the percentages reported by other investigators. For example, in the Stirling County Study about 57% were found to be possible or probable cases, and in the Midtown Manhattan Study about 75% had at least some degree of impairment (2, 3). Conversely, in the Florida Health Study, about 72% were considered to be well; in contrast, only about 40% were found to be "well" in the Stirling County Study and about 25% were rated "well" in the Midtown Manhattan Study (4, 5).

Our 28% figure is very close to that cited by the President's Commission on Mental Health in April, 1978, which reported that "25% of all Americans (about 55 million people) suffer from mental problems and that 15% need some form of mental health services" (6).

The drastic differences in the percentages reported to be at risk in the Florida Health Study, compared to other major investigations, can be attributed to differing theoretical and methodological approaches. As we saw in Chapter 4, the most formidable obstacle confronting psychiatric epidemiologists is the lack of a consensually agreed upon definition of mental illness; consequently, investigators develop measures for assessing risk from differing frames of reference. As a result, case definition and the methods utilized to identify those at risk vary considerably. Furthermore, the populations studied were very different. Stirling was a rural county with a pastoral character, and Midtown Manhattan covered a limited area in a teeming metropolis. In contrast, our County was typical of the Southeastern United States—it was being transformed by rapid social change and it contained a representative black population as well as poor whites and many apparently affluent suburbanites.

CONCURRENCE OF MENTAL, PSYCHOSOMATIC, AND PHYSICAL DISORDERS

A major reason for differences in the percentages reported to be at risk by various investigators is that they have difficulty not confounding symptoms of physical and mental illness; therefore, some of the physically ill are likely to be placed in the mental health risk group. In designing the instruments to measure SPI, we made a serious attempt to limit them to the measurement of mental and interpersonal problems primarily; in particular, we tried to exclude indicators of possible psychosomatic or physical illnesses. But in the real world, in contrast to the researcher's mind, mental disorders, psychophysiologic distress, and physical illness are often concurrent conditions, existing in a variety of possible combinations. Extensive analyses showed that just 9.2% of our sample were in the SPI Only category. Of the 463 respondents (28.1% of the sample) in the SPI category, about 67% had reported psychosomatic ailments and/or physical illnesses as well. Thus, less than 10% of the total sample were in need of mental health care only; the remainder also required medical attention.

These findings have significant implications for health planners and those concerned with the delivery of health services. In many instances, it is possible that mental symptomatology or interpersonal distress is indicative of psychosomatic and physical illnesses; consequently, physicians' greater attention to their patients' emotional reactions to physical illness is warranted. Moreover, we think that the primary physician "on the front line" will be called upon increasingly to practice holistic medicine by treating the patient's mental and emotional as well as physical ailments. Primary physicians will be compelled to develop working alliances with mental health professionals to whom they can refer patients needing a level of mental health care beyond the general practitioner's or internist's level of skill and available time. Physicians, therefore, need to develop their referral procedures and their skills for identifying those patients who can be treated in various settings—physicians' offices, Community Mental Health Centers, other clinics, psychiatrists' offices, or the hospital.

"INCIDENCE" AND "REMISSION"

Findings from the three-year follow-up study allowed us to report data on "incidence" and "remission," topics about which there is scanty knowledge. The three-year incidence rate for risk for mental disorder, as measured by HOS caseness scores, was 14.1%; the three-year remission rate was 29.0%. Those who changed from low to high risk during the three years tended to be the respondents in the age groups 45-59 and 60+, the blacks, those who were poor, or the widowed or separated.

Remission tended to occur relatively often among the respondents aged 23-29, whites, those in the middle or highest SES quintile, or the divorced.

We searched for biological, interpersonal, social, and spiritual factors related to either incidence or remission, but found only a few significant relationships. Incidence was associated mainly with physical illness and low SES. Many respondents in the incidence group had social support systems as indicated by their reporting that they had relatives or friends nearby, but our socioanthropologic analyses of the County revealed that this finding should be interpreted in light of Oscar Lewis' description of "the culture of poverty" (7). When confronted by stressors, many poor respondents in the incidence or continued caseness groups could rely on relatives and friends only for consolation. Their relatives and friends usually were enduring the same conditions of life and had neither material resources with which to help nor access to professionals and institutions other than the pastor or the welfare worker.

RISK AMONG THE YOUNG

The prevalence data showed that disproportionately larger percentages of the young respondents were at risk than are usually reported by other major studies. Our research was conducted at a time when the generation gap was a prominent issue. The protests of the young, the Vietnam

Conflict, the Civil Rights Movement, and women's lib were highly publicized societal concerns. Whether these were meaningfully, not just coincidentally, related to our finding that unusually large percentages of the young were at risk can neither be proved nor disproved. In 1973 as well as in 1970, large percentages of the young were at high risk. Thus, their distress cannot be viewed as ephemeral. We think that this finding is related to our nation's extensive sociocultural problems, not just transitory issues. In particular, as Margaret Mead has noted, American youth have little status and few rites of passage. Their dependency position is prolonged, consistent with a technological society's needs for, and rewards given to, the highly skilled (8). The problems of the young, therefore, probably cannot be resolved nor significantly diminished in less than a generation's time, if then. The magnitude and severity of the problems of the young are recognized not only by scholars in this field and the news media, but also, in a somewhat backhanded way, by the lowering of the voting age. Implicitly, the belated change in the voting age from 21 to 18 is prima facie evidence that the young in this generation needed status.

Concern about the mental health problems of the young, as supported by the results of our study, is substantiated by the rising rates for "social" causes of mortality—suicide, homicide, and accidents—among those aged 15-24. As has been noted, a shift in the frequency of any condition toward younger persons presages a rise in its prevalence in the future.

THE HEALTH STATUS OF THE BLACKS

The health status of the blacks in the County was poor. In 1970, significantly higher percentages of blacks than whites were in the SPI category and in the HOS caseness range, and had reported concurrent psychosomatic and physical ailments. Moreover, the results of the follow-up study showed that the health of the black respondents had deteriorated.

Mortality data reveal that black males and females have significantly lower life expectancies than their white counterparts, particularly in the South (9). Furthermore, the morbidity and mortality rates of young blacks for accidents and homicide are extremely high, possibly accounting for much of the difference between the whites' and the blacks' life expectancies (10).

We think that the deleterious effects of the caste system, and even the roots of the problem in slavery, have endured. The blacks were not only seen as inferior, but treated as inferiors. The political wrongs to which they have been subjected have been redressed only fractionally by enfranchisement and desegregation. For those without status, political changes seldom bring concomitant sociocultural changes within a short period of time. Thus, the blacks in the South who had been denied access to social and economic opportunities often obtained only political rights.

Moreover, the younger blacks were torn by competing value systems. On one hand, those who did not become militant were scorned by those risking their lives in the cause of equality; on the other hand, the older blacks, often more conservative (and necessarily suspicious and vigilant), cautioned forbearance out of fear of reprisals. They had been conditioned by the past.

The plight of black females was especially grievous. Repeatedly, they were the race-sex group with the highest scores on indices of risk for mental disorder, psychosomatic distress, and physical illness. For years, the black females, particularly in the South, had maintained the family structure, often struggling against formidable handicaps to nurture the children. In Alachua County, large percentages of adult, black females worked as maids or in menial jobs to obtain the necessities of life for their own offspring and sometimes the children of others. Frequently, the black female was the principal breadwinner. At the same time, they had high aspirations, envisaging that they would be located higher on the "ladder of life" five years in the future than did the other race-sex groups. The discrepancies between aspirations and achievements were painful to observe. The black females located themselves in the present in 1970 at 6.0 on Cantril's Ladder, but perceived that they would be at 8.6 in 1975. Although three years had elapsed, their perceived present position in 1973 was only 6.1; nevertheless, they projected that their position in 1978 would be at 8.2. Their perceived present position had scarcely changed between 1970 and 1973—the optimistically envisioned much better position in life was still agonizingly far away.

We think that the social and material deprivations experienced by the blacks in conjunction with the deleterious aspects of the psychology of oppression have had traumatic effects on the black respondents in our study. Although some of the political trauma had been lessened, the wounds, if healing, were still inflamed in the early 1970s.

SOCIOECONOMIC STATUS (SES) AND RISK

We examined a number of sociodemographic variables to find possible associations between them and risk for mental disorder. This is one of the epidemiologist's major tasks. In numerous analyses, we found that lower SES was significantly related to risk for mental disorder as measured both by SPI and HOS scores in the caseness range. Consistently, this same relationship has been reported by most investigators in Western nations (except in Sweden). During the past century the hereditary versus environment argument—propounded by the pre-Socratics and formulated by Plato—has developed at times into a vicious controversy. Does one have only one's self to blame for poverty and its associated adversities? Or, do social inequities and the quality of the social environment determine the quality of life for the person?

However, we should recall that in the 1880s, Darwin's cousin, Sir Francis Galton, termed the "nature versus nurture" dichotomy too simplistic. Geneticists agree that the expression of the genes is modified by the environment. Although we can do little about the genotype, our society has both the power and the resources to assure that people are decently fed and can live secure from the indignities of poverty. Whether the necessary social action programs will be effectively mounted is dependent almost solely upon our society's values.

INTERGENERATIONAL AND GEOGRAPHIC MOBILITY AND SPI

Social mobility, as measured by differences between respondents' and their fathers' levels of education and occupation, was more weakly and inconsistently related to SPI than simpler variables such as age, race, and SES. A detailed analysis of our respondents' intergenerational mobility patterns revealed that, as compared to their fathers, about 70% of them were educationally upwardly mobile and about 10% were downwardly mobile. Slightly more than 50% were occupationally non-mobile. We were surprised that there was not more upward intergenerational mobility in view of the rapid social change that was occurring. Downward social mobility was associated with higher risk for mental disorder, consistent with other investigators' findings. Women under the age of 44 tended to have higher educational levels than their fathers but lower educational levels than their husbands.

It appears that some degree of status incongruity (differences between educational and occupational levels) is related variably to risk for mental disorder. Respondents in the upper-middle SES quintile, the most upwardly mobile group, tended to score in the high-risk range on the Impairment of Functioning scale. This scale included questions about difficulties with work resulting from feelings of worry or nervousness, suggesting that their upward occupational mobility may have been stressful. In clinical medicine, psychosomatic illness is observed frequently in men who have risen to higher socioeconomic levels, but we found no evidence to support that observation.

Migration, geographic mobility, also was inconsistently related to SPI. The social structure within the County was being transformed by an influx of newcomers from other parts of Florida, adjacent states of the Deep South, and especially the Northeast and the Midwest (Elsewhere in the nation). SES appears to be the significant intervening variable associated with migration and risk for mental disorder. Within the low SES stratum, higher percentages of migrants from the Deep South were in the SPI category or in the HOS caseness range than those from Elsewhere, Other Florida, or the native Alachuans. Within the middle and upper SES strata, there were no significant associations between geographic origin and risk for mental disorder, although a somewhat small percentage of high SES respondents from the Deep South were found to be at risk.

SOCIAL CHANGE AND SOCIAL ORDER

Our major hypotheses reflected our concern with the rapid social change that was sweeping the County and the apparent disruption of the established social order that had been maintained for a century by vicious social control mechanisms such as the Ku Klux Klan, as well as by legitimate mechanisms.

As presented in Chapter 9, most of our respondents reported that they perceived most of the social changes we had studied; and many of them were "upset" about the changes. But contrary to our hypothesis, there were few significant associations between perception of and concern about the social changes on the one hand and being in either the SPI or the Not-Impaired groups on the other. However, more respondents in the SPI category reported that they were "upset very much" about the processes that had a personal and interpersonal character, such as racial unrest, young people leaving, outsiders moving in, and a faster pace and pressure in everyday life, than those in the Not-Impaired group. But about equal percentages in the two groups reported concern about major, realistic problems such as the rising crime rate, increased use of drugs by the young, pollution, and crowding in the schools.

A significantly large number of the Alachuans were in the low SES stratum. Also, they tended to be either non-mobile or downwardly mobile intergenerationally and were found to be at risk on our Psychopathology scale and symptom pattern subscales (anxiety, depression, etc.). In contrast, most of those from Elsewhere were in the middle and upper SES strata and upwardly mobile; relatively few had high scores on the psychopathology and symptom pattern scales. But our hypotheses about changes in the social order were difficult to test scientifically. SES cropped up repeatedly as the most significant variable associated with SPI or HOS caseness scores. Therefore, we were compelled to look at social order within SES strata. Arranging the geographic groups according to percentages in the low, middle, and upper SES strata showed that within the low SES stratum, the group with the largest percentage in the SPI category consisted of those from the Deep South, followed closely by the low SES Alachuans and Other Floridians.

Within the middle and high SES strata there were fewer Alachuans than those who had moved into the County. In fact, the only point at which the percentage of those in the SPI category in the three SES strata did not follow the SES lines strictly was that the percentage of the high SES Alachuans in the SPI category was about the same as that of the middle SES Other Floridians. We think that the "upper class" Alachuans who had once occupied preeminent positions in the social order and controlled the County's political, economic, and social life for generations were losing status. Occupying the top positions in the social order were the well-educated, technologically oriented newcomers who were able to capitalize on the expanding business and other opportunities that were associated with Gainesville's becoming a regional center for education, medicine, science, and technology.

ASPIRATIONS AND SATISFACTIONS

When we began our research, we were especially interested in our respondents' aspirations and satisfactions. The original construct of SPI included aspirations and satisfactions as one of its dimensions, but later we found that we could not synthesize aspirations and satisfactions with our overall measures of psychopathology, impairment of functioning, and interpersonal distress.

However, the results of our study of the respondents' aspirations, as measured by perceived locations on Cantril's Ladder five years in the past, at present, and five years in the future, showed that most of them believed that their positions in life had improved somewhat between five years ago and the present. Those in the lowest SES quintile and the blacks placed themselves lower in the past and also in the present than did their counterparts. But almost all of the respondents envisioned a brighter future, expecting to attain a significantly higher position five years in the future. Hope springs eternal!

In 1973, the follow-up sample positioned themselves on the Ladder at 6.9, exceedingly close to the 1970 position in the present, 6.7. But, in 1970 they envisioned that their position on the Ladder in 1975 would be significantly higher, 8.4. Although three of the five years had elapsed, their present positions in 1970 and in 1973 had changed only slightly. Their optimism continued despite the lack of perceived major advances between 1970 and 1973. In 1973 they located themselves five years in the future at the 8.3 level on the Ladder, a position almost identical to that (8.4) envisaged in 1970 for five years in the future.

Such optimism should be heartening. And we found that "great expectations" for the future were not associated with risk for mental disorder unless they were "grand"; a significantly large percentage of those with high aspiration scores (differences between the present and the future) were in the SPI category. Also, the pitiful group who perceived their future position as lower than the present contained a significantly large percentage of those in the SPI category and were found in the follow-up study to be significantly over-represented in the incidence group whose health statuses had worsened between 1970 and 1973.

In viewing the rapid changes in the County, we wondered whether life characterized by the outward trappings of success was also inwardly satisfying. We found that most employed respondents (87.4%) expressed satisfaction with their work, but that a disproportionately low percentage of those in the SPI category expressed the same degree of satisfaction. This same finding was true for the housewives and the married respondents. However, there were no significant differences in the percentages of students reporting degree of "satisfaction with life as a student" whether they were in the SPI category or the Not-Impaired group; slightly more than 75% of the students expressed satisfaction. Over 90% of the upper SES respondents stated that they "enjoyed" their work; about 90% of the upper SES housewives expressed satisfaction with being a housewife. The major trend, therefore, was the direct relationship found between higher socioeconomic status and a greater degree of satisfaction. For example, over 90% of the upper SES respondents expressed satisfaction with their work in contrast to slightly less than 80% of those in the lower SES quintiles. And this relationship was much stronger for the married respondents; over 90% of those in the upper SES groups were satisfied with "married life" in contrast to 70%

or less of those in the lower SES groups. Thus, satisfaction with one's activities, especially marriage, was related to SES. In general, the wealthier, the better educated, and those at the top of the occupational ladder were more satisfied than their counterparts.

SPI AND MODELS OF MENTAL ILLNESS

We conducted a number of multiple regression equations to determine variables associated with SPI. We found six significant variables; they explained 15% of the variance. Listed in the order in which they entered the equation, they were:

1. Nervous or emotional problems in the family	.0005
2. Lower SES	.0005
3. An unhappy childhood	.0005
4. Being separated	.0005
5. Being a sickly child	.005
6. Having grown up in the Deep South (Florida excluded)	.025

The strong association between a history of mental illness in the family and SPI points to the importance of possible genetic influences. The importance of marginality is shown by the strong relationship between lower SES and SPI, and that of role by our finding repeatedly that the separated were a high-risk group. The predictive significance of childhood factors supports, at least to some extent, developmental and psychoanalytic concepts of the etiology of mental illness. Then, we classified possible predictive items into three groups in order to test, in somewhat crude form, the applicability of different models of mental illness—biological, developmental, and social—to SPI.

These models had been formulated by astute clinicians whose observations of their patients disclosed the interplay between dynamic forces—individual and social—that determine the cause and course of mental illness. But, since these observations had been gleaned from work with patients, a selected group, we were curious about the extent to which the various models would be applicable to the general population, including the emotionally disturbed who had never received treatment. Therefore, we conducted a series of multiple regression equations using items relative to the various theories as independent variables and SPI as the dependent variable. Awareness of the complexity of the human situation precluded our thinking of almost any of the independent variables as being truly independent; but some, such as race or a family history of mental illness, are beyond the individual's control and can be conceptualized as semi-independent.

The three models tested were labeled: 1) the biological (containing items related to mental illness in the family, physical health, etc.); 2) the developmental (containing items related to childhood); and 3) the social (containing items about roles, migration, mobility, etc.). The three models explained about equal percentages of the variance in SPI: the biological—16.6%; the developmental—14.1%; and the social—15.8%. To test the models with various groups in the population we first compared the whites and blacks. The results were:

Model	Social Psychiatric Impairment (Percentage of Variance Explained)	
	Whites	Blacks
Biological	15.0	18.5
Developmental	13.4	12.6
Social	14.8	19.9

Then we carried out the same procedure for the three SES strata. The results were:

Model	Social Psychiatric Impairment (Percentage of Variance Explained)		
	Low SES	Middle SES	High SES
Biological	17.9	12.3	15.9
Developmental	9.6	10.9	18.3
Social	10.2	12.0	16.5

The differences in the amount of the variance explained by the three models are relatively small except in a few instances; we think that not finding many major differences, in itself, is important. The obvious conclusion is that different models have been formulated and that they have some degree of utility because no single model adequately explains that complex condition we term mental illness. There was a great deal of overlap among the models; when combined into one equation, the predictors for all three models explained 20.4% of the variance in SPI.

The exceptions deserve comment. The social and the biological models explained more of the variance in SPI among the blacks than did the developmental which contained many items related to psychoanalytic theory. Finding that the social and the biological models explained about equal percentages of the variance in SPI among the blacks points to the importance of SES and role factors for mental illness in the blacks. The biological model also fitted the blacks better than it did the whites. The variables contained in the biological model were mainly items related to physical illness in childhood, at present, and in the family.

The developmental model explained a much larger percentage of the variance in SPI for the high SES group than for the low SES group. This finding substantiates opinions that the developmental model was a product of clinical observations of "upper class" patients and that its applicability to the many low SES persons appears to be very limited. Finding that the biological model fitted the low SES group much better than the other two models points to the importance of conditions such as concurrent physical illnesses that are prevalent among the poor and the deprived.

These attempts to test some theoretical aspects of psychiatry and psychology in general populations are rudimentary but they indicate that the data obtained from studies of mental illness in the community give the psychiatric epidemiologist an opportunity to make contributions to our often elaborate but generally insufficient theories of mental health and illness.

Finally, as Beiser has noted: "Epidemiological inquiry usually produces data about association among variables, rather than a definitive understanding of the process. Though only partial knowledge, the data may nonetheless suggest methods of control" (11).

We think, however, that well-designed, prospective studies of families and other household aggregates that include medical and genetic, as well as psychiatric and socioanthropologic, investigations could shed light on the etiology of mental disorder. The epidemiologist's task for the future, therefore, is to obtain information that advances knowledge. But whether that knowledge will lead to wisdom is a question that can be answered only by those concerned about the human condition and committed to its improvement.

REFERENCES

1. Eliot, T. S., "Choruses from 'The Rock.'" In: *Selected Poems.* New York: Harcourt, Brace and World, Inc., 1936, 107.

2. LEIGHTON, D. C., HARDING, J. S., MACKLIN, D. G., MACMILLAN, A. M., and LEIGHTON, A. H., *The Character of Danger*. New York: Basic Books, Inc., 1963.
3. LANGNER, T. S., and MICHAEL, S. T., *Life Stress and Mental Health. Vol. II of the Midtown Manhattan Study, T.A.C. Rennie Series in Social Psychiatry*. New York: The Free Press of Glencoe, 1963.
4. See Reference 2.
5. See Reference 3.
6. *President's Commission on Mental Health Report*. Louisville Courier-Journal, 28 April 1978, A3.
7. LEWIS, O., *La Vida: A Puerto Rican Family in the Culture of Poverty—San Juan and New York*. New York: Random House, 1966, xlii-lii.
8. MEAD, M., *Culture and Commitment*. Garden City, N.Y.: Natural History Press/ Doubleday & Company, Inc., 1970.
9. SCHWAB, J. J., CHALMERS, J. M., CONROY, S. J., FARRIS, P. B., and MARKUSH, R. E., "Studies in Grief: A Preliminary Report." In: B. Shoenberg, I. Gerber, A. Wiener, A. H. Kutscher, D. Peretz, and A. C. Carr (Eds.), *Bereavement: Its Psychosocial Aspects*. Irvington-on-Hudson, N.Y.: Columbia University Press, 1975.
10. SCHWAB, J. J., and SCHWAB, M. E., *Sociocultural Roots of Mental Illness: An Epidemiologic Survey*. New York: Plenum Publishing Corp., 1978, 10.
11. BEISER, M., "Psychiatric Epidemiology." In: A. N. Nicholi, Jr. (Ed.), *The Harvard Guide to Modern Psychiatry*. Cambridge, Mass.: The Belknap Press of Harvard University Press, 1978, 610.

Subject Index

Author Index